Believe in the beautiful future
of your own dreams

Dreaming OF YOUR Future

About the Author

Theresa Cheung is a *Sunday Times* bestselling dreams author. She has a degree in theology and English from King's College, Cambridge University, and a master's in English from King's College, London University. She is the author of numerous titles that have been translated into over forty languages, including the bestselling *Dream Dictionary from A to Z* (HarperCollins) and the *Dream Decoder* card pack and *Dream Rituals Oracle Cards* (Hachette).

Theresa works closely with scientists researching consciousness and has contributed features about dreams to national and international newspapers, websites, and magazines, including *Bustle, Vice, Cosmopolitan, Good Housekeeping, InStyle, Red, Grazia, Heat, Metro, Glamour,* and many more. She has been interviewed by Claudia Winkleman on BBC Radio 2, Nicky Campbell on BBC Radio 5 Live, Roman Kemp on Capital Radio, Regina Meredith on Gaia TV, George Noory on Coast-to-Coast AM, Piers Morgan on ITV, Terrence Lee on Fox News, Chicago, and by other leading media outlets, including KTLA, Today Extra, Channel 4 and BBC Radio.

The subject of a night poet episode on Nicky Campbell's BBC Sounds 5 Live podcast, *Different,* and a frequent dream-decoding guest on ITV's *This Morning,* Theresa has hosted numerous national dream call-ins live on TV and radio decoded dreams for numerous celebrities and influencers. She has given dream-decoding talks and webinars to leading companies and brands, such as Action Coach, Anthropologie, Beauty Bay, Dynavision, Immediate Media, Shiseido, Kiss Cosmetics USA, Premier Inn, Olympia Mind Body Spirit, and the Hearst magazine group. She also hosts her own popular podcast, *White Shores.*

You can message, share your dreams with, and follow Theresa on Instagram @thetheresacheung and via her Facebook and X author pages, and learn more about her dreamwork at www.theresacheung.com.

Dreaming OF YOUR Future

Unlock the Precognitive Secrets of Your Mind

Sunday Times Best-Selling Author
THERESA CHEUNG

LLEWELLYN
WOODBURY, MINNESOTA

First Edition
First Printing, 2025

Cover design by Shira Atakpu

Library of Congress Cataloging-in-Publication Data (Pending)
ISBN: 978-0-7387-7938-6

Llewellyn Publications
A Division of Llewellyn Worldwide Ltd.
2143 Wooddale Drive
Woodbury, MN 55125-2989
www.llewellyn.com

Printed in the United States of America

Other Books by Theresa Cheung

The Dream Cure

The Dream Dictionary from A to Z

Dream Decoder (card pack)

Night Vision

The Premonition Code with Dr. Julia Mossbridge

Dream Ritual Oracle Cards

Empower Your Inner Psychic

How to Catch a Dream

The Element Encyclopaedia of Birthdays

The Afterlife Is Real

Haunted World

21 Rituals to Ignite Your Intuition

Forthcoming Books by Theresa Cheung

The Akashic Records

For the ghost of what is yet to come

Contents

Introduction

You are, always have been, and always will be a precognitive being.

You may not know it (yet), but it is a truth universally unacknowledged that precognition is a natural-born ability hidden deep within everyone, including you. Sixth sense is hardwired into your DNA. You already can sense what is way ahead of your time. You just haven't been noticing it.

This book will show you how your sleeping precognitive ability is always waiting for you to wake up to its visionary presence in your very own dream time. The overwhelming majority of precognitions occur in the nocturnal dream state. This doesn't mean waking precognition isn't possible. It most certainly is, and you'll learn how you can sense your future with your eyes wide open too. But by far the swiftest, simplest, safest, and sweetest way to see your future first is in your dreams, a.k.a. your night vision.

It's Your Dream Time

The mindfulness movement preaches that fulfilment can only be found by focusing all your attention on the present moment—the power of your now. Given the undeniable truth of this, you may wonder why I'm suggesting that you consider diverting some of your precious attention to what hasn't happened yet in real time.

I'm suggesting it because the meaning of your life may well depend on it.

To reference Viktor E. Frankl, psychiatrist, Holocaust survivor, and multi-million-selling author of the enduring masterpiece of survival literature, *Man's Search for Meaning*, the inability to see the future is linked to "dangerous giving up." With "loss of belief in the future," you risk losing your mental, physical, and spiritual "hold."[1]

Trusting in the hope of your tomorrow matters. It brings you meaning. This may sound like a direct contradiction to the mindfulness mantra until you start to experience the life-changing power of conscious precognition for yourself. And when you do experience it, you realise that it doesn't contradict being mindful at all. Rather, it complements and enhances it, because you understand how your future is always being created by your present.

This book will help you directly experience the life-enhancing power of precognition. Your direct personal experience is the game changer.

To paraphrase a quote commonly attributed to the ancient Chinese sage Confucius, what you hear, you forget, and what you see, you remember, but what you do, you understand. That's why this book has been designed to be as practical as possible, offering things you can do immediately to help you not just see and believe in the future but also lovingly hold onto it. It will show you that your future is already alive and bringing infinite reassurance and meaning to your present. And although it is possible to glimpse your future ahead of time when you are awake, most typically your future will reveal itself to you first while you are sleeping.

Dreams Really Can Come True

You have likely experienced the elements of a nocturnal dream mysteriously playing out in your waking life a few days later so that you have that sensational moment of *déjà rêvé*, or a dream remembered (literally "already dreamed"). For instance, you dream about someone you have not heard from in years and then a day or so later you get a surprise text message from them. But despite the normality of déjà rêvé, it is only recently that scientists and psychologists stopped dismissing predictive night visions as random.

1. Frankl, *Man's Search for Meaning*, 79.

I was born into a family of dream-loving psychics and spiritualists and from an early age was encouraged to explore the futuristic potential of my dreams. My passion for dream power led to my career as a dream author, and for decades I have been writing best-selling dream titles informed by my own dreams and research and the countless dreams sent to me by my readers. I'm grounded in academia, having studied theology and English for my bachelor's degree at King's College, Cambridge University. But I'm not a scientist, and in my university days I swiftly discovered that precognitive dreamwork was considered unscientific. I gave up on the science of precognitive dreamwork being out there, but my belief in and passion for precognition never diminished.

You can imagine my elation when, about a decade ago, I discovered there was ongoing credible research into the very real possibility of dreams being predictive. There were visionary scientists willing to take an active interest in the precognitive dreams of people all over the world, which I have devoted my writing career to collating. These scientists were studying these dreams as the data they are, and I began to collaborate with them to create books, blogs, podcasts, and presentations. Forgive the pun (the dreaming mind loves puns, as you will learn later), but it was a dream come true! From that moment on, I have referred my readers not just to the future they can glimpse in their dreams and waking hunches but also to the science.

And the science is revealing that there is convincing statistical evidence to suggest that precognition—the ability to know the future before it happens—is real. It is an innate ability within us all, but one most of us have lost touch with and faith in.

Dreams foreshadowing the future, a.k.a. precognitive dreams, have been reported throughout time in every culture and belief system. Precognition can certainly happen when you are awake (and this book will explore that, too, and what you can do to increase the chances of it happening more often), but it is most likely to occur when you are deep in slumber. Indeed, I'm taking a giant leap of faith and proposing to you here, for the first time in my career as a dreamwork author, that every dream has (seriously overlooked) precognitive themes foreshadowing a potential future for you.

That is why the second, larger portion of this book is a directory of the most common dream threads and how to start interpreting them as premonitions. It draws on the latest science as well as my own precognitive dreams and those sent to me by my readers over the last three decades. It also encapsulates my decades of research into the very real possibility that the future can be glimpsed night after night, and time and time again, in our dreams.

I want this book to wake you up so that you can fall asleep and dream bigger. Like a vividly recalled precognitive dream, I want this book to surprise you in every possible way. In hindsight, I can see now that this is a book my future has always wanted me to write. I just needed to catch up with that future and believe in it.

Dream Directions

Since childhood, my dreams have repeatedly revealed glimpses of my future to me. I could write an entire book about those precognitive dreams, but I will restrict myself to the following two examples, as this book is hopelessly devoted to you. This is because by far the best way for you to understand the precognitive power of your dreams is not to read about the dreams of others, however precognitively accurate they may be, but to directly experience your own dream power. I am simply sharing these two personal stories because I believe they can help set the dream scene for you.

The first example happened many moons ago when I was just starting out in my writing career. I woke up one morning with the memory of the voice of my departed mother speaking loud and clear to me. In my dream, I was in a magical forest and unsure of which direction to take, and she told me to take the right path. I heard her say it in the dream. I did not ponder the meaning of the dream too deeply upon waking. I simply thought it meant "follow your heart," as that is what my mother always told me to do when she was alive, and I really needed to be reminded. At the time, my heart was calling me towards a career in spiritual writing, but my pocketbook was calling me to return to school teaching.

That same day, I was driving towards a busy junction intending to turn left to get to a radio interview. But then I spontaneously recalled the clear and present directive from my dream to "turn right," and without understanding why, I instinctively obeyed. Later, I discovered that if I had turned left as originally planned, I almost certainly would have been involved in a fatal pileup.

Had a precognitive dream warning saved my life?

Whether it did or not cannot be proved. But it proved to me that listening to my dreams could open the door to my future in a way I had not fully experienced before.

My dreams also protect and prepare me in less dramatic but always empowering ways. Indeed, the inception of this book was appropriately marked by a clear vision in a dream.

In the final days of 2023, although I didn't realise it at the time, my inner precognitive revealed itself loud and clear. As is often the case, it surfaced first in my dreams and then in my intuitive waking response to a memory of those dreams.

Over the course of several nights, I had a series of vivid dreams featuring images of cherry blossoms, the national flower of Japan. I had recently been teaching precognitive dreamwork to an online Japanese spiritual growth company, so this was unsurprising. The deeper meanings behind sacred symbols of Japanese culture, such as the cherry blossom, had already found a welcoming home in my heart.

With New Year's 2024 a few days away, I assumed that my dreaming mind was drawing upon the beautiful symbol of the cherry blossom to aptly remind me of the fragility of life and the poetic potential for rebirth and new beginnings that can be found in every ending.

As I believe my dreams are a richer, more alive, and more creative version of myself, living out the wisdom of my night vision and proactively incorporating elements of a dream into my waking life (if safe to do so) is something I instinctively do. Cherry blossoms featured strongly in my dreams, so I felt called from within to promote to my readers and podcast listeners the intriguing Japanese tradition of *hatsuyume*.

Hatsuyume

Hatsuyume is the Japanese term for the first dream recalled in the new year. In Japanese culture, it is traditionally believed that your hatsuyume is strikingly precognitive and can often foretell your luck in the ensuing year.

I felt that referencing hatsuyume would be an enchanting way to motivate my readers and listeners to make dream journaling a New Year's resolution and to consider their dreams as potentially precognitive.

As January approached, I drew on the metaphor of hatsuyume to remind anyone willing to listen to me of the life-changing significance of writing down and reflecting on the meaning of their new year dreams.

Then, in the early days of 2024, Japan was uncharacteristically and for distressing reasons dominating the news cycle. The country was hit without warning by an earthquake and then an air disaster.

Given that I had so heavily promoted hatsuyume a few days before tragedy struck Japan, I found myself invited out of the blue to discuss hatsuyume and the meaning of new year dreams on major media channels. This unexpected media spotlight encouraged more people than I could have dreamed of not only to learn something fascinating about Japanese culture and send loving prayers to Japan during a time of need, but also to reflect on the precognitive potential of the first dream they recalled in the new year.

There are some who would call all of this random, down to chance, but I believe otherwise. For me, it is a "meaningful coincidence," or what Swiss psychiatrist and psychoanalyst Carl Jung, the godfather of psycho-psychic dream interpretation, termed *synchronicity*.[2] I believe that precognition, whether it manifests personally, for others, or in global events, is synchronicity in disguise.

After what felt like a striking vote of confidence from my precognitive mind to write this book, the words flowed through me in the weeks and months that followed. I channelled without hesitation, doubt, or fear my lifetime of precognitive dream research into the pages that follow.

My aim throughout is to help you notice, decode, and fully experience the precognitive potential of your dreams and waking hunches for yourself, but most important of all, to empower you to practise simple precognition-boosting techniques that will—if applied daily—ignite your natural-born precognitive ability, when your eyes are shut tight and wide open.

---

2. Holmes, "Carl Jung on Synchronicity."

What Lies Ahead?

To help you clearly see what lies ahead in this book, here's a heads-up on what to expect.

Part 1 sets the timeless dream scene for you. You'll be immediately introduced to your essential precognition-boosting action plan.

To get the most out of this book, you are strongly advised from the onset to start incorporating these simple, effective precognition-boosting actions into your daily routine. They are the essential foundation stones that will ignite all of your future visions. Don't overthink. Just start doing them, and let the understanding and validation of them emerge in the days and weeks that follow. Aim to consciously do them every single day, so that over time they become unconscious and feel like a natural expression of who you are.

Following your precognition-boosting daily plan, which firmly lays down the solid foundations needed to process and progress to the time-travelling revelations that lie ahead, the rest of part 1 will jump right back into your future. You will dip into the scientific theories of time, discover the likely personality traits of visionaries, and explore optimal methods of precognitive dreamwork. You will also be encouraged to experiment with a series of supplemental exercises designed to enhance the precognition-boosting action plan set out in chapter 1.

All of the techniques shared here have just one clear vision: to dramatically increase your chances of accurately reading your future, in both your waking life and your dream life.

Part 2 is your ahead-of-time dream decoding directory, featuring the most common precognitive dreaming threads. For easy reference, there is also a handy index in the back of the book listing the most common symbols to appear within those dream threads. This dream symbol directory differs from other dream-decoding resources available both in book form and online because all of the themes and symbols are interpreted not just from a psychological, self-help perspective but also primarily precognitively.

Using this directory on a daily basis will help you effortlessly interpret the future-forward meanings of the most common dream threads—the dreams that research shows you are most likely to have. The word *thread* is used here deliberately, as every dream is like a thread connecting it to all of the other night visions used by your precognitive mind.

From now on, you can immediately refer to this precognitive dream directory when a dream memory surfaces upon waking, whether you have read part 1 or not. Just make sure you have started to incorporate into your daily routine the precognition-boosting action plan set out in chapter 1.

Repeatedly interpreting your dreams precognitively will absolutely kick-start, train, and strengthen your future vision. I foresee that after reading this book, applying the techniques suggested, and using the dream directory frequently, you will never lose sight of your lifesaving future again and the sense of meaning it can bring you. In your own dream time, you will prove to yourself time and again that your dreams offer you guidance, clarity, and purpose because they know your future direction long before you do.

You will never again say or think "it was just a dream," because you will have fallen deeply in love with the infinite time-travelling potential of your very own dream time. Falling asleep will become the greatest adventure and waking up the greatest joy.

Ah, what future-forward dreams, what revelations and infinite eureka moments, are coming your way!

Part One

It's Dream Time!

Chapter 1

Powered by Your Dreams

The issue with mainstreaming the reality that we all have precognitive ability is that we are so indoctrinated in the belief that time is linear. This book will dramatically challenge that belief and help you rethink your own perception of time in a radical new light.

The science of precognition, and trying to explain how the future can dip into the present, is a head crash, but the science matters and the coming chapters will not shy away from presenting some of it and key findings for you to reflect on. However, I'm fully aware as you begin reading this book that when it comes to processing the reality of precognition, the theory feels abstract—impractical and impersonal. There is nothing as convincing or real as your own direct personal experience, so from this moment on you are strongly urged to start gathering your own proof that you are a precognitive being and do all of the suggested exercises in this book.

Your future is ready and waiting for you to catch up with it. There's no better time to begin dreaming your future-forward life than right now. Let's dive right in.

Your Daily Precognition-Boosting Action Plan

Precognition, like life itself, can only be understood or recognised as the miracle it is backwards, or in hindsight. But it must be fully experienced and lived forwards.

The more attention you pay in the present moment to your waking hunches and night visions and the future they are constantly pointing you towards, the more you will learn not just to "see" the future of your dreams but also to attract or manifest it.

Start incorporating the following precognition boosters into your life every single day. In time, perhaps even before you finish reading this book, these simple techniques, if you repeat them daily and consistently, might just prove to you once and for all that your dreams really can and do come true.

Make sure you have this precognition action plan marked for handy reference, as it is going to be your future-forward catalyst from this moment on. Don't worry if it feels like a lot to immediately take on board. Let me reassure you that all of the suggested actions are far easier to incorporate into your daily life than you might initially think. And even if you start to practise only one of the recommended actions, rest assured that you will still be seriously sharpening your future vision.

Part 1 will revisit these techniques and offer more detailed insights and targeted ways to overcome common roadblocks to sticking with them in the long term, but for now you are encouraged without hesitation to leap right into the unknown.

Remember Your Nocturnal Dreams

The first rule of empowering your precognition is to recall and write down your dreams upon waking. The second rule is to recall and write down your dreams upon waking. If the only thing you take from this book is to remember and write down more of your dreams so that you can consider in hindsight how much they have foreshadowed a future event, situation, or mindset, your time travel adventure will have begun in earnest.

Recalling your dreams is crucial because most of your dreams contain precognitive themes, whether that be in showcasing potential future events, emotional reactions, situations, or mindsets. If you have ever experienced déjà rêvé (a dream remembered) on the day after a memorable dream or a few days, weeks, months, or even years later, and you had the foresight to write it down, then you already have your personal proof that you are a precognitive being. This is the perfect moment to stop dismissing this experience as random and to shine a light directly on it. The only way to do that is to make recalling and writing down your dreams a top priority every time you wake up from a sleep or nap.

Prove Yourself

Be sure to keep a written and date-stamped record every time you notice something in your waking life that you have experienced previously in a dream. This could be an object, event, situation, symbol, person, or location or even a feeling, reaction, or mindset. It's your personal proof—the scientific data you need—that you really are a dream oracle.

One thing I've learned from collaborating with scientists over the last few years is the importance of collecting evidence that can be verified. After-the-event anecdotes are compelling, but their impact is weakened if there is no proof that you recorded your precognition before it happened.

Note: Be mindful that your precognitive dreams showcase potential futures, so never fear recording them. If you don't like the future foreshadowed in your dreams, remember that you have free will and can change that potential future by the choices you make in the present. Your future is out there, but it is also always hiding in your own hands and endlessly being created by you in the present. (More about dreams as powerful manifesting tools in chapter 4.)

Live Your Dream

As your dreaming mind transcends the laws of everyday life, logic, and reason, your dreams can show glimpses of your future. This entire book is designed to help you to fall in love with the precognitive (psychic) potential of your dreaming mind, encouraging you to consciously seek out déjà rêvé in your waking life so your future is constantly guided and inspired by the feelings of your own dreams and the flash forwards they are revealing to you every single night.

To reassure your dreaming mind that you really are taking it seriously as a precognitive asset and that you want to live its wisdom, upon waking when you recall a dream, choose a colour, object, sound, or any other safe/ everyday symbol that featured in it. Then during the day, actively notice, seek out, or follow the associations you make with that symbol, as I did for my cherry blossom dreams. Create your own déjà rêvé synchronicity until you don't have to anymore.

For example, if you dreamt of a bicycle and own one, go for a ride on it. If you don't own one, notice bicycles more during the day or search online for a video of one to see what associations it triggers in you. If you noticed the colour blue in your dream, wear something blue the next day or make sure the pen you write with has blue ink and so on. If you were walking up some stairs in your dream, then every time you climb stairs during the day, take your mind right back to your dream staircase.

This "live your dream" exercise is super helpful because your precognitive mind has got used to being ignored over the years. It needs reassurance not just through your intention to recall and record your dreams upon waking but also through your actions—just as you learn to trust others because of their actions and not their words. You need to show, not just tell, your dreaming mind that you are authentic, that you want to connect to it and live its wisdom in your waking life.

Observe how actively connecting to your dream symbol and bringing it to life (consciously seeking out déjà rêvé) makes you feel, and what sacred/ creative associations are triggered by that feeling of familiarity and interconnection between your inner and outer worlds.

Trust in You

Believing something is possible is key. Nothing illustrates this better than that watershed moment for human potential on 6 May 1954 when British runner Roger Bannister smashed the four-minute mile barrier. Knowing the four-minute mile was no longer impossible inspired other athletes to do the same. The key to their success was believing that what was previously deemed impossible was now possible.

The power of collective belief is strong. It illustrates how interconnected we all are on an energetic level.

In much the same way, belief in your own precognitive potential is the single most important factor when it comes to precognitive experiences.

Repeat this affirmation daily out loud or in your thoughts: "I am a precognitive being. I see the future I am attracting clearly in my dreams and in my waking hunches."

Your belief that precognition happens and is real will inspire others to smash through doubt and fear and awaken precognitively too. Your belief will change not just your life but the lives of others as well.

Meditate

Most of us have experienced a hunch that proved to be correct or had a dream that played out. This is normal and not exceptional, but if you are in the minority and feel you have never had a precognitive experience, a daily course of meditation could very well do the trick.

Meditation can stimulate the parts of your brain associated with empathy, intuition, and creativity—all doors to unlocking your innate precognitive potential. That's why just a few minutes of daily meditation (or, if you struggle with meditation, some calm alone time to simply clear your mind and notice your thoughts but not interact with them) is highly recommended for every budding precognitive.

Let Your Body Talk

Although precognition is most likely to occur in the dream state, it can happen when you are awake as well. When it does happen, precognitive signals tend to be experienced first in your body, most especially in your gut and your heart rate.

The term used for physical foreshadowing is *presentiment*. Notice what your gut and your heart tell you immediately upon waking and throughout the day, especially when you meet someone new or visit a place for the first time. Let your body do the sensing.

Daily and Consistent Practice

Keep repeating the precognition-boosting techniques in this chapter every day until they feel entirely natural.

A positive sign that you are heading in the right direction with your precognition training is how much you enjoy or look forward to doing these exercises and how excited they make you feel about your own precognition. Notice how the shift in perspective they offer raises your vibration and reminds you that whatever is happening in your life right now, you always can rise above it, see the bigger picture, and transcend time.

Everything, Everywhere, All at Once

Never lose sight of the fact that precognitive experiences and dreams happen, and when they do, they make a nonsense of the traditionally accepted concept that time is linear. They suggest that your past, present, and future might just be happening all at once and there is a part of you that is infinite.

Here's another instantly vibration-raising thought for you to consider. It's well known among psychologists that if people feel they are being observed, they instinctively perform better. This phenomenon is known as the "observer effect." Well, you are being watched all the time. Your future self is here watching you, meaning it really is always the right time to go ahead and impress yourself!

Your future self is already way ahead of you and eagerly absorbing this new insight. You may as well read on now and catch up with yourself ahead of time. Now that you have begun your future-forward life in earnest, it's the perfect time to answer to some frequently asked questions that may well be running through your mind.

FAQ

Q: Should I know what the future holds?

A: Your ability to dream or sense a potential future carries great responsibility. The power of suggestion is strong. When you start developing your precognition, it is vital that you do so with feelings of unconditional love for yourself and others and make a promise with your future self to share and act on only the empowering information it sends to you.

Should you sense something potentially negative coming for yourself, you now can mend your future, choose a different mindset or approach, and avoid a potentially toxic scenario.

Things can get more complicated when you sense something negative in the future for others. My advice would be to share your concerns if you can to the person or people involved, but do so with a lightness of spirit and a reminder that this is a probability you sense ahead for them. The direction of another person's future is always their choice. Then let it go.

If you can't share your precognition or you feel anxious about doing so, be sure to write it down with a time and date stamp so you have proof should anything play out in the future. This proof will perhaps give you confidence to reach out to others, if need be, in the future.

Q: Can anyone dream or sense their future?

A: Yes, but rather like learning to play the piano, those who practise their scales daily are more likely to excel.

Q: Are dreams literal or symbolic in their predictive potential, and how can you tell the difference?

A: Your dreams can be both literal and symbolic. But literal dreams—where the meaning requires no decoding—are exceedingly rare. Most of your dreams should be interpreted symbolically rather than literally, in that it is the personal associations you make with your dream symbols/scenarios that are predictive and not the symbols themselves.

Given most dreams are symbolic, the dream directory in part 2 will help you interpret their symbolic meanings from a precognitive perspective. However, as dreams can on rare occasion be literal, it is always worth ruling out any literal interpretation. This is often easily done. For example, if your teeth fall out in your dream, have you been to the dentist for a checkup recently? If you are still anxious about whether an accident-themed dream, for instance, is literal, there's no harm in doing personal safety checks or reaching out to people you dreamt about to ask if they are okay. Then let it go, and if it does unfortunately play out, it is not your fault.

The only surefire way to know if a dream is speaking to you literally is if the dream plays out in waking life. Should that happen, see if you can detect any patterns or signs that might help you determine the next time if a dream is literal rather than symbolic.

Literal dreams often feel uber-realistic, and there is likely to be a clear storyline, or a beginning, middle, and end. Symbolic dreams tend to have a fragmented, incoherent feel, rather like a music video. You typically find yourself right in the middle of the action, with no awareness of how you got there, and the storyline (if there is one) is all over the place. Curiously, dreams of departed loved ones often have this uber-realistic, linear narrative feel, too.

Just because you dream something does not mean it will happen. It just means that, with your current mindset, this is the potential future situation, event, or emotional response you are attracting. If you don't feel happy about that future, now is your opportunity to reset by changing your mindset and approach.

In some rare cases your precognitive dreams can be literal rather than symbolic. You can only find out if this is the case in hindsight, so here is another reason to faithfully record all of your dreams. Should you recognise a dream that was more literal than symbolic in its depiction of your future, study everything about it and what you were doing in the days before you dreamt it to see if you can detect a pattern.

Q: Is precognition the same as intuition?

A: Intuition is your gut instinct, your inner voice. It is "thinking without thinking." Intuition is the more socially acceptable term for inexplicably knowing or sensing the future. It draws on your unconscious stored knowledge and, unlike precognition, can sometimes, but not always, be explained rationally. However, the similarities between intuition and precognition are super strong. Precognition and intuition are both unconscious or spontaneous insight informed, but not entirely made, by your rational mind. In my humble opinion, intuition is precognition, or at the very least, a surefire precursor or path to precognition.

Q: What is the difference between a premonition and precognition?

A: *Precognition* is using an alternative sense (your sixth sense) to tap into the future. It encapsulates all of the different ways you can know the future, such as precognitive dreams, thoughts, visions, sensations, feelings, and so on, but it does this without drawing on information from your five senses, memory, or logic.

Premonition is the term used to describe just one way of knowing the future, via a specific feeling, which means that precognition is the umbrella term that includes premonition.

Q: Are remote viewing and telepathy the same as precognition?

A: *Remote viewing* is the ability to accurately visualise a location or target that you have never seen or experienced before or been given any information about. *Telepathy*, or mind reading, is the ability to empathise so much with a person that you literally know what they are thinking and feeling as they are thinking and feeling it.

Both remote viewing and telepathy are therefore the ability to inexplicably see or sense something in the present moment. They spill over into precognition only if whatever is glimpsed or sensed is unknown or has not occurred yet and is then proved to be accurate at a future date.

Q: Can I consciously control my precognition?

A: Most precognitions happen randomly in your dreams and in waking life. In other words, they tend to happen when they want to happen. There are things you can do to induce precognitive dreams and hunches (and this book offers training techniques for that), and you can train your precognition to make it more likely to happen and to help you notice when it happens, but you can't operate it like an on-off switch, because its natural state is to be spontaneous and unpredictable. Like the ocean, you can learn how to sail and navigate it, but you can never fully control it.

Q: Why does the future I accurately sense or dream about often concern trivial or insignificant things?

A: It's true that many of the dreams you have that predict future events will foreshadow things that on the surface appear relatively trivial. This is especially the case when you initially start training your precognition. For example, you may dream about a colleague at work wearing a distinctive pink scarf you have never seen them wear before. The following day they are wearing a scarf similar to the one you saw in your dream!

These kinds of precognitions can feel like a waste of time, but the deeper you go with precognition, the more you will understand that no sensing about your future, however trivial, is ever a waste of time. Your dreaming mind is simply showing you that you can see your future in a way that is not going to alarm you. It is drawing your attention to the present moment being one of great significance, even if you don't think it is.

If you do experience a "trivial" precognition, whether as a waking hunch coming true or a dream playing out in waking life, seize the moment to reflect on your current mindset. You may not understand why, but your precognition is surfacing at this moment in time for a reason. It is a power point, an opportunity to change your present reality and the future you are busy attracting.

Q: Why can't I recall my dreams?

A: Poor dream recall happens to us all from time to time. For advice on how to reactivate your dream recall muscle, see page 73.

Q: I am diligently writing down my dreams but not making any progress. What am I doing wrong if everyone is precognitive?

A: If you are not having any precognitive dreams, thoughts, or feelings, this is unusual. Your mind must work hard to block its natural predictive tendency. If you have given the daily precognition-boosting action plan on page 12 in this chapter at least three weeks, paid special attention to the advice about meditation in chapter 3 on page 45, and tried the additional techniques listed at the end of each chapter, then it's possible your mind is saying no for a good reason. There may be things stored in your subconscious that right now may be too challenging or overwhelming for you to process, and you may need to switch off totally and come back to your training in a few months. Or, if you still want to train your precognition, you may need to do so with the assistance of a trusted therapist or mental health professional.

Typically, though, once you really start to believe in your inner precognitive, you may end up with the opposite problem: dream-overcrowding. An overwhelming number of random images and sensations surfacing in your awareness when you are awake may make it tough for you to distinguish between negative thinking and wishful thinking, which dovetails neatly into the next question.

Q: How can I tell the difference between negative thinking and precognition?

A: Both anxiety and wish fulfilment dreams leave you in a rich emotional state upon awakening, thinking things such as "OMG, I actually flew!" or "I have lost my job." One potential marker to help you determine whether a dream is precognitive is that your emotional response upon waking will be more muted, almost neutral. It will feel like a *fait accompli*, like what you dreamt about has already happened.[3] For instance, you wake up thinking "I know I won't get the job today" and then you get the call you just knew was coming.

It's the same with precognitive dreams that showcase positive outcomes for you. You will not have a shadow of doubt that something great is coming your way.

Now that you know precognitions happen, you should always start with the assumption that your flash forward could potentially be true. But you also need to know how to internally differentiate genuine precognition from negative self-talk and bias.

The way to do that is to practise the techniques in this book daily and patiently and accurately record your results. You need to study your results, both the successes and the failures, like a scientist and become the scientist of your own precognition. And should you wake with a feeling of calm knowing or inner certainty, pay close attention, as your dreaming mind may—and I stress *may*—have sent you a literal precognition.

Chances are you will notice a pattern when your future thinking is proved correct or incorrect. For example, in addition to an inexplicable inner certainty, you may notice that precognitive thinking tends to be specific and one-track or focused around one event, goal, mindset, or experience, whereas anxiety tends to jump wildly and incoherently from one different and unconnected or unrelated scenario to another.

You may also find that precognitive experiences motivate you to take some kind of positive action, to do something about it. You don't feel helpless or passive or want to remain inactive anymore. And precognition feels calmer, less wordy and more supportive. It motivates and inspires you,

---

3. Stowell, "Precognitive Dreams: A Phenomenological Study."

whereas negativity is highly self-critical chatter rattling around in your head. Precognition raises your vibration, while negative thinking drains you. But although these are likely indicators of precognition, you still need to work out how precognition speaks to you.

Note: If you have many negative precognitions, please seek immediate advice from your doctor or a trained counsellor or therapist.

Q: How can I tell the difference between wishful thinking and precognition?

A: If the precognition comes true, it's the real deal. Before that, it is always best to treat any kind of future forward as a probability that could be right but could also be wrong. So use your common sense and always do your own research if you need to make important decisions. Don't rely on your precognition alone, especially at this early stage in your awareness of it.

One characteristic of positive premonitions that turn out to be true is that they don't tend to be consciously induced. In other words, they appear out of nowhere and with strong conviction. You don't know how or even why you know—you just *know*.

Q: Can you use your precognition to win the lottery or predict the stock market?

A: I've lost count of the number of times I've been asked this question, and the short answer is yes, you can.

In 2022 I interviewed an inspiring filmmaker/journalist named Timothy Schultz on my *White Shores* podcast. In 1999, at age twenty one, he became the youngest-ever winner of the Powerball lottery in the US, winning around 28 million dollars. He got in touch with me after reading *The Premonition Code,* a 2017 title I coauthored with neuroscientist and leading presentiment researcher Dr. Julia Mossbridge. He told me that before he won the Powerball, he had a vivid and realistic dream that he would win it. That dream played out precisely, and you can listen to his remarkable true story on my White Shores podcast[4] or his popular *Lottery, Dreams and Fortune* podcast on YouTube.[5]

The long answer is that if you have a precognitive hunch that you are going to win the lottery, follow it through and buy your ticket if you can, but please don't count on it and remind yourself that it is a probability, not an actuality. The same applies if you have a lottery-winning dream, although lottery-winning dreams are exceedingly rare.

It sounds clichéd, but the goal of your precognition training and dreaming is your inner rather than outer wealth. The more you look within to find answers, the more you will evolve into a wiser and kinder version of yourself. Happiness gained from the outside is fragile and fleeting. There is no point gaining the world and losing your soul.

This search for inner answers is continuous and has no destination, but it is a search that is never tiresome, because along the way, you open your mind to new possibilities and learn so much of value about yourself, others, and the world. Curiosity drives you forward and reminds you what a thrilling adventure your life is.

As far as the stock market is concerned, I believe that many covert precognitive dreamers work there. They may not be aware that they are using their precognitive skills, but ask any successful trader and they will talk about following logic but also an inexplicable gut instinct—precognition by another name. Indeed, any career that requires predictive or forecasting skills or intuitive decision-making, such as healthcare professionals, may well be using premonition in plain sight. I know for a fact that many highly successful global businesses, as well as detective organisations, hire undercover psychics and consider their predictions.

Q: Is precognition the same as déjà vu?

A: *Déjà vu* ("already seen") is the feeling of having already lived an event or experience. *Déjà rêvé* ("already dreamed") is seeing an event or experience in the dream state and then noticing when that event or experience happens in your waking life.

---

4. Cheung, "Lottery Dreams and Your Fortune with Powerball Winner, Timothy Schulz."

5. Schultz, *Lottery, Dreams and Fortune.*

It is possible that déjà feelings have been ignited by memories of past events surfacing because they feel so much like an event occurring in the present. Precognition, however, carries with it a feeling of something wildly unexpected and unknown rather than something familiar. Having said that, I believe that spontaneous déjà feelings are typically highly precognitive.

Q: Is precognition the same as synchronicity?

A: There is a school of thought that believes that *synchronicity*, the spiritual term for meaningful coincidence, when unrelated events or circumstances inexplicably concur at just the right moment, is precognition. For example, you think about a person and then they call out of the blue. It is as if you knew or had a predictive hunch that they would call. And there is that goose-bump, synchronistic feeling when you realise you have pre-experienced an event or circumstance in a dream.

It could also be argued that your subconscious, the place where all of your dreams and intuitions originate, is entirely precognitive. To take another big leap from here, all other psychic abilities, such as telepathy, could also be described as precognitive.

Q: What is the future of precognition research?

A: Precognition is establishing itself in scientific circles as worthy of investigation, but the number of scientists currently studying it remains small. The important thing, though, is that it is being studied and is no longer immediately dismissed as pseudoscience or woo-woo.

Some scientists are investigating precognition for its ability to potentially predict global events. They do this using international dream databases. Another line of inquiry is to test and identify people who consistently score high in precognitive experiments and then investigate their personality traits and brain activity when they're dreaming or doing controlled precognition tests.

I dream of a day when precognitive research and training earns its rightful place in mainstream neuroscience, physiology, psychology, physics, counselling, education, and healthcare. I dream of this because I firmly believe that the more you develop your precognition, the more you connect calmly and lovingly to your own inner world, the place where all creativity, meaning, and inner strength are found.

Your ability to somehow sense the unknown doesn't just aid your own evolution, but also helps you connect with greater empathy to others—because precognition and compassion, a desire to help and heal both yourself and others, go hand in hand.

Chapter 2

A Natural-Born Precognitive

Your brain is a predictive force.

The founder of modern neuroscience, Santiago Ramón y Cajal (1852–1934), once described the countless neuronal firings in your brain that enable you to think and dream as "mysterious butterflies of the soul."[6]

Despite extensive research, close to a century later the infinite mystery surrounding the workings of the human brain lingers on. But one clarifying development is that cognitive scientists are increasingly drawn to the theory that those mysterious butterflies, which create your perception of your waking and your dreaming world, are inherently predictive. Much of your reality is determined by your mindset, demonstrating the transformative power of perspective. The scientific term for all this is predictive coding, or predictive processing.[7]

In a nutshell, your brain is constantly making and then updating predictions about what your future might hold. It draws on your past expectations and beliefs and combines them with incoming sensory signals and, in the process, shapes itself into a finely tuned prediction machine.

Sensing your future isn't going against the linear code. It is a perfectly natural process for your brain, so natural that you aren't even consciously

6. Santiago Ramón y Cajal, in his autobiography, *Recollections of My Life*.

7. Ficco et al., "Disentangling Predictive Processing in the Brain."

aware that it is happening all the time. Contrary to what you may think, precognition is going with your neural flow, not against it. It is how your brain wants you to interact with and perceive the world.

Mindfulness encourages us to believe that the only reality to fully savour is the present moment. While your power is in your present and the choices you make there, this should not mean that dreaming about your tomorrow is self-limiting. Far from it. You can fully appreciate the power of your now and at the same time dream about future possibilities spiraling from your present.

The truth is that your incredible brain simply cannot be limited or constrained to experiencing just the present. It is far more infinite, deep, and expansive than that. Reflecting on tomorrow, on what might be, what if, is the source of all creativity. It is also your natural brain state. All brains are wired predictively, not just those of the gifted few.

I hope this will give you renewed confidence in your own predictive potential and underline to you that your perspective doesn't just create your present experience but is also constantly creating and signposting your future.

Episodic Future Thinking

Here's another gift from the world of science that I hope will help you look ahead of your time with greater assurance.

Consciously tuning into your brain's natural ability to sense your future is terrific news for your brain health. Research suggests that your brain absolutely loves it when you free yourself from your addiction to linear time and simply allow it to do what it naturally wants to do all the time: anticipate and dream up your future.[8]

Future thinking lights up areas of your brain that are not used when you remember the past or ponder the present. According to fMRI studies, in scans that reveal patterns of brain activity, imagining your future involves increased activity and connectivity in eleven or more different

8. Schacter, Benoit, and Szpunar, "Episodic Future Thinking."

brain regions. By comparison, remembering your past or reflecting on your present ignites just six of the same brain regions.[9]

Every time you mentally time travel into your future, you wake up additional regions of your brain. The academic term for mental time travel into your future, the ability to pre-experience it in your mind, is EFT, or episodic future thinking.

EFT is your innate ability to mentally time travel and pre-experience or visualise your future in advance when you are awake. It is your vivid and realistic future imagination, the world of tomorrow that you already see in your mind's eye.

EFT forces your brain to create something in your mind's eye that you haven't yet experienced but could. It must conjure up possibilities and fill in the blanks. EFT isn't just terrific brain training; it can change your life for the better.

EFT helps you decide whether the future you imagined is one you want to experience. Pre-feelings will automatically kick in when you consciously predict your future. If your imagined future feels unpleasant, you will instinctively move to make changes in your present to ensure it doesn't manifest.

But once your brain has visualised or described to you a future that excites you, it naturally wants to keep the positive momentum going and starts to do what scientists call *opportunity detection*. As soon as an empowering future memory is created, your predictive brain will actively search for ways to help you prepare for and achieve your future goals.

Note: Visualisation is a technique where you consciously create mental pictures in your mind and bring those mental pictures alive by bringing your physical senses of sight, touch, taste, smell, and hearing into it as much as possible. However, you may be someone (like me) whose mind often goes blank when asked to form mental pictures. This is a condition called *aphantasia*, and it is more common than you may think. The good news is it doesn't inhibit your ability to see and recall images in your dreams, and there are ways around it when you are awake. Instead of forming mental pictures, you can create word pictures. Write it down. Describe

9. Stawarczyk and D'Argembeau, "Neural Correlates of Personal Goal Processing during Episodic Future Thinking and Mind-Wandering."

the future vision to yourself like an art critic discussing a painting, or a literary critic analysing a book, or a film critic reviewing a movie.

Be Ready for Your Future

Precognition is most likely to strike spontaneously when you are dreaming, because when you are dreaming, you transcend linear time. So you may be wondering why I am encouraging you here to start consciously predicting your future, EFT style, when you are awake. I'm doing so because I want to drill down on the fact that science is proving that your brain has a future-forward bias, and sensing your future is not just good for your mental well-being, but is the way your brain wants to flow.

EFT should not feel dissonant. It should feel totally natural and every day for you. You just need to relax, suspend your disbelief, and let your future thoughts guide and energise you.

Repeatedly cultivating a futuristic mindset during the day will filter through and empower your dreams to reveal ever clearer potential futures to you. Your waking perspective influences your dreams, as your waking life and dream life are intimately connected. Of course they are. You don't stop being the same person when you fall asleep and dream. You just enter a different state of consciousness where there is no time, no logic, no reason, just infinite intuition and creativity.

A bonus is that EFT is also an instant mood booster. In recent years, thousands of peer-reviewed studies on EFT have been published.[10] Here's a speedy roundup of their promising conclusions.

People who regularly engage in EFT are more likely to feel motivated, to self-direct their lives, and are also less likely to feel depressed and anxious. This is because when you practise EFT, you play an active part in creating the future you want, in contrast to people who suffer from depression and find it hard to mentally time travel into the future. Their minds are filled with uncertainty, making it hard for them to imagine a future distinct from their current reality. For those struggling with anxiety, the obstacle is different. Their minds are hyper-focused on vivid negative possibilities for the future. They miss a crucial element of effective EFT train-

10. Atance and O'Neill, "Episodic Future Thinking."

ing, which emphasises the power of envisioning a positive future and how cultivating a sense of optimism energises and sharpens their ability to spot new opportunities.

The growing body of evidence linking EFT to mental and emotional well-being could result in EFT techniques being used to treat depression, anxiety, and cognitive decline. People who can vividly imagine their future selves thriving are more likely to make a long-term investment in themselves and take small but vital healthy steps each day in the direction of their dream future. You don't even need to be specific in your future dreams. Imagining anything positive about your future realistically and vividly primes you to do things today to increase the likelihood of a happier future.

Last but by no means least, there is a natural bond between EFT and creativity. The more you practise EFT, the more imaginative and therefore creative and visionary you are going to feel and be.

As the White Queen says to Alice in Lewis Carroll's *Alice's Adventures in Wonderland*, it really is a poor sort of memory that only works backwards. Scans show that when your brain is visualising the future, it is far more alert and active than when it is remembering the past or experiencing the present. In short, consciously thinking ahead of time is great news for your brain health. And the more you do it during the day, the more you prime your dreams to reveal the future ever more clearly at night.

Now that you know what EFT is—and how your waking brain is predisposed to it and how good it is for boosting your brain health, motivation, mood, creativity, and visionary dream potential—I hope that from this moment on you will fully nurture your EFT skills every day. Let go of resistance. Suspend doubt and indulge in a spot of futuristic daydreaming or mind wandering for a few moments each day. Treat yourself. You are worth it.

Predict Away

At some point each day, spend just a minute answering in a notebook or file or in your mind's eye the following questions about how you will wake up the next morning.

Answer these questions briefly. Don't overthink; just intuitively write down what first comes to mind and bring it alive in your imagination.

Ponder how you feel and what you smell, hear, and sense in this mini mental time-travel exercise. See and pre-experience your tomorrow morning as clearly as possible in your mind's eye, as if it were happening right now.

If visualisation (forming mental pictures in your mind) doesn't come easy to you, talk to yourself about your tomorrow instead. Describe out loud or silently in your mind exactly how you will wake up. You can also write it down.

- What room or space do you wake up in?
- What wakes you up?
- Do you wake up naturally?
- What is the exact-to-the-minute time at which you wake up?
- Is it light or dark outside?
- What is the weather like?
- What are you wearing?
- What mood are you in?
- What dreams bubble to the surface?

Repeat this exercise every morning and keep a record of how accurate your predictions are. Over time, you will surprise yourself.

Become a Frequent Time Traveller

Once you are comfortable practicing the EFT exercise to predict how you will wake up the next day, try predicting how you will wake up one week ahead to really give your brain a visionary injection. Or better still, try for one month ahead, and from there, take a giant leap of optimistic faith in your future and EFT for one year or even five or ten years ahead. When you do this exercise, you might just find that you switch from a first-person perspective when visualising your near future to a third-person perspective when the future is more distant. And with that observational third-person perspective comes a dose of loving empathy for yourself and others, according to research.[11] It seems that when we focus on the near

11. Macrae et al., "Turning I into Me: Imagining Your Future Self."

future, we are more inside our own head, but when the forecast is long term, we become more open-minded and less ego-identified.

Get into the daily routine of creating living and breathing memories of your future. Make it a future you feel optimistic and happy about and one you love to revisit repeatedly in your daydreams.

Be as vivid and realistic in your future visualisation as possible. This won't happen every time, but your aim is to feel that you are pre-experiencing the event. When you recall your past, you can experience it and see yourself there, so do the same with your future. When you are in that imagined future and it is a future you love, accept it as real in your mind's eye. Fully experience that imagined future with all of your senses and believe completely in it. Pre-live it as if it were already happening.

Greet Your Future Self

Record a short voice message for your tomorrow self on your phone or a recording device, say around thirty seconds to a minute long. Make sure the message is unconditionally loving and positive. Then the next day, be sure to listen to that message from your past self.

This simple exercise, if repeated daily for several weeks, has been proven to boost well-being. It is also great for helping you connect with unconditional love to your future self, or the part of you that can mentally time travel. Always speak with kindness, respect, and positivity to your future self. Indeed, the more lovingly you hold onto your perception of your future self, the more vivid your ability to see your future will be. Promising research has shown there is a link between unconditional love for yourself and precognitive dreaming.[12]

Here is yet another reminder that when you do this exercise every day, make sure you speak to your future self with unconditional love. Double down on the positivity. Become a magnet for the energy you want to see in your future.

Love and time are both mysterious, unseen forces, and because of their similarity, they are at their most potent and transformative when you value

12. Mossbridge, Cameron, and Boccuzzi, "State, Trait, and Target Parameters Associated with Accuracy in Two Online Tests of Precognitive Remote Viewing."

their interconnection. Recording unconditionally loving messages for your future self can help you harness the infinite potential and power of both. To help you learn how to use unconditional love to connect with yourself over time, you may want to experiment with the free Time Machine app (https://www.timemachine.love).

Precognition Time

EFT sounds very much like precognition, and practising EFT techniques will almost certainly boost your precognition and, most important of all, help you feel comfortable sensing what is to come, but there is a subtle difference between the two.

EFT flows with your brain's natural predictive state and draws inspiration from your memory and imagination as well as your five physical senses. EFT is also something you consciously direct or choose to do.

Precognition, however, is perhaps the most mysterious brain butterfly of all. It is the largely unconscious ability to know or be influenced by information about the future without drawing on information from your memory, sensory information gathered by your five senses (sight, sound, taste, smell, texture), or information deduced from logic or even conjured up by your imagination. Precognition is sometimes described as an inner voice, a future knowledge, and often it happens spontaneously in your dreams and waking hunches. In lab tests for precognition, experiments ensure that all alternative explanations, including chance, are excluded. Scores must be above chance over time for scientists to confirm the explanation as precognitive.

Phrases such as "I just knew" or "I trusted my gut" and terms such as sixth sense, hunch, or intuition are typically used to describe precognition. In essence, precognition is knowledge of the future that is informed but not made by your rational mind. It is just knowing something will happen without knowing why you know it.

The reason precognition is most likely to happen first in your dreams is because when you are dreaming, your conscious mind is asleep and can't throw up logical barriers to receiving information from your future. In dreams, your intuition and creativity reign supreme and are no longer restrained by the chains of reason and addiction to linear time. Everything is possible, and the only things missing are logic and reason. You connect to the deep mystery of your inner space, your infinite essence or soul, where time is irrelevant and past, present, and future collide.

This sounds deep, but there is a growing body of visionary science behind it.[13] Indeed, precognition may well be the place where science and spirit can happily converge. If you would like a little more insight into the very real science of precognition, you can find more of my reflections in Appendix: The Science of Precognition.

Stress-Free

Yes, the serious scientific research proving you are a precognitive being is happening, but another really helpful thing for you to know right now is that this research also suggests that the greatest enemy of precognition is anxiety.[14] Stress kills intuition and can lead to poor decision-making. It stops precognition in its tracks, because when you feel anxious, this instantly short-circuits your brain's unconscious predictive preference.

Precognition and stress, like love and fear, cannot coexist. Bear this in mind moving forward when practising your precognition-boosting action plan. Make stress management and finding inner calm a top priority. This is yet another reason why precognition is more likely to occur in the dream state. Not only is disbelief suspended when you dream, but so is the stress response.[15] During the REM (rapid eye movement) stage of sleep, when most dreaming occurs, your brain seems to enter a unique state. There is an absence of the flight-or-fight hormone noradrenaline, which is present during the other non-REM sleep stages as well as during waking hours.

Noradrenaline is like your body's adrenaline. It is a chemical that stimulates stress and anxiety. With this hormone absent and with the limbic (emotional and creative) parts of your brain active, your dreaming mind is free to relive and process memories in a uniquely stress-free environment.

---

13. Bem, Tressoldi, Rabeyron, and Duggan, "Feeling the Future: A Meta-Analysis of 90 Experiments on the Anomalous Anticipation of Random Future Events."
14. Remmers and Zander, "Why You Don't See the Forest for the Trees When You Are Anxious: Anxiety Impairs Intuitive Decision-Making."
15. Walker, *Why We Sleep: The New Science of Sleep and Dreams.*

This allows your brain to process trauma and safely role-play possibilities and distressing scenarios without any accompanying emotional distress.

In the next chapter, I will cover more about the importance of easing anxiety to boost your precognition, the key role that self-love and self-belief play in training your precognition, and simple techniques to help you get there faster.

Your Clear and Present Case for Precognition

Hopefully what you have read so far will have set the precognitive scene for you. You will have seen that scientists are researching it actively and that meta-analysis results (data examined from numerous studies) show that precognitive experiences happen, and when the circumstances are right, your future really can be glimpsed in your dreams and waking hunches. However, despite the data looking promising and consistently being backed up by anecdotal reports, for many people the biggest stumbling block, apart from not yet having experienced precognition for themselves, is their ingrained belief that precognition can't be possible because time is linear.

Modern physics is more comfortable than you might think with time potentially being nonlinear. Check out the recommended resources section if you want to dig deeper and follow the research, as you will find some of my further reflections there as well as key studies and recommended additional reading.[16] Bear in mind, though, that as mind-opening as modern physics is, by far the best way to convince yourself that precognition is possible is to harvest your own personal experience. The more you experience precognition for yourself, the easier it will be for you to free yourself from conditioning to linear time and the disbelief roadblock that can set up.

If you consistently practice the techniques in this book, I predict that however sceptical you are, you will soon have a clear precognitive dream experience to call your own. Above everything else, this and this alone will convince you that you are a precognitive being.

---

16. See *The Premonition Code*, a book I wrote with Julia Mossbridge. See also the recommended resources section in the back of the book.

Every person who wakes up to the reality that their future really can be glimpsed becomes a bright light for others when all other lights go out. Their wise foresight inspires others to look within, understand their own precognitive instincts, and grow towards their best possible future selves.

Precognition Happens

From now on, operate calmly from the assumption that precognition happens within you 24/7. It happens in your dreams every night and is happening right now in your waking life. Noticing, trusting, and training it every day will support your happiness and personal growth.

The journey into your future begins not in the science lab or a physics equation but from the inside out. It begins with that aha moment when a dream or hunch really does come true and you no longer need convincing that your future self is alive within you and doing what it can to reassure you that your best is always yet to come. You can't explain why yet, but you just know the future is yours to create.

Supplemental Precognition-Boosting Techniques

In addition to your precognition-boosting action plan set out in chapter 1 on page 12 and the daily EFT exercises in this chapter, here are some supplemental exercises well worth doing to complement your program.

Daily Micro Preparation

Your future is built on your history, the lessons you learned from your experiences in the past. So get curious and experiment doing new things each day, because today is tomorrow's past. Give your future the inspiration it needs to pull you forward. Take a minute or two today to learn about or try something you've never done before. This can be as simple as taking a different route to work, eating a new dish, or listening to music you wouldn't normally choose.

Shift your perspective and start to think of your life as continuous learning and information gathering for your future self. Ensure that your precognitive brain has plenty of insight to draw upon when looking ahead to your future in both your waking life and your dreams.

Back to Front

Sometimes it's hard to imagine that your life can change. If this is the case for you, then this backwards-facing exercise might unblock your ability to mentally time travel.

To believe change is possible in your future, it can help to recall how much change has already happened in your life. Just as your mind can reach into your future and create a memory there, you can also mentally time travel into your past.

Go back mentally in time now to the person you were around five years ago from today. Picture yourself or describe yourself. What were you doing? What were you wearing? How were you feeling? What were your hopes and fears?

What would surprise your five-years-ago self about the person you are today? Think on it. Have you surprised yourself yet? If not, why not? Make sure that five years from now, your future self is pleasantly surprised by the positive changes you have made.

Memory Games

Though it hasn't been proven yet, precognition research does strongly appear to suggest that people who do well in controlled precognition tests tend to have detailed short-term memories. This makes sense because remembering details of your dreams upon waking is key, so consider how accurate your short-term memory currently is.

There are plenty of simple and free memory tests online, but here's one you can do every day to see how you improve. Listed below are twenty unrelated words. Study them for around forty seconds, then set this book aside and write down as many words as you can remember.

Nine	Plug	Sword	Table	Apple
Book	Ring	Cry	Fire	Navy
Bird	Rock	Clock	Lamp	Desk
Ball	Horse	Baby	Take	Phone
Pen				

How many words did you recall? Don't be surprised if you only remember around three to seven words, as that is what most people will recall. But if you do this exercise each day and choose twenty new words, because you are testing your short-term memory here, not your long-term memory, you will find that your short-term memory improves. Make sure the twenty new words you choose each day are unconnected (for example, choose only one and not two animals or colours, etc.) and keep practising until you get closer and closer to twenty new words correctly recalled. If you ever hit close to the mark of twenty words recalled, congratulations! Keep that short-term recall consistent and extend your next memory list to twenty-five words and so on.

Your predictive brain will thank you for your effort because it is always trying to notice details that are significant for your future. But as these details are often subtle, not only do you often fail to notice them, but even if you do notice them, the chances are high that you will fail to recall them! With a little daily short-term memory training, you can change all that.

Take Note

Don't forget the vital step for all precognitive dreamers in training, which is returning to those predictions when the date you predicted comes around to see how accurate you were. When you notice that you are correct, please take a moment to seriously congratulate yourself. Just don't beat yourself up when you are not correct or have not predicted correctly.

Scientists learn more from their failures than their successes and consider failures to be stepping stones to creating the formula for success. Remember that the act of observing and accurately reporting your own precognitive data—both the hits and the misses—will transform you into a citizen scientist researching the reality of precognition. Imagine if Thomas Edison (1847–1941), who famously took over 1,000 attempts to invent the light bulb, had given up on the 200th attempt or even the 999th attempt! Combine your recordkeeping with your daily precognition training and over time you will prove to yourself (and all those willing to listen) that you are a precognitive being.

Keep Going

When you create a future memory, remember it is right out there now. It has been born and needs to be nurtured with lashings of love if it is to survive. You have birthed it into existence, but it isn't yet fully grown or set in stone, and you, being the creator, can revisit it at any time to add or modify it as you wish.

You are the architect of your future. What you are looking forward to has already been born and is real within your mind, heart, and soul. You are getting way ahead of yourself, and that isn't self-centred or escapist. It's a selfless, courageous, and truly visionary way to experience your life.

Chapter 3
Precognitive Living

It's time now to explore what is known about the most likely personality traits of highly precognitive people. Understanding where you fit in on the precognitive personality scale is revealing, because it can help you find the optimal way to nurture your natural-born precognition.

The Norm, Not the Exception

Sensing things beyond time and the material realm is far more common than you may think. Indeed, many researchers and scientists in this area are concluding that precognitive experiences are the norm and not the exception.[17] Our sixth sense is encoded in our DNA.[18] Also encoded in our DNA is an instinct that we are part of something greater than ourselves.[19]

In ancient times when we were at the mercy of super predators, our lives depended on our innate sixth sense, but the march of industrialisation, technology, and rationalism has made us forget how to use it. We place our physical senses on a pedestal, as if they create our experience of life, but this could not be further from the truth. We create the world

---

17. Travers, "New Psychological Research Says Paranormal Experiences Are the Norm, Not the Exception."
18. Murphy and Prentice, "Humans Have a 'Sixth Sense,' and It's Actually Vital to Our Health."
19. Hamer, *The God Gene: How Faith Is Hardwired into Our Genes.*

through our invisible senses. Precognition is an instinct within everyone, and we all can remember and activate it. The problem is the barrier of doubt and fear that has built up over the centuries and made us mistrust it and therefore ourselves.

What You Believe

Research strongly indicates that those who believe precognition is real are far more likely to have accurate precognitions than those who doubt it.[20]

The clear message here is that you dramatically increase your chances of having precognitive experiences if you believe in precognition, or at the very least keep your mind open to the possibility.

Precognitive Personality Characteristics

Although belief in precognition is by far the most dominant characteristic of people who have accurate precognitions, certain other characteristics have come to the fore in studies.[21] I'll share them here because they are intriguing, but do bear in mind that the association is slight. They are just potential indicators from small rather than large-scale studies and are by no means written in stone.

There seems to be no bias when it comes to gender differences and precognitive accuracy, although some preliminary data suggests that hormonal changes in women may impact their precognitive performance.[22]

One leading characteristic to emerge is an adventurous approach to life, which means being open to new experiences: a seeker of knowledge who believes change, rather than routine, is the spice of life.

There could be a connection between accurate precognition and extraversion, assertiveness, and sociability. Rest assured, though, if you are (like me) more of an introvert who values your quiet, that there really is not

20. Hitchman and Roe, "A Re-examination of Nonintentional Precognition with Openness to Experience, Creativity, Psi Beliefs, and Luck Beliefs as Predictors of Success"; Luke, Delanoy, and Sherwood, "Psi May Look Like Luck: Perceived Luckiness and Beliefs about Luck in Relation to Precognition"; and Rattet and Bursik, "Investigating the Personality Correlates of Paranormal Belief and Precognitive Experience."

21. Honorton, Ferrari, and Bem, "Extraversion and ESP Performance."

22. Mossbridge and Bem, "Reproductive Hormonal Status as a Predictor of Precognition."

enough evidence yet from research to suggest a one-size-fits-all precognitive personality type.

Tentative research suggests a link between sixth sense and being born into a spiritually/religiously inclined family as well as childhood trauma, autoimmune disorders, and being left-handed.[23]

There is a demonstrable link between unconditional love for yourself and precognitive experiences in dreams and waking life.[24] In other words, self-compassion and self-respect are key in both your precognitive dreamwork and your life.

Over the decades that I have been collating true life stories about precognitive experiences, I have noticed that many people who contact me fall squarely in the introvert category. I have also noticed, in my non-scientific analysis of data sent to me, that many of these individuals are empathetic, compassionate, and creative people who would probably score high on the Highly Sensitive Person Scale, a scale that psychologists use to identify people with highly sensitive traits, namely empathy, intuition, and creativity.

Sensitive Souls

According to psychologists, around 20 percent of people identify with highly sensitive personality traits.[25] They live their lives constantly alert to what they can't see or explain rationally but that they sense empathetically and intuitively, a.k.a. precognitively.

This doesn't mean the remaining 80 percent are a lost cause. It just means there is a spectrum of sensitivity. Even those labelled insensitive experience times in their lives when their innate sensitivity is activated, typically by acute stress or loss.

Sensitive personality traits have likely evolved and remained innate because they are crucial for survival, with intuition helping us be alert to potential threats and empathy encouraging us to take care of each other.

---

23. Beischel, "Mediumship Research at the Windbridge Research Center by Director of Research, Julie Beischel, PhD."
24. Mossbridge, Cameron, and Boccuzzi, "State, Trait, and Target Parameters Associated with Accuracy in Two Online Tests of Precognitive Remote Viewing."
25. Aron, *The Highly Sensitive Person.*

High sensitivity can also run in families, but whether you identify strongly with highly sensitive personality traits or not, be aware that the potential for sensitivity is always there in your DNA, even if it is hidden or you don't quite believe in it yet. Highly sensitive people will likely be more instinctive in their precognition, but a serious challenge for highly sensitives is setting boundaries to limit sensory overload. They need to filter out what is relevant from what is not in the endless flood of invisible potentially precognitive messages they pick up on.

The challenge for those who identify as less sensitive—and therefore less inclined to believe precognition is real—is to awaken precognitively in the first place. But when so-called insensitive individuals do open their minds to the reality of precognition, the messages they sense tend to be clearer and more convincing than for those who are highly sensitive.

In a nutshell, whether you consider yourself highly sensitive or not, whether you believe in precognition or not, you can still awaken precognitively. You just need to approach your precognition training in a different way. The game changer for everyone, especially those who consider themselves to be insensitive, appears to be meditation.

Inner Calm

When the brains of people who say they are not precognitive are studied, it seems that the parts of the brain associated with being highly sensitive (in the right hemisphere) don't light up in the same way they do in those who are more open to precognition. But when a simple course of daily meditation is followed for at least three weeks, those "precognitive" brain parts do start to ignite with greater intensity.[26]

Research on monks shows that there is a correlation between the number of years of regular meditation and precognitive brain activity.[27]

This is incredibly helpful research to know about if you are sceptical and want to find a way to start trusting in and activating your own precognitive potential. A course of daily meditation might just do the trick.

---

26. Penberthy, Hodge, et al., "Meditators and Nonmeditators."
27. Roney-Dougal and Solfvin, "Exploring the Relationship between Tibetan Meditation Attainment and Precognition."

While meditation, or calming your mind, sounds simple, it can be anything but, as our minds have a natural tendency to roam. That's a great thing, as mind wandering is often the door to precognitive insight, but only if you know how to notice and then observe that insight. That's where meditation comes in. It helps you detach from your thoughts without judgement so you can notice whatever precognitive guidance and feelings arise.

Not only does meditation activate the creative parts of your brain, but it can also boost your concentration and problem-solving abilities. Students who meditate regularly are more likely to graduate.[28]

Other studies show that meditation can change how your mind works and help you deal more calmly with stress[29]—more reasons why it is so good for your precognition training, as stress and poor concentration are precognitive roadblocks.

If meditation doesn't come naturally to you because your mind is constantly preoccupied, you are not alone. Many people struggle with meditation. I struggle with it, and the reason for my struggle is that I tend to focus too much on the end goal of clearing or calming my mind and not on the experience itself.

I constantly need to remind myself that meditation isn't the absence of thought, as thoughts never cease to flow, but rather it's being aware of those thoughts but not identifying or interacting with them. It isn't zoning out of your thoughts or controlling them or stopping their endless stream in your mind; it is observing them, watching them flow past, without interaction, expectation, or judgment. Compare it to sitting beside a stream and simply watching the movement of the water as it flows by.

Your Daily Meditation

You are strongly advised to meditate every day. It's a key part of your precognitive-boosting action plan, but don't panic if it feels like another item on your to-do list, as it need only take a few minutes.

You'll find a bewildering array of meditation techniques out there, many of which make it sound far more complicated and time-consuming

---

28. Flaherty, "How Mindfulness Helps Grad Students."

29. Walton, "Seven Ways Meditation Can Actually Change the Brain."

than it is. Experiment if you like, but if you find yourself forcing or straining for results, please stop. There really is no right way to meditate.

If you are new to meditation, just think about it as your time to recharge. You plug your phone in every day to recharge, so do the same for yourself. You don't need to set aside acres of time or go on a retreat or learn complicated techniques. You can meditate effectively in under two minutes. Give it a try now.

Simply set a timer for two minutes and then find somewhere safe and quiet where you can sit comfortably. Now close your eyes gently and observe your thoughts and feelings without judgement or interaction.

Your thoughts won't stop during those two minutes, but your internal dialogue with them will, because you are choosing to notice them but not answer or expect anything from them. Watch those thoughts, and the energies they create within you, fly by.

When the two minutes are up, congratulate yourself. You have taken some time out from the tyranny of your thoughts and reminded yourself that you are not your thoughts. They do not define or control you. Your thoughts are separate from who you are. You decide which thoughts you are going to entertain or not. You get to choose what you want to think about.

You can extend your meditation time to five, ten, or twenty minutes, but this is not essential.

You can also try a two-minute breath meditation, where instead of observing your thoughts, you simply focus all your attention on the flow and feel of your breath. It's well known that deep breathing from the stomach rather than the chest is optimal for our holistic well-being, so setting aside two minutes to simply make a conscious effort to breathe more deeply can be an instant calmer.

As you slowly breathe out from your stomach and through your mouth, imagine you are exhaling tension. Totally empty your lungs, and when they are empty, pause a bit before inhaling. Then, as you inhale deeply through your nose, imagine you are breathing in calm. Focus your thoughts on the different feelings of your inhale and your exhale. If your mind wanders (and it will, because that is what our minds are programmed to do), just bring your attention back to the flow of your breath.

Alternatively, you can choose a calming mantra—typically one word, such as peace, love, or future—to say out loud repeatedly for two minutes. Concentrate your attention on how saying that word feels and the energy of it. When your mind wanders, bring it gently back to your focus word.

During your meditation time, you can also make use of ambient sounds, gentle music, or calming essential oils known to boost dream recall, such as lavender and frankincense. Find whatever calming combination works best for you.

Into Your Body

Sensing the future through unexplained physical changes, such as increased heart rate, sweating, butterflies in the stomach, dryness in the mouth, vocal changes, goose bumps, etc., is known and being demonstrated in scientific circles as *presentiment*.[30] Here is a legendary example of it.

British acting legend Sir Alec Guinness once shared a personal story of his presentiment on the *Parkinson* talk show, and you can still watch that chilling interview on YouTube.[31] In it, he describes a chance meeting he had for the first and last time in September 1955 with fellow actor James Dean, the Hollywood heartthrob of his day.

Dean recognised Guinness and bounded up to him like a puppy. Even though they had never met, he was eager to show Guinness a new sports car he has just bought but not driven yet. As soon as Guinness saw the car, with the bow still tied around it, he experienced what he described in the interview as a "strange feeling, almost like a different voice" physically coming over him. There was also a certain knowing that if Dean drove that car, he would be dead within a week. He urged Dean not to drive the car. Dean ignored the warning only to die driving it exactly a week later in a car crash, just as Guinness had predicted.

The moral of all this is to be sure not to dismiss bodily signals, especially those that can't be explained medically or logically. Your body, like your brain, is a precognitive organ, and tuning into your body on a regular

30. Mossbridge, Tressoldi, et al., "Predicting the Unpredictable."

31. "When James Dean Met Sir Alec Guinness in September 1955," YouTube video.

basis to sense what it is trying to tell you is advised. Most of us don't really pay close attention to what our body is trying to warn us about.

Countless leading artists, visionaries, scientists, entrepreneurs, innovators, and other movers and shakers have credited their gut instinct as the reason for their success. The nervous system matrix in your stomach is linked to every organ in your body, including your brain and heart, and this nervous system is deemed so intelligent that it has been called your "second brain." There is also research to suggest that heeding gut feelings can create neural pathways that enhance the mind-body connection activating your intuition.[32]

Like your stomach, your heart is also believed to be highly intelligent and able to know or feel the future before you do. According to the HeartMath Institute, when your heart is coherent and beating in a calm and consistent way, you feel at peace.[33] Given anxiety is the enemy of precognition, heart coherence is the optimal physiological state for your clear vision to shine through.

Now that you know how intelligent and precognitive your gut and heart are, please pay attention to butterflies in your stomach or increased heart rate. Notice all those times you turn away or towards someone or cross your arms or hug a cushion when you feel vulnerable. Your body wisdom is sending you a precognitive warning.

Here is a simple exercise to help you tune into the presentiment of your stomach (gut) and your heart.

Activate Your Body Wisdom

This exercise can help you become familiar with how your body wisdom talks to you through your heart and gut, so that the next time it happens, you are more likely to notice it.

Find a place where you can be alone and sit or lie down comfortably and safely. Set a timer for five minutes if you are pressed for time.

---

32. Krieger, Asker, et al., "Neural Pathway for Gut Feelings."

33. "Heart Coherence," HeartMath Institute.

Close your eyes and tell yourself that you are going to focus on how your body talks to you through the wisdom of your gut and heart rather than through the thoughts in your mind. Slow down your breath.

Shift your attention to your heart and become aware of its beating. Keep tuning into your beating heart until you notice that the beating is steady and calm. Remain still and sense the energy of your heart and how it makes you feel. See if any questions or insights surface.

Then, when you are ready, divert your attention to your stomach. Linger there a while with your awareness and notice what you feel, sense, and think.

If you sense anything while tuning into your heart and gut that has an obvious physical cause, like hunger, promise your body that you will take better care of it and consult a doctor if need be.

When you are ready, open your eyes, stretch, and adjust to your surroundings. Close the meditation time with gratitude for the wisdom of your body.

You can perform this reflection any time during the day when you want to activate and tune into the predictive force that is your own body. You may also want to do it in the first few minutes upon waking in the morning, especially if your dream recall is poor, because memories of the precognitive feelings of your dreams may linger a while in your body's wisdom.

Note: Presentiment can speak through every part of your body, so you can perform this exercise on any body part or organ. The simple reason for the focus on your heart and stomach here is because presentiment research with the most positive results has tended to cluster there.

What a Shower

Here's another body-centred exercise, but you need to do this one in the shower or bath. There's a reason why many people have eureka moments in the shower.

When you shower, you tend to put yourself in a semi-meditative state. You are alone and relaxed and alert at the same time. Your established washing routine preoccupies your conscious mind, leaving your precognitive mind free to wander and make associations free from external distractions.

Doing things that you are familiar enough with to stay engaged but not bored is conducive to precognition. You are doing something, but you are on autopilot and not 100 percent present while you are doing it. Once you understand the perfect combination of relaxation and distraction that your shower provides, and how it can be a great way to focus on both your body and your thoughts and feelings at the same time, you may even find that it is perhaps an even more effective way to boost your precognition than meditation is.

All you need to do is be fully present when you next take a shower, ideally first thing in the morning, as this sets the tone for the rest of the day. Notice how you feel both physically and emotionally as you wash yourself. Waking precognition speaks through your body and through your feelings, and when you shower, it is the perfect opportunity to tune into the wisdom of both.

Please don't make your shower water too hot, as the heat and mist will make you feel too drowsy. Just ensure your water is a little colder than you normally have it. Not ice-cold—that's too much of a shock to your system. But do turn down the temperature to stay alert.

If you can't or don't want to shower, this exercise can be performed every time you bathe, wash, or clean yourself. It can even be performed through the simple act of washing your hands or cleaning your teeth.

Feel Your Future

Alongside body wisdom, feelings are often the language through which your precognition speaks to you during the day. During the night, it speaks through your dreams. In your waking life, everything and everyone will inspire feelings in you, even if those feelings feel random or illogical. Feelings may be able to leave an energetic imprint across time. It is easier to get in touch with and observe your feelings when you feel calm and quiet, hence the emphasis on finding inner calm in this chapter through techniques like meditation. However, writing down how you feel in a daily journal or diary, without accompanying those feelings with judgement or explanation, is another great way to get in touch with the precognitive insight of your feelings.

Emotions, like thoughts, occur unconsciously, but they typically happen before thought. Most of us focus on our thoughts during the day, but focusing just on your thoughts, which are easier to control consciously than feelings are, keeps you from being aware of your feelings and the precognitive hunches they urgently want to share with you.

In the next chapter, you will be strongly reminded of the importance of writing down your dreams in a journal upon waking. Writing down your feelings during the day, ideally in your dream journal too, so you can see how your feelings and your dream life comment on each other and foreshadow your potential future, is optimal for boosting your precognition.

Dreaming Down Your Moon

Lunar living is being aware of the current moon phase and how it may be impacting your emotional life and decision-making. The moon impacts the tides, and the earth and humans consist of up to 70 percent water, so it does kind of make sense to set intentions when the moon is new and waxing and to act and reflect on your plans when it is full and waning.

If this resonates with you, you might also want to make a note of the moon phase in your dream journal. If you do, don't be surprised if you notice that your dreams are more intense when the moon is full and are more precognitive when it is waning. A recent study showed that people were more likely to accurately dream their future when the moon was waning.[34]

Liminal States

Hypnagogia is the term used to describe the state between being awake and falling sleeping. *Hypnopompia* is its between-sleeping-and-waking-up twin. In both of these liminal states, you are not asleep but you are also not fully awake. You are in an impressionable twilight brain wave zone where your waking mind and dreaming mind briefly merge, making liminal states a rich resource for precognitive visions.

Hypnagogia is perhaps the most highly creative liminal state, as hypnopompia is edging towards reality rather than slipping away from it. The

34. Mossbridge, Cameron, and Boccuzzi, "State, Trait, and Target Parameters Associated with Accuracy in Two Online Tests of Precognitive Remote Viewing."

problem is that when you go to bed, you typically fall right asleep and aren't aware when hypnagogia occurs, and if you do experience any pre-sleep visions, they tend to be forgotten. However, there is a brilliant way around that: aim to take a short nap during the day.

The liminal state where you are neither fully asleep nor awake does not have the same potential for precognitive insight as dreaming does, and dreams tend to have a clearer story or theme to decode, Liminal experiences are more random, but it is an egoless state and the prelude to dreaming. You can experience all kinds of potentially precognitive images, lights, colours, sounds, and feelings. What you observe can be a revelation.

Short episodes of light sleep increase the likelihood of waking up in REM, the dreaming stage of sleep, and there is a wonderful way to ensure you wake up in REM and reap the precognitive benefits, and that is to take a nap.

Plenty of studies show that daytime naps, ideally in the early afternoon for around twenty minutes, are good news for your mental and physical well-being.[35] Here is the optimal way to nap to induce precognitive visions.

Lose Your Keys

Hypnagogia, the liminal state just before falling asleep, is a fantastic creativity hack used by visionaries such as inventor Thomas Edison (1847–1931) and Surrealist artist Salvador Dalí (1904–89). Dali famously sat in a chair with a key in his hand hanging outside his chair so that when he fell asleep and his hand went limp, the key would drop to the floor and wake him up. He would then sketch whatever hypnagogic images he could recall.[36]

This is a technique you might want to try for yourself to see what hypnagogic precognitive visions arise for you. I suggest you use a set of keys that will make a clank when they hit the floor, but if you prefer, you can achieve the same effect with an alarm. Just make sure the alarm is one that is gentle or that vibrates on your wrist and not a loud one, as waking up abruptly is not good news for dream recall or your heart.

---

35. Lovato and Lack, "The Effects of Napping on Cognitive Functioning."

36. Saplakoglu, "Sleep Technique Used by Salvador Dalí Really Works."

During the day, ideally early to mid-afternoon, find a place where you can rest comfortably for around twenty minutes. Lie or sit down, depending on whether you are using the keys or the alarm method. Set your alarm for about twenty minutes, and if using keys, make sure your chair has a comfortable and secure back to lean on as you rest. The hand you are holding your keys in must hang by your side outside the chair and ensure that when the keys fall on the floor, they will make a sound significant enough to wake you. If the room you are napping in has a solid rather than carpeted floor, you can use a spoon instead of a set of keys.

Close your eyes and focus on the sounds within you, such as your heartbeat, then switch to the sounds you can hear externally, such as the hum of a heater or the ticking of a clock in the room you are resting in. Then switch your attention to sounds farther in the distance beyond the room you are napping in. Simply notice these sounds. If you can't hear anything, notice the feelings and sensations flowing within you.

When your alarm goes off or your keys drop from your hand, immediately write down and appreciate any precognitive images that surfaced behind your eyes.

Affirmations

Actions always speak louder than words and your brain is influenced by what you repeatedly do, but your brain is also shaped by what you repeatedly think or tell yourself. You need to find a balance between right thinking and right action. That's where daily affirmations come into play.

Affirmations are empowering statements you tell yourself as often as you can. They can help reprogram your subconscious mind and create new neural pathways to boost your self-confidence and belief in your own precognitive ability. They bypass the critical faculty of your conscious mind and speak directly to your subconscious. When you repeat affirmations every day, you are essentially programming your subconscious to automatically think and behave in a certain way.

Incorporating affirmations into your daily routine, alongside meditation and dreamwork, can significantly boost your belief that precognition is real.

Belief in your precognitive ability is essential for enhancing your night vision. Affirmations can play a key role here with their constant reinforcing of empowering statements. The more you repeat them, the more they affirm your natural precognitive state and your growing trust in it.

You can repeat affirmations silently in your thoughts, but it's better to say them out loud and/or write them down.

In a court of law, it's always powerful when someone swears out loud to tell the truth, the whole truth, and nothing but the truth. It's the same for your affirmations. Saying them out loud to yourself feels more empowering than simply thinking them, so any chance you get, say them out loud to yourself, ideally in front of a mirror.

After speaking your affirmation, you may also want to write it down. This has the feel of signing a contract, a sacred promise, with yourself, and your precognitive mind will take note.

If you have never said your affirmations out loud or written them down before, it may feel slightly absurd the first time you do so. But remember what I said about accurate precognition being associated with people who are willing to take risks? Surprise yourself with your willingness to practise daily affirmations.

As far as the number of times you need to repeat an affirmation, ignore what you may have read on social media, as there is no magic number. It's quality, not quantity, that counts. Once a day with absolute conviction is better than a hundred times that are rushed and not deeply felt.

Any time is beneficial to speak affirmations, but by far the most impactful times are upon waking and just before sleep, because your brain is in an impressionable, deeply relaxed liminal state then. What you tell yourself upon waking will set the tone for the entire day ahead. What you tell yourself before sleeping will set the scene for your precognitive dreams to come.

Say It Out Loud, Every Single Day

Here are some affirmations to help you consolidate your belief in your precognitive ability. They are designed to boost your precognition, but feel free to personalise them. Just remember that your affirmations need to be relentlessly positive. As you think, say, or write them, visualise or feel them as if they are already happening. The more consistently you repeat them and the more you believe in their power to shape and predict your reality, the more effective they will be.

Affirmations upon Waking

- *I am a natural-born precognitive.*
- *I sense/see my future clearly.*
- *I am open to receiving precognitive messages.*
- *I have full confidence in my precognition and am guided by its wisdom.*
- *My precognitive abilities are awake and I follow their guidance.*
- *I release all fear and doubt and trust in my own precognition unconditionally.*
- *Good things are coming my way.*

Affirmations Right before Sleep

- *I am a precognitive dreamer.*
- *I see my future vividly in my dreams.*
- *My dreams are a clear channel for precognitive messages.*
- *My dreams reveal the best way ahead for me.*
- *I honour and respect the wisdom of my dreams.*
- *I am guided by my dreams.*
- *I will dream it and then I will do it.*

If you are sceptical about your precognitive ability, you can't simply alter that with a few overnight affirmations. But if you consistently use the precognition-boosting techniques recommended in this book, over time you will steadily increase your chances of proving to yourself (and others) that you are a natural-born precognitive.

Find Balance

Given that anxiety has been shown to inhibit precognition, one of the best ways to boost your precognition is to cultivate inner peace as much as possible.

Whenever there is a healthy balance between your intuitive and creative (unconscious) impulses and your material and rational (conscious) impulses, you feel inner calm. You need both your conscious mind and your unconscious mind to set aside their differences and calmly work together in harmony, rather than constantly trying to cancel each other out. Your intuition offers you the vision, but without practical application, your dreams won't manifest. Likewise, your reason can sort things out logically and put things in place, but without creativity it will feel empty.

Strive for balance between the precognitive and the rational, the spiritual and the material. You will know when you have achieved this balance because you will feel a sense of deep inner calm. That inner calm will in turn inspire feelings of intense gratitude and unconditional love as well as a sense of oneness with everyone and everything. When you feel that joy for yourself and others, you are psychically and spiritually awakening.

It's impossible to always feel centred and calm, and you should not pressure yourself to do so, as getting outside your comfort zone is important for your personal growth. You don't want to fall victim to toxic positivity. But the more you aim to set aside some time to return to your calm centre every day, the more precognitive you are likely to be.

Meditation is one way to achieve inner peace, but it is not the only way. Here are some other suggestions to help you immediately connect to your balanced inner calm centre and the beautiful future it is lovingly holding for you there.

Sound Healing

Inner calm (heart coherence) is the most conducive state for precognition to flourish. Here is a gentle reminder that research shows that anxiety makes it difficult to connect to our intuition. That's why stress management and taking time out each day to centre yourself should feature strongly in your precognition-boosting action plan.

Meditation is one way to find inner harmony and peace of mind, as is mindfulness, which is placing all your attention on what you are thinking, feeling, and doing in the present moment. But there is a delightfully simple way to achieve inner harmony: just listen to music you love.

Listening to music that gives you goose bumps wakes up both the logical and the creative parts of your brain at the same time. The logical, rational part of your brain works on pattern recognition with the notes it hears, leaving the creative, intuitive part free to dream. Activities that use your brain's full capacity in this way boost your precognition.

Like dreams, music can express things that words cannot. Both can energise and carry you far away. As you journey deeper into precognitive dreams, there is no better companion to accompany you than music.

Soothing melodic music, ideally music that gives you goose bumps when you listen to it because it speaks right to your heart, has been proven to calm the body and inspire the brain at the same time. Many of us eject music right out of our lives when we get older. That is a great loss for our brain, our life, and our dreams, because music inspires all three. If listening to music doesn't feel natural to you anymore, think young again and ditch conventional ideas about what is age-appropriate or not. Being willing to shed old mindsets and experiment with new ones is fuel for your precognitive mind.

There are always windows of time in your day when you can let soothing music in like a breath of fresh air. You need only a few minutes, and falling asleep listening to relaxing music is a treat for your body, mind, and soul. If you want to feel energised, you can play invigorating songs, but if your aim is to achieve inner calm, make sure the music is soothing. Don't rule out sad songs or music, as studies show they are cathartic to listen to and have an unexpected mood-boosting effect.

You can take this directive one step further and start to learn an instrument. Your predictive brain will love you for it. Einstein's genius brain certainly did, and a dream inspired his theory of relativity. Yet there was no sign of this genius when he was young. His parents were told that he was "too dumb to learn anything."[37] Everything changed when his mother bought him a violin. He practised diligently and became highly skilled, often improvising for hours when he needed to solve a problem. Could his love of music have been the key to unlocking his genius, his visionary dreams, his belief that imagination is more important than knowledge?

If learning a musical instrument isn't possible, you could always sing or hum to yourself more often to bring some extra harmony into your life.

---

37. Floyd, "How a Mother's Love Transformed a Life."

Toning can bring inner calm too. Repeatedly chanting *Om* or *Ah* immediately feels relaxing. Try some toning for a few moments whenever you feel stressed or just before you go to bed.

There are plenty of free sound apps designed to help you relax. These typically feature nature sounds, such as rain falling or birds singing, or ambient sounds played in a calming loop.

You may also want to experiment with binaural beats, which are two separate sound frequencies played at the same time but entering each ear individually through your headphones. Regularly listening to binaural beats, known as brainwave entrainment, can help induce meditative brain states that lull you into a calm, timeless zone. You can find binaural tracks online. Be aware that they won't sound like a melody or music, because they are sound frequencies created by engineers. If this frustrates you, then it might be best to avoid brainwave entrainment. Spending time with pets or taking a mindful walk in a green place, such as a local park or woodland, where you tune into the living sounds of nature might be a better path towards helping you find your own calm place.

Take 21

If you are doing the precognition-boosting exercises in this book on an ad hoc basis, you are unlikely to progress. You need to do them daily and consistently to achieve clear results. Those results may happen right away, as precognition is unpredictable, but they are more likely to be noticeable around the three- to four-week mark.

The popular idea that it takes around three weeks for your mind to generate a new habit and adjust to a new perspective and/or routine when trying to reach a desired outcome has recently been challenged. Despite this, hitting the 21-day mark remains a significant achievement and a symbolic milestone to aim for. Just don't judge yourself harshly or give up if you hit the 21-day mark and precognition doesn't yet feel instinctive. You are moving in the right direction. It might just take a while longer, all for a reason. There is more for you to learn.

Hang in there. Keep going, but lighten up a little as you do. Forcing something or being too eager comes from a place of lack, which repels precognition. You need to relax, trust in yourself, and smile more when performing your exercises and writing down your dreams. When the time is right, your precognition will flow from a deep and centred place of completeness.

That's easier said than done, but the point I'm stressing here is that the most significant indicator of your progress towards becoming precognitive is if you are enjoying the journey towards that end goal. If you feel good about yourself and are loving the process of recalling your dreams and noticing your waking hunches, you are awakening precognitively.

Smile When You're Dream Decoding

Just keep going one day and one dream at a time. Keep on smiling and looking forward from the inside out. It's just a matter of time before you glimpse your future, and as you know by now, time is always on your side.

When self-awareness and self-love combine, they ignite self-belief, which, in my humble opinion, is precognition by another name.

In many respects, being highly precognitive is not that much different from being a self-confident individual. It is trusting deeply in your own instincts and knowing that you already have within you all that you need to attract a future filled with success and happiness. It is prioritising your well-being above all else. So if you know you have work to do there (as we all do), then perhaps this chapter is your incentive to double down on your self-care. Moving forward makes every precognition-boosting technique you perform an act of unconditional self-love across time.

All of the indications are that your level of self-respect is very much linked to your precognitive abilities, as low self-esteem is associated with intuition-killing anxiety. How much you understand, love, and believe in yourself influences the future you are sensing in your waking life and glimpsing every night in your precognitive dreams.

Those precognitive dreams, and how to recall and understand and work with them, are the sole focus of the next chapter and whatever infinite possibilities lie beyond for you.

Chapter 4

Prepare to Dream Your Future

Welcome to the weird, wild, and wonderful world of your dreams. You are getting ever closer to the beating heart, the timeless soul, of this book. Your future is always looking back at you in your dreams, offering you today's answers to tomorrow's questions.

Most of your precognitive insight is going to occur in your dreams once you understand how to decode your dreams in a future-forward way. This chapter will take you right back to the future you get to glimpse every single night in your dreams. Let's first explore what your dreams are and why they are such a powerful precognitive tool.

Night Vision

Nocturnal dreams are a succession of stories, images, ideas, emotions, scenes, sounds, and sensations that occur behind your eyes when you fall asleep. You spend about two hours dreaming each night and have around five or six dreams every night, whether you recall them or not.

Scientists don't know for sure why we dream, but there is a consensus that dreams are a way for our brains to process information gathered during the day and to learn and develop memories.[38] They are also a repository for unconscious thoughts and feelings, a nocturnal expression of our intuition.

Many people think of the dream state as being somehow separate from the waking state, but this could not be further from the truth. When you dream, you simply enter a different state of consciousness, but it is still all you. Your dreams comment on your waking life and your waking life influences the contents of your dreams.

When you fall asleep, you receive information directly from the intuitive part of your brain, where you can gain profoundly creative insight about yourself, your life, and the future waiting for you—insight that you may not notice or struggle to tune into when you are awake because your conscious logic and reason block it. However, when you fall asleep and dream, your intuition and creativity reign supreme.

Logic and reason are the only things you won't find in the infinite intuitive possibility of a dream, where anything and everything is possible. In essence, when you dream, your precognition, your ability to mentally time travel, is unleashed.

Dream on It

Scientists aren't entirely sure why we sleep either. It isn't to rest, because our brain is active while dreaming and our body twitches when we sleep. I believe the reason we sleep is because we urgently need to dream.

Research proves that there is a strong connection between dream recall and heightened creativity, problem-solving skills, better memory function, and overall mental and emotional health.[39] Dream recall isn't just great for boosting your precognition. It is also positive for your brain health and holistic well-being. Dreaming is also a terrific stress buster, with studies proving its deep healing power for those suffering from PTSD.[40] Problems just seem easier to cope with after a good night's sleep, and in my humble opinion, the sage "sleep on it" advice should really be replaced with the visionary "dream on it" mantra.

---

38. Wamsley and Stickgold, "Dreaming and Offline Memory Processing."

39. Naiman, "Dreamless: The Silent Epidemic of REM Sleep Loss."

40. "Healing Lucid Dream Pilot Study: Origins of IONS First Experiment on Dreams," Institute of Noetic Sciences (IONS).

To quote the opening line of the 2021 blockbuster movie *Dune*, dreams are "messages from the deep."[41] They reveal instant insight into your unconscious state of mind, what you truly believe about yourself deep down. This is significant because what you truly believe is often rather different from what you feel, think, say, and do in your waking life.

In an energetic universe where like energy attracts like energy and beliefs are the most powerful energy of all, what you truly believe on an unconscious level is the future you tend to attract, whatever you consciously tell yourself when you are awake. That's why every dream you have showcases to you a potential future that your current unconscious beliefs are attracting. If you don't like how that dream makes you feel, it offers you a priceless opportunity to heal that future and shift your unconscious beliefs.

Precognitive Dreamwork

Dreamwork can help increase your self-awareness and plant seeds of self-compassion from that self-knowledge. For many people, that is where their dreamwork begins and ends. I am hoping, though, that it won't ever end there for you.

Self-knowledge is the beginning of wisdom, and there is nothing wrong with simply interpreting your dreams from a purely psychological self-help perspective, but it really is just the tip of the vast dream-decoding iceberg. Why not take a leap of faith with me now and dare to explore your dream power deeper than you have ever gone before?

The growing self-awareness and self-love that dream interpretation can foster within you are the essential stepping stones to the ultimate self-belief you need to see your future clearly in all of your dreams.

By far the most transformative way to work with your dreams is to also interpret them as the precognitions they are. Yes, they showcase your current mindset, but they also showcase what future this mindset is busy attracting your way and breathing life into—in other words, what potential

41. Gearan, "'Dreams Are Messages from the Deep': Why a Sardaukar Speaks Dune's Opening Line Explained by Villeneuve."

future event, situation, or emotional response you are going to experience if you continue to act as you currently are.

This is mighty powerful to know, because if you don't like how your dream makes you feel, your insightful night vision is offering you an incredible chance to course correct and avoid the future it is manifesting. Your future is not just out there for you to witness in your dreams; it is also present in your mindset and in your own hands. You can attract a different future by changing your current mindset and your waking choices.

On that futuristic note, the night vision essential reminders outlined in this chapter will not just complement your dreamwork, but will elevate it in every possible way. If you want to see your future ever more clearly in your dreams, be sure to make time to live, breathe, and dream every reminder that follows. They will help you care deeply for your dreams, your future self, and the infinite adventure of your waking life in a radical and exciting way.

Given that all dreams have precognitive elements, not just those that feel vivid, distorted, and memorable, interpret them all as *potentially* precognitive, including the trivial and more mundane ones.

Precognitive dreams challenge you and encourage you to embrace a new perspective. This is important because new perspectives bring with them evolution.

Decoding your dreams precognitively requires a shift in perspective, especially if you are used to interpreting your dreams psychologically. To help you make that shift and kick-start your precognitive dream decoding, part 2 of this book offers you an invaluable and unique directory of the most common dream symbols interpreted from a precognitive perspective. Start using it right now if you haven't already.

Record at least a dozen or more dreams over a period of days or weeks before you start decoding them for their precognitive potential. Precognitive dreams are best interpreted as a series rather than a stand-alone. Too many people get hung up on decoding one particular dream, but dreams comment on other dreams and are a long-running narrative.

Your dreams showcase potential futures that are typically a day or a few days away, but don't rule out the possibility of them showcasing a future that is weeks or months or even years away. That is why it is vital that each dream you recall and write down is accompanied by a date. Be alert to calendrical resonances. You may find that certain dreams play out exactly a year or several years later on a significant date.

Don't forget the importance of reflecting not only on the dream you just recalled but on those you wrote down a few days back. Hindsight is your greatest precognitive dream teacher.

Aim to keep a journal of your dreams and your waking life side by side so you can check for correspondences. If you record your dreams for long enough, you will start noticing foreshadowing surfacing. You may also notice recurring dream symbols. However subtle the foreshadowing is when you do notice it playing out, it's your first documented precognitive hit, so celebrate it as a sign that your precognition is igniting.

Your dreams can foreshadow actual events in your future, but they can also be about future mindsets and emotional responses you may have to future experiences.

Most of your dreams show your future in a symbolic rather than literal way, and that includes dreams of your past. For example, if you dream of being back at school, your dreaming mind is using associations you have with your past to highlight the future. In the same way, a recent experience showing up in a dream is still suggesting a future experience that will have similarities to the current one.

Often it is the personal associations your dreams trigger that are precognitive, rather than the symbols themselves. Equally, the feeling of the dream is key, as chances are the dream is foreshadowing you having that feeling at some point in the future.

Pause and celebrate whenever you recognise something you pre-experienced in a dream manifesting in your waking life. However trivial, this synchronicity is loaded with meaning, a reminder to you that there is more to your life than meets the eye. It is your sacred call to reflect on the direction your life is currently heading in and to make changes if you don't like what is looming ahead.

To quote Napoleon Hill, author of the best-selling book *Think and Grow Rich*, "Some people dream of success, while others wake up and work hard at it." Your dream isn't ever as significant as what that dream encourages you to then do about it in your waking life, or the perspective shifting brainstorming connections it leads you forward to.

Dream interpretation from a psychological perspective fosters self-awareness and self-compassion, and that is perfect. Without self-awareness and self-love, there can be no self-belief. You need lashings of self-belief to manifest success and happiness in your waking life. Precognitive dreamwork gifts you the self-belief required to see your future clearly.

To tap into your incredible night vision, you first need to consistently recall and write down your dreams upon waking. Then you need to learn how to decode them precognitively. The dream preparation, recall, and decoding advice in this chapter will point you in the right future-forward direction and encourage you to start using (if you haven't already) the directory of the most common dream threads that forms part 2 of this book, which will teach you how to decode your dreams as the precognitions they are.

Prepare to Dream Big

There is an ancient tradition of considering dreams to be a source of both physical and psychological healing. The Greek god Aesculapius was thought to visit people in their dreams to bring healing, and those who were sick and wounded would travel from far away to sleep in the Temple of Aesculapius so the god could heal them in their dreams. There is also an ancient tradition of dreams being innately precognitive. Aristotle believed dreams were premonitions of impending illness, and one of the earliest recorded dream premonitions is when Joseph revealed the meaning of dreams to Pharaoh in the biblical book of Genesis.

Psychologists Freud[42] and Jung[43] pioneered the use of dreams in therapy, which has become widespread. Whether people use dreams for physical or emotional healing or to sense or anticipate their future, a common feature is that their dreamwork empowers them. It puts them in contact with a powerful inner wisdom that is actively working for their good. For

42. Sigmund Freud (1856–1939) was an Austrian neurologist and founder of modern psychoanalysis and its use of dream interpretation.

43. Carl Jung (1875–1961) was a Swiss psychiatrist, psychotherapist, and psychologist who founded the school of analytical psychology and its use of dream interpretation.

centuries people have treated sleep and dreams as sacred, and dream temples can be found all over the world, including the dreaming chamber on the island of Malta. These places were meant to incubate both healing and psychic dreams to warn, guide, and inspire the dreamer. Chances are you don't have a local precognitive dream temple to visit, but the idea is an appealing one. Here are some simple steps to help you create a dream temple in your own home.

If you are fortunate enough to have a spare room, you can make it your dedicated precognitive dream space, a place where you can go to nap or whenever you feel the need to incubate a dream to solve a problem or answer questions about your future. If you don't have a spare room, your bedroom will suffice. Just make sure your bed is comfortable, your sheets are smooth, and the room is an ocean of tranquillity. It should have the feel and scent of a sacred and deeply personal place.

Before you go to sleep each night, treat the experience as sacred. Take a warm bath. Eat a light dinner. Avoid alcohol and do everything you can to increase your chances of quality sleep. Focus on incubating the dreams that are to come.

Bedtime Reading

In addition to using the dream directory in part 2 to help you interpret your dreams precognitively, you are advised to make it your go-to bedtime reading. It is highly recommended that you read through the entire dream threads section as if it were a continuous narrative read. When you have read the whole thing, choose a dream thread, or a couple of dream threads, and reread all of the entries you find gathered there. Don't worry about the repetition. You won't ever be bored rereading it, because each time you do, you will have more dreams to work with and new perspectives will appear. It's like how each time you listen to your favorite song, you hear and feel something new, or how each time you encounter a work of art you admire, new feelings are unleashed. It's the same with your dreamwork.

Reading and rereading this book before you go to sleep will give your mind and soul plenty of precognitive food and help you transcend logic, reason, space, and time as you flow towards the tomorrow land of your dreams.

Think Backwards, Dream Forwards

Alongside your nightly dream-inducing reading of the dream directory in part 2, you might also want to experiment with this powerful backwards-thinking technique before you go to sleep or whenever you want to step outside time and daydream. Think of it as your final countdown to help you directly challenge linear time, so you can launch without resistance from logic and reason into your own timeless future, where the only option is to dream bigger.

Precognition defies the linear, logical, and rational laws that govern everyday reality. Just as an arrow is drawn back in its bow before it is set free and can fly, making a conscious effort to think backwards for a minute or so can help you launch directly into a mindset that is receptive to precognitive dreaming.

Precognition belongs to your unconscious world, where there is no sense of order, reason, logic, space, or time. This is the back-to-front, upside-down world you visit every night in your dreams.

Thinking in backwards order blindsides your conscious, logical brain and sends a message to your precognitive mind that you are willing to defy logic and see what it must reveal to you, not just in your dreams but also when you are wide-awake.

Back to Front

At the end of the day before you go to sleep, spend a minute or so remembering your day in backwards order. Start with the present moment and mentally travel back in time to your evening meal, then your afternoon, your lunch, your morning routine, and the moment you woke up and hopefully recalled and wrote down your dreams. Revisit those dreams in your mind too.

Sounds simple, doesn't it? It is anything but. It is a tougher mental challenge than you might think. Your conscious mind will instantly rebel and try to impose logical order. Realistically you may get only five- or ten-second bursts of backwards thinking before your conditioning to linear time shuts it down. My advice is to aim for successful ten-second bursts until you feel confident you can last for longer. A good tip is to focus on the main events of your day and not get bogged down in details.

Make sure you don't strain too much when you try this exercise, as forcing or trying too hard creates stress and self-doubt, both enemies of your precognition. Simply having a go at this exercise is enough. It will stimulate your precognitive mind and remind and reassure it that you are sincere about your efforts to awaken and tune into it.

Remember, anything that encourages you to reflect on your life from a new perspective can wake up your precognition and let it know you are receptive to it. During the day, you can also try writing with your non-dominant hand, learn a new language, shake up your daily routine, and so on. Your precognitive mind will adore your willingness to experience something new and to get comfortable right outside your comfort zone.

Recalling Your Dreams

In your precognition-boosting action plan on page 12, the very first directive is to get in the habit of recalling and writing down your dreams every morning upon waking.

When you wake up in the morning (or if you wake up in the night), keep still for a minute or so with your eyes closed, ideally in the position you woke up in.

Lying still upon waking for a minute or so matters, because any movement upon waking, even blinking, will chase those dreams away. You need to stay in the nonphysical dream state a while longer before fully waking up in order to allow any dream feelings, images, and memories to surface. The musings of your unconscious, which reign supreme in your dreams, can't compete with the dominance of your conscious mind in the waking state and all the control and rationality it brings with it.

When those dream memories surface, make sure to write them down.

Writing Down Your Dreams

Every night just before you go to sleep, place beside your bed a notebook and a pen, or use a recording device if you prefer to speak rather than write down your dreams. A soft night-light is also recommended. As you close your eyes and drift away and your brain enters that impressionable state where the external world begins to ebb away, tell yourself you are going to recall your dreams upon waking.

Upon waking, lie still with your eyes closed for a minute or so until dream memories bubble to the surface. Then when they do, sit up and write down your dreams immediately in your notebook.

The simple act of recalling your dreams is a powerful way to awaken your sleeping precognition, but recalling them isn't enough. You need to write your dreams down clearly so you can refer to them. There is no right or wrong way to journal your dreams. Find what works best for you. Here are some bullet points that I have found to be superbly effective. Experiment until you find what methods work best for you.

- Placing a blank page and pen beside your bedside at night is a great visual cue for your dreaming mind as you fall asleep, and there is something about a blank page that just invites you to write on it when you see it upon waking. Once dream recall becomes more consistent, you can switch to a notebook or journal, or get a file or folder to put all of your blank pages in if the blank page method works for you.
- Be sure to include the date of your dreams when you write them down.
- Use keywords, themes, and bullet points if your dreams are very detailed. You haven't got time to write a novel in the morning. If you experience dream image overcrowding, stick to three or four keywords/themes or the dream that feels most memorable and recent, the one you had just before waking. It is at the top of your dream recall inbox for a reason.
- Don't try to make sense of your dream or create a story or narrative or force meaning into it when you first write it down. Just record and date it and leave the business of decoding it till later in the day when you will be more relaxed and have more time. Trust that when you reread it later in the day, clarity will come.
- Write down your dreams in the present tense, as this helps you reenter the dreamworld as if it were happening now.
- If you prefer to use a voice recorder, see if that method works better for you.
- Draw images from your dream if you feel inspired.

- Don't try to make sense of your dreams or write down every detail when you wake up. This should take no more than a minute or so. You have a busy day ahead to live to the full. Simply write down any keywords, stories, symbols, sounds, or images that come to mind. Don't attempt to interpret your dreams first thing either. Your prime focus upon waking is to establish a sacred routine of recording your precognitive impressions.
- In your dream journal, you might want to record your dreams on one side and your waking activities on the other side of a two-page spread, so you have a day and night journal and can see your waking and dream lives coexisting side by side. Then every evening before you go to sleep, review your dreams from the night before and search for correspondences and foreshadowing of events, situations, objects, and mindsets or perspectives.

I urge you to harvest at least a dozen or more dreams before you get down to the business of precognitive dream decoding, because dreams should be interpreted as a series and not as a stand-alone. Dreams comment on other dreams, and you need to first get in the habit of waking up with them on your mind and recording them without expectation. You have to reassure your dreaming mind that you are serious about working with it and this is not just a one-time thing. You also need to start recognising precognitive themes in your dreams, and you can't do that until you have harvested at least twenty or more dreams.

Déjà Rêvé

Try to consciously meet elements from your dreams in your waking life as often as you can. Deliberately seek out a safe symbol from the night before. For instance, if a colour was strongly noticeable or you were at a nearby location in your dream, wear an item of clothing of that colour during the day or visit the location. Notice how making this dream-to-life connection makes you feel. It might just give you goose bumps. But whether it does or not, your dreaming mind will notice your proactive approach as a sign of sacred commitment to nurturing a loving long-term relationship with it.

Trust and live out your dreams and before long, déjà rêvé will become your everyday experience.

In most cases, you will notice that precognitive elements in your dreams tend to play out in your waking life on the day you woke up with them on your mind or the following day or a few days later. When you sense a feeling of familiarity between your dream and your waking life, this is your moment of inside-out synchronicity, or a dream remembered, your déjà rêvé. However, as your dreaming mind refuses to conform and treats all rules imposed upon it as guidelines, be aware that elements of your dream could play out weeks, months, or even years later, sometimes clustering around significant dates in your calendar or exactly a year later—even more reason to constantly revisit your precognitive dream journal to check for foreshadowing. Your free-spirited dreaming mind works in infinitely mysterious ways.

When/if elements, symbols, or emotional responses from your dream appear to play out in your waking life, conjuring up feelings of déjà rêvé, I immediately encourage you to seize this opportunity to revisit your dream in your mind and rescript it. For example, if you dreamed that you were walking stark naked in a street and the overriding theme of the dream was your feelings of vulnerability/embarrassment, then when/if you feel vulnerable/embarrassed in your waking life, recall that dream and rescript it so you feel great about shedding your inhibitions. In this way, the feeling will transform from inhibition to liberation. Doing this will help reshape your unconscious beliefs about yourself. This is key, because when there are positive shifts in your unconscious, positive shifts in your waking life coincide.

You can get another step ahead of yourself by not even waiting for that moment of synchronicity, or déjà rêvé, in your waking life. The next time you wake up and recall a dream that felt unpleasant in any way, you can rescript it right there and then. It only takes a few seconds, but the impact of this process will send ripples through all of time.

When déjà rêvé happens either consciously (created by you) or spontaneously (whether through a scenario, a symbol, or an emotional reaction you pre-lived in a dream unexpectedly playing out in your waking life), link it immediately to the precognitive wisdom of your night vision. This is your moment in time to see what insight this synchronicity triggers and to remind yourself that much of what you experience is created not by the situation itself but by your own perspective. You can always change your perspective and therefore your future.

Don't Recall Your Dreams

All of the previous advice will help you recall and record your dreams more consistently, but sometimes it is easier said than done.

If you struggle to recall your dreams, this does not mean you don't dream. Brain scans show that we all dream several times a night. The issue is that you can't always remember them. You may have forgotten how to recall them or got into the habit of forgetting them, but there are things you can do to remedy this.

Setting the intention to dream before you go to sleep and keeping still with your eyes closed upon waking for a minute or so can help your brain hold onto the dream. If you still can't recall anything, just let your mind meander as you lie in bed. You will be amazed at how many memories this can ignite. Check in with your body, too, as stored dream memories may be hidden there. Sometimes revisiting a dream memory from the past few nights can help ignite recall.

When images form, immediately open your eyes, reach for your pen and notepad, and write them down. Don't put off writing them down until later when you have used the bathroom or got dressed, because if you do, your brain will be too distracted and your dream memories will vanish. They come from your unconscious world, a subtle, unseen place that doesn't stand a chance against the practical demands of waking reality.

This "write it down immediately" directive remains the case if you wake up in the middle of the night with a dream on your mind. Don't tell yourself you will remember it in the morning. You won't. You need to switch on a night-light and write it down now.

If dream recall still isn't there, write the words "I feel" and see what comes through, because how you feel upon waking is often the result of a dream scenario. The language of dreams is symbols but also emotion. If this still doesn't trigger any dream memories, don't force or strain. Simply write in your journal, "No recall this morning, but I look forward to recalling my dreams either later in the day or tomorrow."

Then let it go. Sometimes memories may filter through during the day. If they do, write them down, but if they don't, that's okay. Trust that you will remember your dreams when you are ready, and until that time comes, your dreams are working undercover on your behalf, healing and problem-solving for you while you are sleeping.

Sleep quality is related to dream recall. The better your quality of sleep, the more likely you are to wake up refreshed, with dreams on your mind. Make sure your bedroom is a sanctuary or a dream temple, a place you associate with sleep and relaxation. Avoid using screens and phones or eating a large meal at least an hour before bedtime. Make sure your bedroom is dark and quiet enough and the temperature when you go to bed is 60 to 68 degrees Fahrenheit (15.6 to 20 degrees Celsius) for the most comfortable sleep.

Go to bed before midnight if you can, and aim to go to bed and get up at the same time each day. If you feel tired during the day, retire earlier rather than having a long lie-in, as lie-ins mess with your body clock and give you jet lag without the holiday.

Pay attention to your diet. Make sure it is healthy, so your brain and body have the fuel they need. Ensure you get enough B vitamins, in particular vitamin B6, which is found in sunflower seeds, tuna, turkey, bananas, and dried fruit and has been shown to be linked to dream recall.[44]

If you can, please aim to wake up naturally on a regular basis. Alarm clocks shock your brain and body into waking reality too violently. They are the enemy of dream recall and heart health. If you must use an alarm, use one that has gentle nature sounds or a watch that vibrates on your wrist to gently wake you up.

Herbal teas, in particular mugwort (*Artemisia vulgaris*), can increase your chances of recalling a vivid dream, but as with all herbal remedies, be sure to consult your doctor to ensure it is safe for you to take.

Placing an amethyst or a rose quartz crystal beside your bed or a spray of dream-boosting lavender scent may also boost dream recall.

---

44. Adventure-Heart, Madden, and Delfabbro, "Effects of Vitamin B6 (Pyridoxine) and a B Complex Preparation on Dreaming and Sleep."

Bear in mind that poor dream recall could be a sign that the balance in your waking life has tilted a little too much towards the material and you need a little more personal reflection during the day. Cultivate a state of inner calm, which, as chapter 3 explored, is conducive to precognition. Meditation can help you find your calm inner space, as can daily yoga, walking in nature, listening to music, and daydreaming—mind wandering really is just another way to dream!

A spot of video gaming can boost your dream recall, as it reassures your dreaming mind that you feel comfortable suspending disbelief and operating in an alternative reality.[45] Just make sure you don't game in the evening, as that will be too stimulating for your brain and keep you awake when you need to sleep. One of the best things you can do to induce sweet dreams is to read some fantasy fiction or poetry just before you go to sleep. It really sets the stage for your dreams to take the lead role when you fall asleep.

Simply reading this book will also serve to boost your dream recall. The more you reflect on dreams during the day, the more dream recall is enhanced, because your dreaming mind draws inspiration from what you focus on during the day. In other words, the more attention you pay to your dreams, the more likely you are to wake up and remember them.

Last but by no means least, if you have been conditioned over the years by your parents, carers, teachers, or peers to dismiss your dreams as random and meaningless, it is very difficult for your dreams to break through that conditioning and make their mark. It is important to change your mindset, take your dreams seriously, and feel grateful for any messages that come through.

You need to let your dreams know they really do matter to you. The next time a dream memory, however slight or trivial, surfaces in the morning or during the day, as you write it down in your dream journal, please do so with feelings of deep appreciation.

Don't neglect the "live your dream" exercise in your precognition action plan (page 13). It's one of the simplest and best ways to reassure your dreams that they feel real to you. Select a harmless aspect of a dream

---

45. Sestir, Tai, and Peszka, "Relationships between Video Game Play Factors and Frequency of Lucid and Control Dreaming Experiences."

that you can re-create or meet in your waking life. For example, if flowers appear in your dream, buy yourself a bunch the next day. If someone you have lost touch with appears in your dream, send them a text to say hi the next day, and so on. Safely and responsibly live out an aspect of your dream. Notice how it feels when you do so and what associations it triggers.

Don't Understand Your Dreams

Not understanding the meaning of your dreams when you do recall them is by far the biggest stumbling block to dreamwork.

Dreams are bizarre—period. The images at first glance seen random, incoherent, and nonsensical, but that is wonderful, as the crazier your dream, the more profound the meaning. There's a simple reason for that. Dream language isn't the same language as the one you use in waking life, because dreams come from your unconscious, which speaks a different language. You need to learn that language if you want to understand it properly, just as you would learn a language if you travelled to a different country and wanted to speak to the people there and truly understand them.

Fortunately, learning dream-speak is much easier than learning a foreign language, as it was once a language that was instinctive to our ancestors. It is the language of symbols, where something represents something else and hidden meanings lie beneath the literal meanings. For example, the cross is typically a symbol of religion, a rose is a symbol of love, a dove is a symbol of peace, a rainbow is a symbol of hope, and so on.

You need to decode the meaning of your dream symbols, and although they have common or universal interpretations, those symbols need to be interpreted personally first and foremost. To illustrate, if you love dogs, then should a dog appear in your dream, the universal interpretation is one of unconditional love and loyalty. However, if you fear dogs and one appears in your dream, it will have a very different personal interpretation.

That is why dream dictionaries online or in book form, although fantastic for kick-starting symbolic thinking, aren't always that useful. They give the most likely universal, archetypal, or generic interpretation, which can certainly complement your interpretation but simply can't give you a unique personal interpretation. The only person who can do that is you. The best dream book is the one you are going to write yourself.

Now that you understand that personal interpretation—thinking of your own associations with a particular dream symbol or image first—is key, here are some simple but highly effective ways to help you start understanding your dreams and, therefore, yourself better.

The morning is not the right time to decode your dreams, as you need to get on with living your day. Save your dream decoding until later in the day, preferably in the evening before you go to bed, so your dreams are on your mind as you fall asleep.

When you are in a calm place, set aside five or ten minutes to free-associate. Think of the first meaning that comes to mind when you reflect on a dream.

Many of your dreams are symbolic, but, as dreams love to surprise, in rare instances they can be literal. Always rule out the literal interpretation first. It is often very easy to rule out the literal interpretation. Let's say you dream that your teeth are falling out. Do you need to visit your dentist? If you don't need a dental checkup, turn your attention to the symbolic interpretation of teeth falling out.

When interpreting dreams symbolically, you need to think like a poet, artist, or visionary. Metaphors, figures of speech, associations, hidden meanings, and even punning are how your dreams love to speak to you about your future. Just as when you were asked at school to interpret a poem line by line, exploring the hidden meaning beneath the surface of the poet's use of symbols, metaphors, puns, and other literary devices, do the same with your dream. Think of it as a night poem or a night portrait with layers and layers of visionary meaning beneath the surface to unpick. You are now the literary critic of your own dreams.

If you still don't have any personal associations with a dream, turn your attention to the emotion driving it. How did your dream make you feel? Did you feel fear, anxiety, frustration, relief, or joy? Just as you are not your thoughts, you are also not your emotions. So observe that emotion and see what it is trying to tell you about your waking life and the choices you are about to make.

Ask your dream questions. Who are you in the dream? Who are the characters? Why are they there? Ask as many questions as you can and see what associations spring to mind. There is always a reason that certain symbols appear in a dream. Your role is to become your own dream detective and find out why they are there.

Dreams are often a symbolic representation of your own mindset and what that mindset is attracting to you. They are like a hall of mirrors offering you your own reflections. For instance, if someone you know appears in a dream, you are not dreaming about them, but about the aspects of their personality that are reflected or required in you. It's all about the amazing *you*. Everything in your dreamscape is a visionary conversation with yourself, with your precognitive mind asking you questions. Objects in dreams tend to represent your abilities and how they are helping or hindering you. If you have ever watched the 2010 movie *Inception*, there is a scene where everybody stops and stares at the dreamer because they are creating the world of their dream. (If you haven't watched this film, make sure you do at some point.)

The exception to this "all about you" method of decoding your dreams is for those people you are super close to or emotionally intimate with. When they appear in a dream, you could be picking up on something related to your relationship with them.

The associations you have with a dream symbol, rather than the symbol itself, will often reveal the meaning.

How a dream made you feel is key to the interpretation, signposting an emotional reaction that is likely in your near future.

Keep going through all of your personal associations with a dream symbol. If nothing resonates, you can research common or generic associations until you get a moment of clarity. Just keep on brainstorming, as meanings will eventually come to you.

When dreams switch from scene to scene, they are often trying to tell you how one thing may lead to another or to make you aware of future-forward consequences rippling out from your current actions. Pay special attention to the final memory or ending of your dream just before you woke up, as it's the final cameo for a reason, the impression or vision your precognitive mind wants to leave most strongly with you.

You will know when you have understood the meaning of a dream because it will be like an aha moment. You will feel a shift, a eureka moment, from within. It will typically be a surprising shift. Dreams love to tell you what you don't already know.

A dream correctly interpreted will lift you up vibrationally. If a dream interpretation drains you or makes you feel anxious or less than in any way, it is not the correct interpretation. Your inner psychic is your higher, timeless, or future self. Sometimes it may use tough love to get a message across, but its aim is always to help you learn, grow, and evolve and live a more fulfilling life.

Should you experience recurring symbols and themes, think of this as your dreaming mind using a highlighter pen. You simply are not understanding their meaning, so your dreaming mind is using the power of repetition to underline to you that you really do need to pay attention now. Once you fully understand their meaning, recurring dream themes tend to stop.

It is easy to focus all your decoding energy on one particularly vivid dream, but dreams complement and enhance other dreams. Consider them a nightly series that you need to tune into for the next thrilling instalment or development in the plot. They are the greatest show on Earth, shining a night-light on the infinite, long-running story of you. That is why you need to harvest at least twenty dreams before you start the business of decoding them. You need to see the themes and stories and symbols of your dreams playing out.

Hindsight

Make sure you look back to your dreams from a few nights before, too. This is a vital step that many dreamworkers neglect to do. It is only in hindsight that you can learn how your dreams are always signposting your way ahead.

Hindsight, looking back at yourself, is your wisest teacher and precognitive guide.

This backwards-looking step is by far the most important one for empowering your precognition. You need to consistently review your previous dreams from several days back to determine when and how they are foreshadowing your waking life.

The more you write down your dreams and repeatedly refer to them to check for foreshadowing, the more you will begin to realise that the greatest precognitive dream book is always the one written by you.

Afraid of Nightmares

Fear of having nightmares can also become a roadblock to your precognitive dreamwork. Nightmares are chilling, terrifying experiences. They may showcase scenarios where you and your loved ones are in grave danger or even dying. Or you may encounter monsters and experience unspeakable terrors, such as paralysis, being buried alive, being unable to speak, and so on.

Nightmares are extreme dreams. They can happen when you are under stress or unwilling to confront aspects of yourself or your waking life that are blocking your progress. But sometimes they just happen, and the reason they happen is the same reason that all of your dreams happen: It's high time for you to learn something vital for your personal growth. Often your previous dreams have tried to teach you this, but for whatever reason, you haven't been noticing or paying attention. So your dreaming mind has no choice but to resort to tough love. It knows you are far more likely to try to recall a shocking dream scenario than a less memorable one.

Remember that nightmares, like all dreams, only showcase a potential future. They highlight a current mindset and the future it is attracting, but you always have the power to change that potential future by changing your mindset. Nightmares are asking you to let go of a mindset that may have served you well in the past but no longer does. They want you to understand that mindset and then release it so you can attract a more positive future.

Nothing illustrates this better than the story of Scrooge told in Charles Dickens's timeless classic *A Christmas Carol*. First published in 1843, it remains as relevant today as ever. It recounts the story of Ebenezer Scrooge, an elderly miser who is visited by the ghost of his former business partner, Jacob Marley, and the Spirits of Christmas Past, Present, and Yet to Come. In the process, Scrooge is transformed into a kinder, gentler man. Although the Spirits of Christmas Past and Present unsettle Scrooge deeply, it is the Ghost of Christmas Yet to Come that he fears the most. Scrooge's transformation can only happen when he has come face-to-face with that fear and seen his future, or the potential future, he is hurtling towards if he doesn't change his present now.

Where your fear is, there is your task. Like Scrooge, the future we are busy creating with our past and present choices is the one we dread seeing the most and prefer to deny exists at all. But the only way for us to learn and grow is to face and heal that potential future.

Nightmares bring hidden fears about the future directly to our attention. There is wisdom in wounds, and it is through the cracks that the light comes in, so treasure your nightmares as the transformative opportunities they are. Your nightmares also showcase negative self-talk and perspectives you currently have that are filling visions of your future with fear.

Nightmares are unpleasant, but they are also incredibly cathartic. Just as a fever is a sign that your body is trying to heal and sweat out toxins that are making you ill, nightmares are doing the same for your inner growth. They are shining a night-light on potentially negative futures your current mindset is attracting that you absolutely need to notice, understand, and safely release in the dream state.

Should your nightmare involve harm coming to you or those you care about, please don't panic. Remember that most dreams, including nightmares, are symbolic. Your dreaming mind is using the shocking symbol of violence to show that your relationship is going to change in some way. Whenever something ends, something new always begins. Some parents have nightmares about their children being involved in a car accident before they head to university or leave home, for example, because their precognitive mind is foreshadowing that their relationship with their child is transitioning to a different phase.

Nightmares also take you safely out of your comfort zone, the place where all personal growth happens, so that you can experience the worst-case scenarios and wake up unscathed the next morning, knowing you have been there and lived to tell the tale. Your unconscious has taken you to your deepest fears so you can be better prepared in waking life.

Nightmares connect you to your shadow side, the emotional part of you that is natural and instinctive but is typically repressed in waking life, such as those unpleasant feelings of irrational anger, jealousy, and so on. But just as there is night and day and a shadow cannot exist without a light source, within you there are both positive and negative impulses. Inner strength is facing, understanding, and learning from what is negative within you, not denying or repressing it. A calm sea does not train a sailor to handle a storm. Similarly, nightmares can help you learn how to manage your dark side so you can choose what is positive in waking life.

Alarming dreams occur and tend to recur until you have acknowledged and dealt with the issues in your waking life that are triggering them. The more you acknowledge and face your emotions in waking life, the less frightening your dreams are likely to be.

The message of all this is that if you find your dreams unsettling and would rather not spend time pondering their meaning, this is more reason to pay attention to them. The future you are currently attracting isn't optimal for you, so your precognitive mind sends you a nightmare to get your attention and encourage you to make positive changes in your waking life. But you don't need to wait for a terrifying nightmare to wake you up to the part you are playing in creating your future.

How to Exorcise Your Night Demons

Did you know that the *mare* in nightmare does not refer to a female horse but is an ancient English word for a goblin or evil spirit possessing you in the night? Should you or someone you know suffer from nightmares, here's how you can exorcise them from your current life and your future.

Write your nightmares down in exquisite detail. The more details you can recall about your nightmares the better, as the details will help you understand and decode them moving forward.

As you write down your nightmares, feel gratitude for them, however ghoulish, as they are transformative opportunities for you. Transform any fear you feel into excitement, because nightmares are a sign that you are about to grow and evolve, and sometimes growth hurts.

Choose one object or image in the dream and ask it why it is screaming for your attention in your nightmares. Listen to what it tells you and then thank it.

Now rewrite your nightmare. It is your nightmare, and you can smile at the end of it if you want to. Change the ending into a happy one. Transform monsters into butterflies.

Remind your precognitive dreaming mind that you are the scriptwriter and creator here. You are not a powerless victim. Reprogram your unconscious to give yourself the ending you want to see manifesting in your future. Remind yourself that changing the future you glimpse in your dreams can change your life.

Problem Power

Even if your dreams don't reach nightmare status, they are more likely to feature a theme of anxiety than of happiness. Up to 90 percent of dreams are anxiety-themed. This is completely normal, so please don't worry if your dreams are anything but sweet. Your dreaming mind is simply shining a night-light on problems in your waking life or negative mindsets you are cultivating that are likely to negatively impact your future.

You may not be fully aware of these problems or negative mindsets in your waking life, but you need to be. You need to notice them, understand them better, and transform them, and that is what your anxiety-themed dreams are wanting you to do. Once you start to regard problems as opportunities to learn and evolve in your waking life, not only will your personal growth fast-forward, but your dreams will become more positive too. Expect fewer monsters and more butterflies, less falling and more flying, in your dreams!

Infinite You

Once you start tuning into your precognition, whether that be through your waking hunches or more likely through your dreams, every day will become a time-travelling adventure. But as exciting as that may feel, perhaps even more astonishing is what the very real possibility of precognition suggests about you.

Precognition suggests that all of your past, present, and future experiences are already encoded within you and there is infinitely more to you than your present self. The true revelation of precognitive living and dreaming is fully experiencing the timeless potential of your own inner space, known as your "long body" in shamanic cultures, a.k.a. the essence or consciousness of you that is infinite, connects you to source energy, and stretches across time.

Your future is right here for you to see. You don't need to wait for it. You just need to write down your precognitive dreams and notice waking hunches and synchronicities to stay ahead of yourself.

If you want to manifest the life of your dreams, you can also try a spot of dreamscaping.

Dreamscaping

Dream incubation, also known as dreamscaping, is often the most neglected manifesting tool. What you unconsciously believe is what you tend to attract in your waking life, but all too often in waking life you aren't aware that you have unconscious roadblocks. Some painful things are buried so deep within you that only your dreams can reach them. That's why outside-in affirmations or positive thinking techniques don't always work. Deep down you don't truly believe them or even know what you believe.

Dreams reveal your unconscious, inside-out beliefs clearly and the future they are busy attracting. Many of those beliefs will be ones you are unwilling to face in waking life, but dreams don't lie to you. They are honest. The beauty of all this honesty is that if you don't like what your dreams reveal, you can influence your dreamscape. If you can dream it, that means your unconscious believes it to be true. Remember, what your unconscious believes is real is the future you tend to attract.

Before you go to sleep tonight, ask your dreaming mind to show you your future filled with happiness and success. If you have an event coming up that you are nervous about, ask your dreaming mind to send you a dream where you ace it. Do the same for all of your future hopes. Ask for dreams where you experience them happening in the dream state.

By setting the intention to dream happier dreams for yourself, you are changing your unconscious beliefs about yourself and your future one dream at a time. Don't worry if it doesn't always happen and those anxiety dreams return or your dream doesn't answer your question as hoped. This simply means you have more growing to do, and that's okay, because growth brings momentum and is what gives your life meaning.

You may think you want happiness all the time, but the uncertainty and challenge that experiencing growth brings, the journey rather than the destination, is where the thrill and meaning of life is to be found.

You can dreamscape when you are awake, too. Indeed, this may be just as powerful a way to create a shift at a deep, unconscious level. The way to do this is to recall a dream that left you feeling anxious in some way. Go somewhere safe and quiet. In your mind's eye, reimagine that dream. Reenter it and change the dreamscape to a favourable outcome. Like a director, reshoot every scene. If you struggle to visualise, as many of us do, you can write down your dream and rewrite the ending. This is extremely effective, as writing things down sends a message to your unconscious that you really mean business.

Lucid Dreaming

Should you find yourself becoming lucid in a dream—that is, knowing you are dreaming when you are dreaming—stay calm and don't let the dream collapse. You have a priceless opportunity to consciously influence your dreamworld and whatever happens there. Seize it.

Lucid dreaming is a rare dream state with tremendous healing potential. Indeed, it has been used successfully as a treatment for PTSD.[46] It tends to happen more in childhood, when it is easier to suspend disbelief. It can be triggered by certain lucid-dreaming techniques, such as the Wake Back to Bed method, but these tend to interfere with your sleep schedule, so are not recommended. Sleep is to the health of your body as dreams are to the health of your mind and soul.

Lucid dreaming gets a lot of attention and is the most researched dream state, but don't get hung up on trying to achieve it. Every dream is extraordinary, not just those rare lucid ones, and when it comes to precognition, non-lucid dreams have just as much potential to showcase your future. By

46. "Lucid Dreaming Study Reveals a Huge Decrease in PTSD Symptoms," PTSD UK.

far the best way to increase the likelihood of a lucid dream, in my humble opinion, is to follow the dream recall and decoding guidelines here and feel gratitude for any dream you wake up with on your mind. Making dreamwork a part of your life will naturally increase your chances of lucid dreaming more often.

Note: Given that psychic abilities often fall in the category of precognition, you may find that not only does your precognitive dreamwork increase your chances of lucidity, but you also experience more afterlife, past-life, telepathic, and other psychic dreams. Awakening your precognitive dreaming potential will sharpen your waking psychic senses, too, because what happens in your dreams doesn't stay in your dreams but also influences your waking life, just as what happens in your waking life shapes the contents of your dreams.

Dream Sharing

When you feel more assured of the validity of your own precognitive dreamwork, you might want to take another great leap into the unknown and use all you have discovered not just to inspire yourself to meet your future with confidence but also to inspire others to do the same. Indeed, if you are on track with your precognition training, this is what you will naturally want to do, because your empathy for others as a dreaming being just like you will sweep you along.

If you encounter someone who is receptive to precognitive dreamwork, offer them a few suggestions but don't immediately try to interpret their dreams precognitively. Tell them that their dreams are not just their inner therapist and can also shine a bright light on their potential future. If they do ask for your interpretation, be sure to remind them that they are the best person to interpret their own dreams and then offer a vibration-rising interpretation. Remember, positivity is the golden rule whenever you interpret your own dreams or the dreams of others.

Over the years, I have found that even the most sceptical person will still have a dream they are eager to understand better. You are now in a prime position to help them understand their dreams. When people write to me asking for help with their dreams, I typically interpret the dream as if I had dreamt it myself and then ask them to reflect on whatever feelings my interpretation inspires in them.

Be conscious that when people share their dreams with you, even though they may not realise it and may even joke about it, they are sharing something sacred and intimate, a piece of their soul. Treat your own dreams and the dreams of others with the utmost respect.

Your Precognitive Dream Thread Directory

It's high time now for you to start actively using (if you haven't already) the directory of precognitive dream threads that forms the remainder of this book whenever you wake up with a dream on your mind. It is designed to complement, not replace, your own personal interpretations, which must take precedence, and to point you in the right direction when interpreting your dream symbols precognitively.

Remember that your self-belief and its unstoppable manifesting power grows every time you interpret your dream precognitively, what it is suggesting about your future. You won't find every symbol or theme that you could possibly dream of in this directory. That would be impossible, as you can dream about literally anything. But you will find the most common dream scenarios reported to sleep and dream researchers, making it a comprehensive and flexible resource.

What makes this dream directory utterly unique to anything currently out there is that every symbol is interpreted not just from a psychological, personal growth perspective, to increase your self-knowledge and self-love (which is what you are used to finding when you search for dream meanings online, in book form, or through dream therapy), but also precognitively, to increase your self-belief. Each symbol is interpreted in terms of the potential future it is revealing to you and the opportunities it is offering you to shape your future in the process. Keep using this directory until it feels effortless to interpret your dreams as future visions.

Part Two

The Precognitive Dream Directory

Directory of Precognitive Dream Threads

Messages in dreams can sometimes feel impenetrable until you learn their secret language. Part 2 of this book is dedicated to helping you learn that language. It will give you the keys to your own precognitive dream power. While the interpretations here are based on the most common or universal symbolism, the true meaning of your dreams will always depend on your personal circumstances, feelings, experiences, and mindset. Here is yet another reminder that the best precognitive dream reference guide is always the one you write yourself. However, because dreams have their own language, it can be hard to know where to begin. What follows will help kick-start precognitive thinking so you can start decoding the predictive symbolism of your precious dreams as the future-forward visions they are.

Common Dream Threads

The word *thread* is used deliberately here, as each dream theme is like a thread connecting it to everything and anything you experience in your dreamscape. Indeed, you will soon notice that some dream themes and symbols referenced, such as falling, being unprepared for an exam, or being chased, make return appearances time and time again in other related threads.

There are suggestions in each thread on how to interpret all of your dreams precognitively. But your dreaming mind is infinitely expansive, and there is never a one-size-fits-all approach when it comes to interpretation. You can also choose to interpret these dreams in the present tense and apply them to situations in your life that are already happening rather than ones that are about to or yet to come. I'm assuming that since the emphasis in this book is on the precognitive potential of your dreams, this approach will lead your dreamwork moving forward. But you need to find what works best for you to increase self-awareness and personal healing.

You'll notice that many of the interpretations in this dictionary are fluid, and instead of providing answers, they encourage you to ask questions of yourself and the future you are busy attracting. This is because questions not only stretch your mind in a way answers never can—as questions open your mind to new perspectives—but also are the future. The words "what if" rather than "it is" have always pushed humanity forward and will continue to do so. Never ever stop asking questions of yourself and your dreams. Your future is right there.

The choice of dream threads listed here is subjective and based on my own research, and within each thread you will find symbols and subthemes that likely deserve categories of their own. It is impossible to list every potential dream thread. Everything you read here is more of a guideline to get you thinking precognitively with your dream interpretation. Use my suggestions as a catalyst for your own forward thinking and to help you better understand your own unique precognitive dream-speak.

Each of the dream threads in this section begins with an introduction to the kind of dreams that fall under that overarching theme, followed by descriptions of the most likely related dream scenarios/symbols/feelings:

- Actions
- Animals
- Body
- Clothing
- Colour and Shape

- Death
- Disaster
- Everyday
- Feelings
- Food
- Houses
- Life Stages
- Metaphysical
- Nature
- Nightmares
- People
- Relationships
- School
- Settings
- Travel

Follow the Dream Thread

Ideally in the evening before you go to bed, take a few minutes to connect the keywords from a dream you recorded in your journal to one thread in the precognitive dream directory. For example, if you dreamt of a lion, the obvious place you need to go for illumination would be the section devoted to animals. However, if you dreamt of a more unusual animal that isn't specifically mentioned in the animal section, such as a buffalo, reading about related animal-themed dreams will still shed light on your unique animal symbol and help you understand its precognitive meaning.

Reading the entire thread that a specific dream symbol likely falls into or is most closely related to, whether that symbol is mentioned in the section or not, will offer you a more expansive precognitive interpretation. But if instant illumination is what you're searching for, you can try looking up a specific dream symbol, feeling, or related theme in the index in the back of the book, which for ease of reference lists all of the dream symbols mentioned in this entire book alphabetically.

The Twelve Most Common Dreams

To help you get started along the right precognitive lines, here are twelve dreams that consistently appear in global dream surveys, with future-forward interpretations. Chances are you've had one or more of these dreams already. If you revisit that dream in your mind now with the benefit of hindsight, see if these instant precognitive interpretations offer any illumination.

1. Being chased—Something is about to catch up with you in your future. Stay alert.
2. Teeth falling out—In the coming days, you may regret something you said or did not say. Watch your words.
3. Car out of control—The future you are heading towards feels out of your control. Get in the driver's seat of your life to avoid a collision.
4. Snakes—You are about to be offered an opportunity to transform or a new perspective that will stretch your mind. Seize it.
5. Pregnant/baby—Your future happiness lies in your ability to be patient and to nurture the part of you that is vulnerable and in need of parenting.
6. Falling or flying—You may soon find yourself in a situation where you feel totally unsupported and like you are at the mercy of things you cannot control. When/if that happens, focus on what you can control, which is your reaction. Transform falling into flying, where you rise above and see the bigger picture.
7. Dying and death—Something is ending in your life, but there is a new beginning on the horizon.
8. Naked—You may soon find yourself feeling exposed in some way. The way forward is to avoid oversharing.
9. Poor performance on an examination—Life is about to seriously test you in the coming days. Forewarned is forearmed.
10. Late or missing a flight or train—You will soon experience FOMO (the fear of missing out) in some way. Let your memory

of this dream remind you to get your validation from the inside out, not the outside in.

11. Cheating—When/if you feel that something is missing in your life and/or your relationships, ask yourself what will inject some excitement into your life.
12. Trapped—You may soon feel like you have no choice in the matter or are trapped in some way, but recalling this dream will remind you in the coming days that you saw this coming and have a choice of how to react.

You'll notice that there are more everyday scenarios in this list than surreal ones. We live in a world where reason often silences visionary hunches. The more people approach dreamwork from a precognitive perspective, the more likely it is that the balance will shift from logic and reason to the highly imaginative, creative, and visionary. I live and dream in hope of this.

Lights Out

Moving forward, the visionary aim of your dreamwork is to place as much emphasis on sensing a positive future as on increasing your self-awareness. Interpreting your dreams both precognitively and psychologically will help remove any kind of disconnection or disassociation between your waking life and your dream life. You will prove to yourself that you really can sense your future ahead of time.

You may notice some repetition of certain key dream symbols and their precognitive implications across several threads, and that is all for a good reason. I'd like you to think of this repetition, and all of the precognitive dreamwork reminders that punctuate not just this directory but also this entire book, in the same way as a recurring dream: as a persistent reminder of something essential for your precognitive awakening that you may soon be in danger of forgetting.

Without further ado, let your future-forward dream-decoding games officially begin.

Actions

You may have noticed that your precognitive mind loves to plunge you right into a dream scenario. You don't know (and often don't care or want to know) how you got there. You just accept that you are right in the middle of the action. Already your dreaming mind is sending you an extraordinarily powerful message.

Moving forward, it is your actions, not your words, that will define you. Your intentions and words have all the potential within them to create the future you want to attract, but without actions to back them up, they are but a noisy gong or a clashing symbol, meaningless and void.

A recurring theme connecting the dream threads is the use of symbols to point the dreamer towards creating a future where actions rather than words are the decisive force. In the dreamworld, just as in your waking world, the actions you experience and observe there speak volumes about what is likely to occur in your near future.

Your brain doesn't know the difference between the dream state and the waking state, so what you do in your night vision matters greatly. Lucid dreaming techniques have been successfully used to practise skills in the dream state and improve performance. For instance, musicians can practise their pieces and athletes can train within a dream. Knowing this, pay close attention to what you or others do in your dream and what actions take place. Even if you hear words and sounds, it is the actions that will speak louder than the noise. It is the actions that are showcasing your potential future loud and clear. Heed their precognitive signs before the potential future you have pre-glimpsed and felt anxious about in your dreams plays out.

At the end of the dream, any activity that is proactive and personal and filled with forward momentum (such as walking, jogging, or running) is generally auspicious, as it points to a future filled with your growing sense of independence. How you feel about this autonomous activity and how agile your dream body is can speak volumes about the direction in which your future self is currently taking you. If you are in a dream race, how are you doing? Don't worry if you aren't winning. Perhaps your future self simply wants you to remember the profound wisdom in the story of the tortoise and the hare.

Moving On

Active/Passive: Another clue to decoding the precognitive message of this type of dream is to determine whether the actions in your dream are proactive or reactive. For example, are you running towards something or away from something? Are you following or are you leading? All will forecast future situations or mindsets and whether they are going to be positive or negative for developing your potential. Sometimes your dream will use frantic action scenarios to encourage you to be more proactive because your future self is doubting you. Much will depend on your personal circumstances and how willing you are to dig deep and find the courage and self-discipline to get in the driving seat of your life.

Activities: Any activity or anything you do in a dream is related to the progress you are making towards attracting a fulfilling future and whether you are on track to positively develop your potential or not. Should you find that your actions are clumsy, destructive, embarrassing, disingenuous, or confusing, this indicates that you are headed towards a scenario in your waking life where you won't live up to your full potential. With this heads-up, you can ensure this isn't the case. If your actions are empowering in your dream, you can look ahead and carry on with great confidence.

Adventure: When you fall asleep and dream, you enter an infinite world of possibility. It is the ultimate adventure park where you can do or be anything. If your dream plants you right in the middle of a high-speed adventure, be that running from wild animals in a jungle, riding in a speedboat to escape capture, or hurtling into space, this is a sign that you are about to experience the thrill of tremendous change in your waking life. Perhaps your life has got too stuck in a rut and your precognitive mind is programming you to seek out more adventure in your waking life. The key to decoding these dreams precognitively will be how you feel about them. This is a clear indication of how you are going to feel when your future life calls you to face a challenge and step outside your comfort zone. If fear is the dominant feeling from the dream, then you need to work on your inner courage. Daydreaming can help you do this, as this will speak directly to your unconscious mind. Take some time to reenter the dream scenario you felt fear in. Perhaps you were being chased or were under attack. Then in your mind's eye, see yourself finding the courage to face your threat and overcome it. If you struggle to form mental imagery, you can simply write down the story of your dream and rescript it. As you imagine or rescript it, know that the braver you are in your dreams and daydreams, the braver you are going to be when it matters in your waking life. Should you dream of escaping a potential threat or discovering the ability to fly or some other superhero power, take this as reassurance from your dreaming mind that you have what it takes. Inject some self-belief into your waking life and you will become unstoppable.

Body Language: How a person's body moves can tell you a lot about their inner world and true feelings, and you can apply this to the way you and other people in your dream move. Does a particular movement stand out? If it does, you are being given a heads-up about something that may happen soon and how you are likely to respond. Is your dream response up to the task? If it isn't, then your dreaming mind is urging you to rethink your stance. For example, if you are sitting in your dream, is that the optimal posture for you or would it be better if you had been standing up in your dream? In the coming days, you may well find yourself in a position where you need to voice what matters to you but are tempted to take a step back. Recall the feeling of your sitting dream and whether it is encouraging you to keep your head down or stand up and be counted. If standing around did feature in your dream, why were you standing? What were you looking at? Did you stay in one position or turn around and look for new perspectives?

Chased: If you are being chased in your dreams, this is forecasting a future response where you feel events are catching up on you. The dream could also forecast you closing your mind to other viewpoints. Or are you running away from an aspect of yourself? Search the details of the dream to see if your flight response is justified. In most cases you probably won't even know what you are running away from, so whenever you feel tempted to avoid, deny, or escape someone or something that disturbs you in your waking life, recall this dream. Let this conscious déjà rêvé remind you that avoidance is self-destructive and futile. What do you need to wake up to about yourself and your life? Face your future fears and understand them.

By doing so, they will melt away. Feeling courage in either a dream or a daydream can have an empowering impact, and the more courage you start to notice in your own dreams, the more courage you will soon discover in your waking life. If you are chasing or pursuing something or someone in your dream, the precognitive message is that your future self wants you to find the courage to catch up with it.

Climbing: If you are climbing stairs or a mountain in a dream, watch out for potential roadblocks but know they can make you stronger and give you a better view or perspective of the right way ahead. Don't avoid them. Climb through them.

Crafts/Arts: In general, dreams with artistic themes foreshadow a burst of creativity on the horizon for you. Dreaming about acting in a play on stage could also suggest you will soon find yourself in a position where others are observing you, and when that happens, you need to play to your strengths and seek out greater recognition in your waking life. Watching a play is warning you not to hide your talents, as you may soon be required to showcase them. It could also be encouraging you to be more objective in some area of your life. If you are studying a picture or reading a book in your dream, this foreshadows a future perspective that will either help or hinder you depending on how you feel about the subject of the picture or book. Any kind of embroidery, knitting, or sewing or the appearance of a needle and thread or a ball of wool in a dream points to the importance of paying attention to the details in the near future. You may be missing something crucial.

Crawling: Crawling in a dream could forecast some kind of humiliation in your waking life. Discovering a dose of humility now might help you avert that potential future.

Creativity: If you don't consider yourself creative or artistic, your night vision shows you that there is an artist within you painting your inner landscape with images every single night. Dreamwork is your opportunity to rediscover the joy and power of your inner visionary. To remind you that you are the artist of your dreams and your future, your precognitive mind will sometimes incubate a dream where the symbolic connection between creativity and dreaming is made crystal clear. You may find yourself painting a portrait, taking photos, or performing creative tasks. Your dreaming mind wants you to find ways to unleash your hidden creativity because your future happiness is waiting for you there.

Dancing: Any dancing, hopping, skating, or skipping in your dream suggests good things are coming your way if the feeling accompanying these dream actions is a joyful one. Keep on singing and dancing from the inside out.

Digging: If you are digging in a dream, your future success relies on your ability to avoid superficiality and look beneath the surface of things for deeper meaning in both your dreams and your waking life.

Exercising: When exercising features in a dream, your future happiness lies in your ability to refine your skills, practise, train, and be more flexible.

Falling: Falling in a dream is a sharp warning that unless you start prioritising self-care and self-respect, avoid oversharing, and put some boundaries in place, the panic you feel may soon play out in your waking life. You will feel unsupported. However, if you felt fine falling from a great height in your dream, this is a more positive sign, as it suggests that you will display a go-with-the flow attitude in waking life at exactly the right time.

Flying: Flying in a dream represents your sense of personal power in the coming days and how well it is going to serve you when tested in the future. It can also forecast that a liberating new perspective or relationship is on the horizon. Believe in your own power and you will attract whoever or whatever your soul needs to grow wings. As always, the key to interpreting this dream, and whether it foreshadows negativity or positivity on the horizon, is how you feel about flying. Fear suggests a lack of faith in yourself that you need to rectify sooner rather than later. If you feel invincible, good things are coming your way. Notice also how high or low you fly in the dream and what or whom you are flying over, as they will all add precognitive insights about future situations or mindsets that are going to raise you up or drag you down.

Kidnapping: Any kidnap or hostage scenario in your dream foreshadows a near future where someone in your life may try to take advantage of you or control you in some way. Forewarned is forearmed. Make sure the hostage-taker in your dream is not a symbol of your own closed mind.

Movements: Any movement you experience or observe in a dream, either your own or that of others, represents how well you are going to adapt to a potential turning point on the horizon in your waking life where you may find that your judgement or abilities are called into question. If the movements in your dream are flowing and natural, this bodes well, but if you are restricted or trapped or your movements are limited in some way in your dream, it is important that you address any self-esteem issues or a closed-minded approach you have sooner rather than later. Doing this now will help you become a better decision-maker. In general, free-flowing dream images where there are no impediments or jarring breaks to your movement tend to be good omens.

Occupations/Work: The work you do in waking life can often express your value to others, so if work-related activities appear in your dreams, your precognitive mind is pointing its dream finger at your self-worth and the potential future your self-worth is busy attracting. If you arrive late or unprepared for work, this suggests feelings of insecurity, but it also encourages you to prepare better and take preventive measures in your waking life so the potential future in your dream doesn't play out. Specific occupations in a dream encourage you to reflect on how certain behaviours and attitudes you currently have are going to either help or hinder your future. For example, if you dream of a scientist, you may need to be more logical and experimental in your waking life. If you dream of a nurse, perhaps you need to be more caring and compassionate, and so on.

Pushed: If you are being pushed in a dream, you may soon find yourself under more pressure than you anticipated. To prepare for that, make sure you don't become a pushover in some area of your waking life.

Puzzles/Problems: This category of dreams includes scenarios where you are lost in a maze, fighting for survival in a jungle, or wading through mud, as well as more mundane problems such as not being able to find a pen or your watch or failing to complete a task everyone else finds easy, and so on. It can sometimes be hard to know what the precognitive indication is here, but in many cases your dreaming mind is suggesting that your future looks confusing and uncertain because you aren't connecting to and believing in it enough in your waking life. It is urging you to find a direction in your waking life and reminding you that it is the journey, not the destination, that matters. There will be twists and turns ahead, challenges and dead ends, but if you follow your instincts, you are always on the right path.

Running: If you are running in a dream, you may find yourself feeling somewhat impatient soon. When/if you recognise that déjà rêvé emotional reaction, let it encourage you to consider if you are trying to run before you can walk in some area of your waking life. Do you need to slow down or do you need to quicken your pace? If you felt exhilarated by your dream running, then it is the latter, but if you felt exhausted, it is the former.

Sport: If you dream of any sport, first consider your personal associations with it. It is possible that the skills required in that sport—for example, teamwork, quick reactions, and so on—might be of use in the coming days, so have them ready to go. Football dreams tend to refer to competitiveness or something you may soon need to tackle in a close-knit group of people.

Standing/Sitting: If you are standing in your dream, then in the coming days you may need to stand up for yourself in some way. If you are sitting, you may find yourself in a situation soon where indecision or a passive response sets you back.

Swimming: If you are swimming in a dream, you may soon find yourself in a situation where you crave emotional support from others. Make sure you want but don't need that support by first nourishing yourself emotionally. If you are diving in a dream, your dreaming mind wants you to stop hesitating and take a safe and well-calculated risk in the coming days.

Throwing/Catching: Any kind of throwing or catching scenario points to discarding a situation or mindset that no longer serves you well in your waking life or the inception of a new idea, relationship, or project.

Unfathomable: Since dreams predict your potential future, and that future has yet to be lived and is deeply mysterious to your present self, it is not surprising that you may wake up sometimes with dreams of doing and seeing things that appear utterly unfathomable. Keep reflecting on them, as meanings will shine through over time. Asking your dreaming mind to send you a clarifying dream the following night can sometimes help when you are at a loss to understand the meaning. Your dreaming mind may simply be using symbols that confound you to encourage you to think outside the box in the days ahead. Even unsolvable problems can be helped by a change of perspective. It is impossible and undesirable to know absolutely everything that lies ahead in your future. Your dreaming mind reveals likely future trends, not absolutes. Mystery should not be feared. Being surprised is the spice of both your dreams and your waking life.

Walking: In a dream, walking, like all forms of travel, is the direction your current thoughts, feelings, and actions are moving you towards. It points to the future you may soon experience in waking life unless you decide to course correct your mindset or some relationship or situation. In most cases, if you are walking or see yourself or others walking in a dream, this is a good omen, because walking is getting somewhere under your own steam. What you walk past, how easily you walk, and any obstacles you encounter will give you a clue to what to expect in the coming days. For example, if you are walking through mud, you may soon encounter a messy or sticky situation. If you are walking on rocks, you may need to protect your boundaries. If you are gliding through the air, your positivity will help you get ahead. Skipping in your dream often forecasts a period of fun ahead, and jumping predicts a surprising leap of faith.

Animals

The appearance of animals in dreams typically foreshadows what is instinctual and primal within you and ready to reveal itself soon. Examples include the flight-or-fight impulse, the urge to find a mate or protect your family, or the desire for standing or recognition within a group. Whenever these primal instincts and behaviours are about to surface in your waking life, your dreaming mind will often alert you with animal-themed dreams.

By understanding the precognitive message, you have an opportunity to prepare yourself and better manage your emotions ahead of time.

The symbolism of animals in your dreams suggests that something familiar is on the horizon, but it carries with it the potential to be wildly unexpected. Should a specific animal appear, the associations you make with that animal indicate what basic instinct is currently unexpressed but about to emerge, and when/if it does emerge, you are at serious risk of finding it hard to control or manage. It cannot be caged any longer. Your dreaming mind is urging you to find some much-needed inner harmony now in your waking life so that when/if pent-up instincts erupt, you are not caught off balance by them. Understanding that you oversee your emotions and not the other way around will push you forward from here.

Animals in dreams represent real inspiration and authenticity, because animals follow their own inner laws. They don't repress their natural instincts. So should you meet an animal in your dreams, you may well find yourself in a position in the coming days where you need to trust your gut and be true to yourself rather than prioritize the expectations of others. Channel the wisdom of the qualities of your dream animal when/if you meet that game-changing moment in your waking life.

Dream animals are a symbol of the relationship you have with yourself (and therefore have with others) or need to have with yourself to thrive. Although wild animal dreams do suggest that your future is more uncertain than do pet dreams, wild animal dreams are potentially more transformative, because if you can develop a healthy relationship with your untamed instincts now, the opportunity for future personal and spiritual growth is immense.

Whatever animal appears in your dreams, regard it as a chance to discover something brand-new about yourself. Here is a reminder again to consider how you feel about that animal in waking life and whether those feelings need to be managed or expressed better. As always, your personal association comes before the universal one. For example, if you love cats, the universal or common interpretation will speak to you, as cats are typically a symbol of independence and mystery. But if you are allergic to cats, their vision in a dream will have the opposite and less positive interpretation.

In essence, all animal themes and symbols in dreams point to aspects of yourself that are getting a little too close to the surface and need to be understood and managed better in your waking life. Something deep and primal within you is stirring and is ready to erupt in your waking life. Should intense emotion indeed surface in the coming days, please don't see it as a negative or try to deny it. Learn the important life lessons your basic instincts must teach you. Then let them serve as an important reminder not just to manage your emotions intelligently, but also to live your life as it was meant to be lived, with passion and spontaneity.

Animal Wisdom

Birds: The distinctive, emotive symbolism of birds, and therefore where their precognitive wisdom lies, is in their ability to rise above and escape the limitations of Earth. They are free to see the bigger picture. If birds appear in your dream, you are on track for some kind of insight, wisdom, or even enlightenment, and the secret to unlocking it in your waking life following this dream will be getting directly in touch with both your imagination and your intuition. Follow your gut instincts in the coming days, and if things get tense or confusing, rather than trying to fly away from a complicated situation, the way forward is to make sure you take a bird's-eye objective overview.

Notice the condition and colour of the bird when looking for symbolic precognitive guidance from this dream. Should your dream offer you details about a specific type of bird, this is valuable precognitive insight, as you can go forth and do your research about the associations and symbolism of that specific bird. In general, bird dreams are considered auspicious signs or good omens for your future, but there are also fewer positive superstitions related to them.

Albatross, black crow, buzzard, or vulture can indicate an impending misfortune of some kind that you need to swerve or duck from. They also warn you to beware of gossip and, in the case of magpies, of losing something that is yours. By contrast, a dove, eagle, goose, hawk, lark, nightingale, jaybird, owl, robin, swan, or yellow bird in dreams projects a bright future. Woodpecker, sparrow, and pigeon suggest that more hard work and persistence will soon be needed, and if you see an ostrich, you may soon find yourself in a position where you can either avoid responsibility or the truth or take ownership. It's obvious which course of action your dreaming mind (which always has your future evolution at heart) wants you to take.

The symbol of a peacock or mockingbird is warning you to avoid arrogance when success manifests for you. Owls suggest that you need to draw upon your own wisdom and knowledge in the coming days or seek expert advice. Turkeys are associated with Thanksgiving and family gatherings, so this dream symbol is warning you to focus on togetherness rather than settling scores when it comes to the next gathering you attend with loved ones. If you hear birdsong in your dream, it has the same interpretation as birds in general, but notice the sound and what feeling it inspires in you. Is the bird's singing sweet or alarming?

Crucial to your precognitive interpretation will be the type of bird in your dream, how healthy it looks, and the symbolic associations you uncover. Caged birds suggest that you may soon encounter some kind of restriction or limitation in your waking life. When/if you notice that feeling or reaction in your waking life, let this déjà rêvé empower you to decide if you are at peace with that restriction or want to break free. If your dream graces you with feathers as symbols to decode, your future lies in taking yourself a little less seriously and consciously relaxing from the inside out when you feel anger or tension in your waking life.

Fish: Dream fish represent the very deepest level of your unconscious due to their early evolution on Earth. Fish are potent precognitive messages alerting you to forces deep within that are just about to surface but that you are not fully prepared for in your waking life. These forces may be healing or threatening depending on the behaviour and condition of your dream fish. For instance, crabs represent the need to protect yourself, but they can also suggest someone in your life being evasive or even the zodiac sign of Cancer. Always brainstorm every association and wordplay to see what they may be suggesting about your future.

Dolphins and whales in dreams suggest that you are on the cusp of experiencing a leap in awareness and personal and spiritual growth. If you are fishing in your dream, this suggests that you are looking for deeper insight in your waking life or hoping to catch an opportunity and that vital information or an opportunity will soon be presented to you. Fishing dreams also point to a much-needed period of rest and relaxation on the horizon in your waking life.

Toad dreams warn of insincere flattery from someone you know appearing in your life, whereas frogs suggest that a whole new phase in your life is about to begin. Remember, frogs experience dramatic change in their lives, starting out as a tadpole. Sharks have a universal significance as deadly predators, so your dreaming mind is warning you to be alert to someone or something that could prove to be potentially dangerous. It could also point to your own fears being your own worst enemy.

How the water behaves in any underwater-themed dream is significant, as you are exploring in the dream the deepest, darkest depths of yourself. This can help you get to the bottom of issues that are likely to prove to be roadblocks to your future happiness.

Insects/Bugs: Should your dream feature insects or bugs, they are signs that you may soon encounter a series of setbacks or frustrations. Your precognitive mind is using this symbol to remind you that even if challenging times lie ahead, insects in most cases are irritating and sometimes alarming but they're not deadly. They are also tiny in comparison to humans, and often our fear is totally unfounded and irrational. Apply this sense of perspective to your waking life in the coming days and don't make mountains out of molehills. Focus on the power of small things to create big results in your future.

Use your common sense and typical associations when interpreting your dream insects. For example, if you dream of a bee stinging you, is this warning you about someone or something in your life that has the potential to drain or disable you? Bear in mind that bees are also symbols of productivity and making honey, which points to potential happiness and success in the coming days. Wasps are a symbol of anger, and ants are connected to your work ethic. Lice, leeches, and maggots suggest that you may soon feel repulsed by something you or someone else has said or done. Dreaming of a moth warns against some kind of damage being done behind the scenes that you may not notice until it's too late. Worms symbolise decay. Whatever the pest that appears in your dreams, more attention to detail and greater self-awareness are what your precognitive mind demands from you in the coming days.

Flies in dreams suggest that you may soon feel mildly annoyed by someone or something or that you could well find yourself wishing you were a fly on the wall or feeling invisible in some way. When/if you experience that déjà rêvé, don't waste your energy trying to get everyone's attention. Stay undercover and bide your time until you are ready to be seen.

Scorpion dreams suggest that a situation may soon occur in your life that feels painful or harmful in some way. Perhaps it is stinging criticism from others or your own negative perspective. Whatever it is, it is self-defeating and the way forward is to shine a light into the darkness and stop it in its tracks before it can cause any real harm.

Insects also represent irritations that are likely to crop up soon but that you can effectively deal with if you just keep your cool. Swarms of insects could portend malicious rumours suddenly appearing in your life that need to be contained. They can also point to instinctual urges within you that have the potential to upset you and others if you are caught off guard by them.

Magical Creatures: Should any creature that appears in your dreams take on monstrous qualities, this is a symbol of your shadow or aspects of yourself that may come to the surface over the next few days unless you deal with them now.

The appearance of a giant or an ogre in your dreams suggests an uphill struggle or problem that might make you feel small or something that may soon blow up out of all proportion. Just remember that nobody can make you feel inferior without your consent. Dream goblins also suggest potential trouble and mischief on the horizon unless you find ways to protect yourself against it.

By contrast, the appearance of magical creatures such as fairies, mermaids, dragons, unicorns, the phoenix, or any surreal impossibility—for example, pigs flying or animals talking—can suggest that either you will soon find that some situation in your life is unworkable or you will soon need to think outside the box, depending on the feeling of the dream.

Should you encounter any creatures or characters from ancient myths and legends or from fairy tales, treat them as you would any other dream symbol. Brainstorm your personal associations and the traditional ones and see what future lessons or blessings they are pointing you towards.

Every dream has surreal/fantasy elements, but when the images and scenarios in your dream feel so fantastic or impossible to understand, here is your best approach. First, try to see if the meaning is obvious. For instance, if you encounter a creature in your dreams that has eyes in the back of its head, is your dreaming mind telling you that you need to watch your back in the coming days? If this does not work, brainstorm all of your personal associations and then have fun researching all of the common ones. If that doesn't give you any insight, sit down with a pen and paper and start to draw/doodle to see what insights flow from your unconscious.

If none of the above helps and the dream continues to nag at you, then before you go to sleep the following night, revisit your dream so the last thing you are thinking of before you go to sleep is that dream. Your precognitive mind will take the bait and likely send you another dream that has the same message about your future but is easier to understand. This technique is one you can use for any dream you can't make sense of, not just dreams that are filled with fantastical creatures.

Pets: Animals represent drives within you that are free from convention and expectation, but the main difference between wild animals and domesticated animals in your dreams is that in general, pets, such as cats and dogs, are a sign that when your instincts surface in your waking life, you will likely have much more control over them and they will feel less threatening. The qualities of the domestic animal in your dream will suggest the best way to manage and learn from those instincts.

Be aware that pets featuring in your dreams is also a sign that you may soon feel a deep need for unconditional love, attention, and affection and a longing to give and receive love. Feelings of responsibility and caring for someone else or others are about to take centre stage in your life.

Pets need daily love and care, so the loving message of this dream is again to prioritise self-care. However, if the pets in the dream are neglected, this indicates that soon you may find yourself feeling overly dependent on validation from others in some way. Guard against that by offering yourself lashings of unconditional love and care. A sick or wounded pet is a clear warning from your precognitive mind to take better care of your physical and emotional needs in the coming days.

Should your dream feature domestic animals and/or pets and they are well cared for, you are discovering within yourself the ability to take care of your emotional needs, and this will serve you well.

If you are lucky enough to have a pet and dream of them, make sure you recall your dream the following day when spending time with your pet. This conscious déjà rêvé will speak directly to your precognitive mind because of the feelings of unconditional love your pet inspires within you. Remember, it has been shown that feelings of unconditional love dramatically boost precognition, so the more time you spend with loved ones and pets, the better.

Reptiles: Should a reptile appear in your dream, this is a heads-up urging you to keep your emotional cool in the future. Something potentially dangerous may surface soon that could unsettle you, or you could encounter biting comments from others, but if you approach it rationally, you will not be harmed. Timing will be everything. Because crocodiles and alligators are masters of disguise, an intense situation or revelation may suddenly appear, so you need to be prepared. Should your dream feature snails, turtles, or tortoises, the way forward is to proceed at your own sweet pace. Take small but steady steps in the direction of your dreams each day.

Scenarios Involving Animals: Dream animals can appear in an infinite number of scenarios, but if they are wounded, in pain, or dying, this is warning you of a potential defensive or reactive emotional response upcoming in your waking life. Should you notice this response in the days ahead, take time out to pause and reflect on what is happening. Your precognitive mind is using the symbol of a neglected animal to remind you of the importance of tending to your basic physical needs. Your future self can't pull you forward until you take better care of yourself.

Killing and/or eating animals in a dream is a strong precognitive sign. Your animal instincts should neither fully control you nor be destroyed or killed. You need to find positive ways to express and manage them in the coming days.

Should an animal be watching, attacking, or chasing you in a dream, this is a sign that in your waking life you may soon find yourself in a position where your instincts take over and throw you off balance. It could also be a sign of potential power moves behind the scenes at work or in some area of your life that you need to be on your guard against. More likely, though, some area of your personality longs to be expressed and is tired of being repressed. The way forward is to face and deal with any fear or doubt you have about your ability to intelligently manage your emotions.

If you hear animal sounds in dreams, figure out what feeling or emotional reaction those sounds suggest to you in waking life, so you are better prepared if a future situation or mindset links you back to them. For example, if you hear roaring, this could reflect pent-up anger within you or towards someone or something else surfacing in the coming days.

The wilder and more dangerous the animal in your dream is, the greater the precognitive warning about aspects of yourself that are eager to break free from control by your conscious mind. Such dreams are again offering you an opportunity to learn to manage your instincts sooner rather than later.

If you dream of animals in a lab, this suggests future limitations, and the way to avoid that restrictive potential is to acknowledge the emotions and qualities represented by the animal. Caged animals predict that when the need arises, you will remain firmly in control of your instincts, but depending on the feeling of the dream, they can also suggest a desire to free yourself and go with the flow. Whenever you feel a desire to break free in the days ahead, return to your animal dream, tune into your intuition, and let the déjà rêvé inspire you to make a well-thought-out decision.

Should you take the form of an animal in your dream, this is a sign of future inhibition. Notice the animal concerned and focus on the traits and wisdom of that creature, as they indicate what you need to assimilate or learn from for your personal growth. Should you encounter a wise or talking animal in your dreamscape, it suggests that you will soon discover in your waking life an inner wisdom and strength you didn't realise you had.

Snakes: This is one of the most common symbols to surface in dream surveys in recent years and for good reason. Snakes are potent symbols of personal and spiritual rebirth and the importance of shedding old mindsets (skins) if you want to heal your present and attract a happier future. There is also the implication of dishonesty to consider, so should you dream of a snake, make sure in the coming days that you are ruthlessly honest with yourself and others and watch out for people whose actions do not match their words.

Specific Animals: If you don't feel anything about your dream animal, think of the qualities typically associated with it. The following list of keywords for some of the most commonly dreamt-of animals will help kick-start those associations for you. Be sure, though, to brainstorm your personal associations first and stay alert. These animals are starring in your dreams for a reason. They want to get your attention ahead of time, as you may need to utilise these basic impulses in your waking life very soon.

Ape/Monkey: Inquisitiveness, mischief
Bat: Blindness, secrets
Bear: Overprotective, volatile
Beast or Mixture of Animals: Memories, regrets
Bull: Aggression, bullishness
Cat: Independence, mystery, stealth
Cheetah: Speed, stealth. Any wild cat in a dream suggests that you will soon find the drive to go out and get what you want, but remember that dreams love the precognitive power of puns. Watch out for someone or something cheating in the coming days.
Cow: Empathy, receptiveness
Deer: Gentleness, vulnerability (*Stag:* virility)
Dinosaur: Primitive, underdeveloped, outdated
Dog: Loyalty, companionship, spontaneity. Take a good, long look at your relationships in the coming days, especially the one you have with yourself.
Donkey: Humility, stubbornness
Elephant: Wisdom, memory, good luck
Fox: Stealth, deception

Frog: Transformation
Goat: Survival, resilience
Horse: Nobility, adventure
Lamb: Innocence, vulnerability
Lion: Pride, predator, strength. Remember the precognitive potential of the dream pun here: Are you lying to yourself or is someone lying to you?
Mouse: Timid, dull
Rabbit: Creativity, sexuality
Rat: Disloyalty, intelligence
Sheep: Conformity, calm
Tiger: Unpredictability, sexuality
Wolf: Greed, freedom
Zoo Animals: Restriction, observation

In every case, remember that dream animals represent your unfiltered instincts, the beast within you. Reflecting deeply on what aspect of yourself that animal represents to you will help you immediately identify, understand, and therefore manage it when those instincts ultimately rise to the surface.

Bear in mind that because we tend to assign certain personality traits to animals, this type of dream can sometimes point to people you are emotionally close to in your waking life who may soon act in an unpredictable or uncharacteristic way.

Finally, be sure to consider the archetypal, mythical, and spiritual associations with your dream animal as you do your precognitive dream interpretation, as well as puns using animal qualities to describe a feeling or situation, for example, feeling badgered, and so on. Whatever the scenario, when it comes to animal dreams, some aspect of your personality and your life is straining at the leash to get your urgent attention and alert you to an exciting opportunity for transformation that most definitely lies ahead.

Spiders: A spider is a symbol of a small issue coming up in your waking life that could become a serious one if you don't pay attention. The devil is in the details. However, a spider is often a positive sign showing you that the way ahead is to be patient and work hard. The dream could also be a warning that you may soon feel like an outsider or that there is going to be a dominant female energy arriving on the scene that could unsettle you.

One way to understand what your spider dream is trying to tell you about your future is to talk to it. In your waking life, hold the image of your dream spider in your mind and ask it what it wants to share. It is possible that you may soon feel trapped by someone or something or by your own lack of self-confidence. Take heart that dreams of spiders, like all dream symbols, can have positive interpretations. In this case, the dream is telling you to make sure you can demonstrate your truth through your actions—the things you repeatedly do—rather than just talk about your truth when the time comes. In other words, walk your talk. You have within you the capacity to create something utterly unique and beautiful that has not been seen before.

Body

Your body, parts of your body, and themes related to health and well-being featuring in dreams are all related to how well you are likely to perform in the future, not typically your physical performance, but rather your mental and emotional performance—for example, your ability to remember or your ability to be compassionate and so on. Your precognitive mind seizes on the associations linked to the body or body part to give you a heads-up about areas of potential concern and what emotional or mental abilities you are going to have to work on, discover, or understand better in the coming days.

Having said that, in rare cases your dreaming mind can precognitively draw attention to bodily ailments before you consciously recognise anything is wrong and sometimes even before there are any physical symptoms. I have had numerous people message me over the years about warning dreams that encouraged them to visit a doctor and literally saved their lives. This is exceedingly rare, but if you do have a vivid or recurring dream memory of a part of your body that is injured or diseased or you receive a warning of some kind about your health in your dream, there is no harm in getting a checkup with your doctor.

Sometimes dreams about the body can reflect how you are going to feel about yourself physically in the near future. If your dream body looks and feels beautiful, carry this body positivity over into your waking life. It will serve you well. If the opposite is true, be especially alert to feelings of insecurity in the coming days, and when/if anxiety strikes, remind yourself that your dreaming mind sensed this might be an issue moving forward and draw self-confidence from that inner wisdom.

Should injuries and broken bones feature in your dream, this symbolises a potential loss of parts of yourself in order to fit in or please others. If/when you notice this kind of fragmentation trending in your waking life, consider the reasons behind it. Ask yourself how much you are willing to compromise or give away parts of yourself. Let this questioning remind you to value your energy, time, and attention more. What you are freely giving away could be irreplaceable.

In essence, any dream that features your body or feelings about your body is always worthy of serious reflection. How you feel about your body is a vital part of how you feel about yourself overall as a person. How you feel about yourself is the future you are busy creating and attracting. Moving forward, whenever you write down your dreams, dig deep into your recall, and if your body or body parts or the bodies or body parts of others featured in your dreams, be sure to make a note, as it is an element you may not have paid close attention to before.

When your dream features body themes or body parts, look especially for puns, as that will likely give you the best interpretation, for example, being unable to stomach something or not having a leg to stand on. Then in your waking life, when you notice a situation or an emotional reaction that resonates with this dream, brainstorm all possible meanings. This is your opportunity to change your future for the better.

Above all, aim to symbolically associate whatever body part or how your body looks or feels like in a dream with your inner world and whether your precognitive mind is sensing that your current mindset is putting you on a path to future disorder or health.

Note: As body dreams are typically about your emotional and psychological well-being rather than your physical health, should you have recurring dreams about your body that are disturbing and unpleasant, your dreaming mind may be pointing you towards counselling to boost your self-esteem.

Your Body Counts

Blood: Blood is a profound symbol of the life force and of moral and physical strength. If there is blood loss in your dream, it's a sign that you will soon feel drained and are placing yourself at serious risk of emotional pain unless something about your current mindset changes. In much the same way, dream wounds relate to things that you have kept hidden coming to the surface or aspects of your personality that you have neglected demanding your attention in the very near future. There is often great wisdom to be found in those wounds.

Body Parts: It can be helpful to remember that we often use body parts as metaphors in our waking lives to express certain intentions and emotions, for example, getting a foot in the door, losing your head, and so on. In the coming days, you may be able to apply the metaphor from a dream body part to your waking circumstances and let it help guide, motivate, or centre you.

When precognitively interpreting body part dreams, view the images as symbols of your abilities and/or performance in some area of your waking life that will almost certainly take or need to take centre stage in the coming days.

Below are some suggested keyword associations and potential questions to ask yourself regarding various dream body parts to help you get started with your own research. You will notice that each body part has a psychological, emotional counterpart.

Head: Decision-making, intellect, logic

Face: The persona or mask you will soon find yourself presenting to the world, what you will face, and, if you see a face in the mirror, secrets to be revealed. If there is dream acne or pimples, something in your life may soon need to be cleared up because it has been festering too long.

Chin: The ability to take things on the chin or keep your chin up

Neck: The neck symbolises the connection between body and mind, but remember the puns here, such as sticking your neck out or being neck and neck.

Heart: Loving feelings for yourself and others

Chest: Your ability to be honest and protect your feelings

Ears: The importance of listening and paying attention to both your own gut instinct and the guidance of others

Eyes: Observation and judgement, the windows of your soul, the way you see ahead, the vision you have for yourself

Mouth: Communication, sensuality

Nose: Curiosity, intuition

Hand: Expression, details, and creativity and how well you may soon handle a situation in your waking life. Pay attention to the gesture of your hands. If your dream hands are dirty or blood-stained, this suggests that something potentially inappropriate is coming up and you may need to clean up your act. Should you wash your hands (or any body part) in your dream, be sure the following day to reconnect with your dream mindfully when you wash your hands. Reflect on what pain, regret, or guilt your dreaming mind wants you to release and heal from.

Fingers: A new direction to point towards. The index finger suggests that you may soon need to make a point, the ring finger is commitment, the middle finger indicates assertiveness, the thumb symbolises self-confidence, and the little finger is empathy.

Arms: The ability to reach out and connect to or protect yourself from others

Shoulders: A responsibility that will require emotional courage could soon be heading your way.

Breasts: Feeling that your privacy is being invaded or that you need to get something off your chest

Back: Something in your waking life needs to be put behind you.

Stomach: Repressed emotion, things you may find difficult to stomach or tolerate in the short and long term, and the importance of finding middle ground if you are to progress

Genitals: A penis suggests that assertiveness will soon be required, a vagina indicates the importance of receptivity in the days ahead, and the anus is all about the power of leaving things behind and not allowing the past to dictate your future.

Ankle/Knee/Elbow: Adaptability and flexibility. You may soon find out if you need to be more flexible or if you have been too accommodating.
Heel: Something that may make you feel vulnerable in the coming days
Legs and Feet: The need to move or stand up for yourself
Nails, Teeth, Hair, Skin: Any body part that you constantly shed and replace symbolises the ongoing need to let go of limiting mindsets and evolve.
Hair: Strength, vitality, intelligence, self-esteem, sex appeal. Dreaming about a haircut or brushing or washing your hair represents a reshaping of your self-image or perspective in the coming days.

Should any part of your body be cut or bruised, this can be a warning of criticism in the coming days or a feeling that you want to cut something or someone out of your waking life.

Body Talk: Precognitive wisdom speaks through your body when you are awake, most notably through your heart and your gut, so if your dreaming mind shines a night-light on your entire body, pay extra close attention.

A cold or frozen body predicts a loss of creativity and passion ahead unless you find ways to reignite your enthusiasm for something or someone in your waking life. Cold feet indicate that a potential fear of making decisions will impede your progress. Dead bodies represent potential that is not going to be expressed unless you find a way to breathe some much-needed energy into it. Should your body disappear or you shrink to a tiny size in a dream, watch out, as you may soon find yourself feeling ignored, lonely, or isolated. Let the warning in your dream empower you from the inside out and remind you that you deserve to be seen and heard.

The left side of your body in dreams and in waking life highlights the power of intuition and creativity to shape your future, and the right side highlights what is more practical and rational. If your body is diseased, dismembered, sick, or unwell in your dream, you are in danger of pushing the limits in waking life, physically, mentally, and emotionally, and when you sense this happening in your waking life, make sure your drive to succeed does not tear you apart. Heal the crisis instead.

A loss of limbs does portend a growing sense of inadequacy unless you make a change in your waking life. You are also at risk of giving away too much of yourself, so guard against that. Anxiety and depression may follow if you don't protect your boundaries now.

If you are burnt, cut, bruised, or scarred in your dream, this warns against reacting to a future hurt in a self-destructive way. It also suggests things you carry with you that will negatively influence your decision-making progress.

Bones: Dream skeletons reference how supported you are going to feel soon by both yourself and others. They also hint at memories or people from your past that may soon reappear in your waking life. Notice how you feel about your dream bones, as this will arm you with more information about what area of your life needs to be brought back to life or laid to rest. Alternatively, is the way forward getting to the bones of the matter?

Breathing: Should you struggle for breath in your dream, this suggests that you may soon feel a need for more personal freedom. Anxiety about work or a relationship or a difficult situation is likely to drain your creativity and passion if you don't allow some fresh new perspectives into your life.

Kissing: The precognitive theme here is longing for more intimate communication. Pay attention to who is doing the kissing and who is being kissed and how the kiss makes you feel. The associations you glean from this will tell you what you need to get up close and personal with for your personal growth.

Restroom Dramas: Unless you need to use the restroom in your waking life and your dreaming mind is tuning into that bodily need, the precognitive symbolism here is strong. Needing to find a restroom, or any faeces or urine imagery, suggests that something that no longer serves you needs to be urgently released for your future well-being. This could apply to a situation or a relationship, but it is more likely to refer to a mindset or to emotional waste, such as regret, guilt, shame, frustration, or anger. It will soon become clear to you that there is something you must let go of in your waking life. Retrace the story of your dream. Did you find a restroom? How did you feel when you found it? If you didn't find one, then let this dream be your catalyst or outlet giving you the permission you need for emotional release.

Be aware that toilet-themed dreams can also indicate a growing sense that you don't have enough time in your waking life for your own intimate needs. Should you feel tempted in the coming days to overcommit, let the memory of this precognitive dream empower you to say no more often. A lack of privacy or personal space could also be a factor you need to consider. Alternatively, this dream can predict saying the right thing at the wrong time, so be on your guard against this happening and check your impulses if you feel tempted to speak without thinking in the coming days, as your words and actions have an impact on others. Vomiting in a dream carries similar precognitive warnings, but this is more likely to do with something you said that was toxic to you or the person you said it to.

Sickness: Dreams that spotlight sickness, unless you are currently ill, are forecasting that your holistic well-being may be at risk if you continue to think, feel, and act the way you currently are. They clearly pinpoint areas of potential conflict and concern that you need to focus on now to attract a more balanced future. You need to nurse yourself back to wholeness and health.

Follow up with your doctor if the dream features images and sensations that feel disturbing, as such dreams may foretell actual illness if you don't take better care of yourself. In most cases, dreams use body symbolism to point to your psychological health and how this is going to impact your ability to perform rather than to your physical health. Traumatic memories that are holding you back can surface in such dreams, suggesting a conflict with some aspect of yourself that you haven't acknowledged or can't accept, and the priority for you moving forward is to identify the part of you that is unwell. Inner troubles are about to surface unless you address them now.

Should you be blind in your dreams, you may soon find yourself in a position where you struggle to see the truth or face reality. Will you turn a blind eye or will a new perspective help open your eyes?

Silent Screaming: Not being able to speak in a dream suggests that you may soon find yourself unable to express your opinion or get your point across effectively. Prepare ahead of time for that so you aren't tongue-tied when you need to speak. If you are deaf in a dream, the spotlight in the coming days will be on your ability to listen.

Should you have a dream about having a stroke or cancer or some other life-threatening disease, again it is always worth getting your health checked by your doctor. In most cases it is unlikely you have any disease, but this dream does point towards future frustration or feeling that something or someone unhealthy is eating away at you. It needs to be exorcised. Some discomfort or uncertainty is on the horizon, and this will challenge you, but challenge is not to be feared. Crisis is opportunity.

Feelings of powerlessness may lie ahead if dismemberment is the theme of your dream. Should a body part be deformed in some way, self-criticism and fear of what others think about you is most likely to stop you from succeeding in the future. Paralysis in dreams is a nightmare scenario referring to things not progressing. When/if you notice that stuck feeling in your waking life, let your dream warning put you in touch with your inner compass.

Teeth: Dreaming about teeth falling out or crumbling is one of the most commonly reported dreams all over the world. The first step is to make sure that a trip to the dentist is not overdue. Your dreaming mind could be warning you about a problem with your teeth, but when you have ruled out that possibility, feel free to fully explore the precognitive meaning.

Toothless dreams often forecast times of change ahead, and your precognitive dreaming mind may have conjured up this image to prepare you for that transition and to remind you that change is inevitable and part of the flow of life. Babies losing their milk teeth is entirely natural. This dream could also indicate a potential loss of innocence. Should you discover something in the coming days that changes your perspective forever, be sure to reflect with gratitude on this déjà rêvé helping to prepare you ahead of time for the revelation.

Losing your teeth in a dream can suggest that concerns about your appearance and/or ageing are limiting your personal and spiritual growth. In this social media age where everybody is a star constantly presenting images of themselves to others for likes, it is not surprising that toothless dreams have becoming even more commonly reported. This dream also predicts issues with communication potentially coming to the fore. You may soon find yourself in a position where you feel unable to express yourself effectively. Let this dream warning empower you to assert yourself. Or perhaps you will soon regret something you said or what you didn't say. Teeth in the animal world often communicate anger, so the symbolism of losing teeth for some reason in the near future speaks loud and clear here.

Clothing

In real life, clothes hide, reveal, protect, and create a perception. They also express your personality and influence the first impressions others have of you. If you have read Jane Austen's novel *Pride and Prejudice,* you will know that first impressions can be decisive, but they can also be wrong.

The precognitive symbolism here could not be more obvious, with dream clothing representing your self-image. If you have a dream where clothes feature, this means that soon your reputation and/or self-esteem is going to be on the line.

The condition of the clothes will suggest whether this dream is warning you to protect yourself against exposure or reassuring you that you are heading in the right direction. Putting on clothes suggests you will soon move forward. Undressing is also a promising sign, as it suggests you will soon shed mindsets or relationships that are holding you back. If you find yourself unable to get dressed or undressed for whatever reason in the dream, this is a reminder that the biggest roadblock to your future happiness and success is your own perspective and how you feel about yourself.

Buying or shopping for new clothes in a dream suggests a fresh start is on the horizon. Look forward to it. If you are washing your clothes in the dream, your precognitive mind is telling you that the way you present yourself may need a refresh and negative mindsets need to be purged. Towels in a dream suggest that you will soon throw in the towel or wipe the slate clean in some area of your waking life.

Inappropriate Clothing

Should you find yourself wearing the wrong or inappropriate clothes in your dream or clothes that don't belong to you, this dream is urging you to change your perspective, because if you don't, you may soon find that your self-esteem takes a hit. This dream is highlighting the distance between who you truly are and what you feel others want from you. Alternatively, depending on how relaxed you feel in the clothes, it could suggest a new perspective or that you need to get out of your comfort zone.

Pay special attention to the colour and texture of the clothes in your dream, as this will offer you precognitive clues.

If you find yourself partially dressed in your dream, your precognitive mind is urging you to plan and prepare better for the future. If you notice any other problems with your dream clothes, such as them being too tight, too big, too formal, too shabby, and so on, heed the signs. Your precognitive mind is telling you that very soon your self-image will be called into question and you need to find ways to get ahead of yourself and build your confidence from the inside out. View problem clothing dreams as positive, because they are making you aware of a tension or conflict within you that you may not be admitting to in your waking life. This conflict is limiting your future potential. Forgive the pun (even though your dreaming mind loves puns), but it is time to change.

Specific Items of Clothing

Should your nocturnal precognition highlight an item of clothing for you, thank your dreaming mind for getting down to specifics. The key to discovering the implications for your future will lie in the strong associations with that item of clothing. As always, let your personal associations lead the way before jumping into the common, universal ones listed here:

Apron: Are you about to undertake a messy but creative task?

Bag: A bag can suggest that you may soon be asked to keep a secret, as in don't let the cat out of the bag.

Belt: Is this dream about support or restraint being required in the coming days?

Coat: Keywords to brainstorm here are protection, formality, your public image, and so on, as some or all of them are likely to surface soon in your waking life.

Dress/Trousers: You may soon find yourself questioning gender stereotypes in both yourself and others. If the dress or pants fit, you are going to feel in charge of a situation or relationship. If they don't fit, is this a warning of being caught with your pants down or feeling out of your depth?

Fabrics: Brainstorm all associations if your dream spotlights a particular fabric, such as leather, silk, etc.

Footwear: You may soon feel the need to keep your feet on the ground or stay in touch with reality. When you do recall your dream footwear, it will typically point to aspects of your personality that will either help or hinder you in making the best decisions, so put your best foot forward. Notice the colour and condition of the shoes, as this will contain insights you can use to help you move forward. If you are wearing someone else's shoes, your precognitive mind is saying that in the coming days you need to see their point of view.

Gloves: Should you notice gloves, a symbol of intimacy in Victorian times, appearing in your dreams, you may soon find that a desire to be honest with someone washes over you. Perhaps someone or something in your waking life needs to be handled with extra special care or treated with kid gloves. To help you sense what your dream is foreshadowing, mindfully put on a pair of gloves and recall your dream. See what associations and/or future visions this conscious déjà rêvé triggers.

Hat: A hat in a dream is a clear vision of personal growth or new perspectives on the horizon. It's also a symbol of intelligence or what will set you apart in some way. If it's a helmet, this is more about the need for greater protection.

Jewellery: Jewellery symbolises a priceless inner beauty that you need to reconnect with in the coming days, for example, loyalty or compassion.

Makeup: Makeup has a similar precognitive interpretation to clothing in dreams. It's all about what you need to conceal or hide or reveal, but with the added emphasis on your ability to make changes swiftly. Don't forget wordplay. You may soon find yourself in a position where you need to make up with someone or something in your waking life.

Mask/Costume: This is a clear warning about some kind of deceptive behaviour to watch out for from someone or perhaps yourself in the coming days.

Nightwear: Your dreaming mind could simply be warning you here to prioritise your sleep quality so you don't end up with serious sleep debt.

Shirt/Tie: Puns may help with the precognitive interpretation here, for example, rolling your sleeves up, losing the shirt off your back, tying up loose ends, and so on.

Suntan: A suntan is a potential warning from your precognitive mind to wear more sunscreen.

Swimwear: Perhaps a vacation or some time off should be planned.

Tattoo: You may soon find yourself drawing on the wisdom of a lesson or memory from your past to help you make a significant decision.

Umbrella: Any protective item in a dream is urging you to protect yourself against future emotional overwhelm.

Underwear: This is a potential precognitive symbol of deeply personal assumptions that are hidden but are about to confront you in your waking life. You need to decide if these attitudes can help or hinder you moving forward.

Wallet/Purse: These are highly personal items that suggest you may soon feel anxious about your identity in some way. They could also be warning you to make sure you keep your personal items safe when in public and your personal details safe when online.

Perhaps more than with any other type of dream, and because clothes are relatively easy to acquire, should your precognitive mind draw your attention to a particular item of clothing, try to wear it or something that closely resembles it in the coming days. The resemblance could simply be the colour of the item if the dream clothing was outlandish.

It doesn't matter what the resemblance is. Just be sure to make that connection soon after recalling the dream. For example, if you wore a blue jumper in your dream, then wear a blue jumper if you have one. If you don't, then make sure an item of your clothing is blue. When you make that dream connection through an item of clothing, let the conscious déjà rêvé remind you that you are constantly creating your future through your mindset and your actions in the present. Is it time to go back to the drawing board or are you on track?

Mirror: If any of your clothing-themed dreams feature mirrors, this is a precognitive warning that your core values or beliefs about yourself are going to play a vital part in your future success. If the mirror is cracked or dirty, watch out for self-deception in all areas of your life. Honesty is your key to a clearer future. The time may soon come when you need to hold yourself accountable to something higher.

Nudity: Should you expose yourself in a dream, either deliberately or by accident, this is a warning against oversharing or being too trusting in the coming days. Pay attention to how you feel in the dream, because if the exposure doesn't make you feel embarrassed, this suggests you will soon feel called to be more honest and direct in some area of your life.

Being naked or partially clothed predicts fear of some kind of exposure as well as concerns about what others think of you. Should you recall this dream, give yourself a helping hand by focusing on why you feel the need to hide. Are you being true to yourself? If not, why not? Are you trying too hard to impress or are you concerned others will see through you? These are the tough questions your precognitive mind wants you to ask yourself in the coming days.

The key to interpreting this dream will be the reactions of others. Often other people in your dream just carry on as normal and don't even notice. This is your dreaming mind telling you that you are worrying needlessly, and whenever you feel anxious about the opinions of others, you need to revisit this dream in your mind. It will remind you that most people are too preoccupied with worrying about what other people think of them to worry about you! The only person you need to impress is yourself.

Should you find yourself in a dream strip club, this predicts you will soon be given the opportunity to reveal and express yourself. Just make sure that when that happens, you are authentic and your motives are not misunderstood.

Colour and Shape

Although some people do dream only in black and white, most of us dream in technicolour. You may have got into the habit of focusing on the story, symbols, or images of your dreams and not the colours of your dreamscape. I hope that reading this thread will encourage you to pay far more attention to the colour themes in your dreams, because just as colour has been shown to impact your mood and behaviour in waking life, it plays a significant part in the creation of your dreamscape too. As with everything in your dreams, your dreaming mind is trying to convey a precognitive message to you through the emotive symbolism of colour.

For example, if you dream of a green statue crashing to the floor, you may focus your precognitive dreamwork on the symbolism of a statue breaking, and you may soon break free from a restrictive or limiting mindset or situation, but the colour green will tell you what that restrictive emotion might be. Perhaps a feeling of envy, either your own or someone else's, is the roadblock to your future happiness?

Colour always evokes emotional reactions. To help you decode the symbolic meaning precognitively, reflect on how you would describe a specific colour to someone who can't see. What thoughts and feelings would you use to describe it? Those thoughts and feelings are about to surface in your waking life. Prepare ahead of time for them.

The next time you recall a dream, see if you can recall any colours or if a specific colour stood out. Then brainstorm all emotional associations, leading as always with your personal ones. What feeling does a specific colour inspire in you? Chances are you will soon experience that emotion, or you may find yourself in a situation where the associations with your dream colour help you make better decisions. For instance, if blue is the colour you recall, the need to stay calm and objective is being highlighted. The next day, be sure to seek out that colour in your waking life and notice what that conscious déjà rêvé inspires in you.

If you believe that you dream in black and white, first consider whether this is because you have not paid enough attention to colours or considered colour to be relevant in your dreamwork. If that is not the case, know that dreaming in black and white does not in any way diminish the precognitive potential of your dreamwork. In fact, it may infuse it with greater clarity. Black is associated with negativity, but it is also the colour of transformation. It symbolises what is hidden in the shadows but is crucial for your personal growth. White, by stark contrast, is traditionally the colour of wholeness, clarity, purity, potential, and innocence.

Look Around You!

If you have grown used to disregarding the colours, shapes, and patterns of your dreams as incidental to the main action, you have been missing out on a wealth of potential precognitive dream-decoding insight. From now on, when you wake up with a dream on your mind, see if you can recall any colours, shapes, or patterns. This may not happen right away if you have got into the habit of forgetting those details upon waking, but now that you know how important they are, you are on the right track. Since your dreaming mind always notices what you are doing in your waking life, one way to bring more colour and shape into your dream recall is to pay more attention to the emotional impact of the colours and shapes in your daily life.

Look up from reading or listening to this book and take a moment to gaze around you. What colours jump out at you? What shapes speak to you? What calms you? What annoys you? What inspires you? There is so much in our daily lives that we are not aware of. Let your precognitive dreamwork inspire you to drink in the details whether your eyes are wide open or shut.

Traditional Colour Meanings

The precognitive potential of a dream colour will always lie in your personal reaction to that colour in waking life, but the following traditional associations can help kick-start symbolic thinking. You'll notice that the interpretations below lean towards the positive, because your dreaming mind always wants you to expect the best for your future self, but be aware that every colour can also carry negative warnings. For example, the downside of yellow is cowardice/caution, green is envy, brown is dullness, red is danger, and so on.

Beige: Objectivity, neutrality
Black: Mystery, endings
Blue: Calm, intellect
Brown: Grounded, practical
Gold: Wealth, abundance
Green: Harmony, nature
Grey: Ambiguity, serious
Orange: Creativity, warmth
Pink: Compassion, love
Purple: Spirituality, transformation
Red: Passion, intensity
Silver: Intuition, opportunity
White: Purity, innocence
Yellow: Change, hope
Colouring: If you are colouring in a picture or using colouring pens in a dream, you may soon find yourself in a position where your ability to look on the bright side and see the positive will be a game changer. Dreaming in colour suggests that there may be many answers or approaches to consider moving forward. In other words, keep an open mind. Dreaming in black and white suggests a clear right-and-wrong or black-and-white approach.

The strength of your dream colours will indicate just how strong your emotional response is going to be to a future situation or mindset. Rich and vivid colours suggest that a sense of well-being is more likely, whereas weak or faded colours suggest oncoming fatigue.

Dark conditions in your dreamscape point to confusion and potentially being in the dark about something but also to transformative potential, as it is in the darkness that everything grows. Light suggests that there is clarity at the end of the tunnel. Just keep going one small and careful step at a time and you will get there.

Shapes

The shapes and patterns may also not be the first thing you recall when you write down your dreams upon waking. But like colours, they carry precognitive messages for you. I hope you will now pay far more attention to both the colours and the shapes in your dreams, because both the colour and the shape of a dream symbol or image can totally illuminate the meaning. For instance, if you dream of a house, the shape of the house can speak volumes. It will show you how you can shape or change an anticipated outcome.

There is a whole world of potential meaning to uncover in shapes and patterns. Just as absent-minded doodling can suggest a great deal about your mindset, the shapes and patterns of your dreams predict the future you are creating with your current approach in waking life.

Crosses in dreams forecast carrying a burden of some kind. Make sure that burden is one you are willing and able to carry and is not one that drags you down.

Triangles literally point to the achievement of your goals being in sight. They also imply spiritual enlightenment.

Squares can predict a period of stability but can also warn against an impending sense of tedium and limitation that you need to be on your guard against when/if you notice it manifesting in your waking life.

Star shapes almost always carry with them optimistic associations. Your future looks bright if you keep your head up and your mindset positive in your waking life.

Circles in dreams forecast completion and feelings of satisfaction. Does the circle feel like a secure or a restrictive place, or is it in danger of breaking? If the latter, what can you do to make sure the outcome is satisfying? One of the most common circles to appear in a dream is a ball. Are you trying to throw the ball or are you catching it? If you are trying to throw it, perhaps you need to ask for advice from others in your waking life to help you move forward. If you are catching it in your dream, you will soon find yourself in a position where you need to take action. The time for talking is over.

If the circle in your dream has knots, does this portend a future setback or roadblock or the tying up of loose ends? It is your dream and your future you are creating. You decide.

Crescent shapes in your dreams may forecast a burst of intuition and creativity in the coming days.

The appearance of mandala shapes, typically a square inside a circle, suggests that the best way forward is to be an individual and to stand out from rather than merge with the crowd.

Should the shapes in your dreams appear irregular or random, your dreaming mind is urging you to look for precognitive signs and patterns not just in your dreams but also in your waking life. They will point you in the right direction. The same applies to any patterns you recall. For example, dots urge you to pay more attention to the small details in the coming days. Lines predict that a decision is on the horizon and/or the best way to achieve your goals is to focus clearly and stop meandering. Spirals anticipate repetition in your waking life, but also steady progress being made with that repetition.

Death

Images of death or dying in a dream can understandably cause great alarm upon waking, especially when interpreting your dreams precognitively. You may worry that the dream is a bad omen foreshadowing an actual death or misfortune, but rest assured that this is rarely the case. It is almost always about the upcoming death of some external or internal issue and the birth of a new phase.

Death is inevitable. It will happen to us all. But it is also the great unknown, shrouded in mystery and uncertainty, as none of us can know what will happen when we die, when it will happen, and how we will deal with the death of loved ones. All of the questions that death inspires are so harrowing and impossible to answer that our instinct is to deny or repress them from surfacing into our awareness when we are awake. But our dreaming mind is not in the business of repressing or denying. It will force on us numerous different death and dying scenarios for a variety of different healing purposes.

It is important to point out from the onset that dying and death dreams are rarely literal. In extremely rare cases these kinds of dreams have precognitive elements, but in the overwhelming majority of them, the dreaming mind, being the artist that it is, simply uses the shocking and memorable symbolism of death to wake you up to the power of the choices you make in your waking life. Above all, never fear death and dying dreams, because when it is really a question of death, your dreaming mind will not be so obvious; it will speak another symbolic language.

However nightmarish the death and dying themes are in your dreams, celebrate them as the transformative gifts they are. They are a powerful call for inner healing and personal growth in your waking life. You need to let go of one phase in your life and welcome in the next. It is the necessary end of one phase of your life, because life is a constant shedding of old skins. That is how we learn, grow, and evolve. Nothing stays the same. Death, of course, is the biggest change and the one that can give every moment of our lives meaning. In the profound words of Jung, death is "an archetype, rich in secret life, which seeks to add itself to our own individual life in order to make it whole."[47]

As we don't like to dwell on death when awake, sometimes our dreaming mind will dwell on this imagery simply to prepare us for our ultimate future, and those of our loved ones, so that when the time comes, the grief is not unfamiliar and we are better prepared for the sense of loss we feel. Be aware, too, that those dreams of loved ones dying or dead can also be a simple reminder to tell them how you feel about them while they are still alive. This is especially the case when you feel great emotion in the dream. If there is no emotion, then it is possible the dream is pointing to aspects of your own personality that you need to say goodbye to.

Afterlife Dreams/Ghosts: Dreaming about a departed loved one is believed by some to be an afterlife sign, a reminder that death ends a life and not a relationship in spirit. There is research to suggest that those who dream of departed loved ones feel comforted and the experience is incredibly healing and eases the grieving process. From a precognitive dream interpretation perspective, this kind of dream is pointing the dreamer towards a future where they have come to terms with their loved one being in a peaceful place, whether they believe in an afterlife or not, and this acceptance can help them move through and beyond their grief.

Your dreaming mind may also conjure up images of departed loved ones to suggest that a problem you are dealing with can be solved by fol-

---

47. Jung, *Memories, Dreams, Reflections*, 302.

lowing an example or approach you associate with the personality traits of the departed loved ones who visited you in your dreams.

In some cases, people report having the most rewarding conversations with departed loved ones in their dreams, a reminder yet again that in our waking lives we should not wait until a person has literally died to tell them how we truly feel.

Cemetery: Should a cemetery feature in your dream, it could suggest a desire to remember or value your past. It could also point to a need for closure in some area of your life and urge you once again to let go of mindsets that no longer serve.

Cemeteries commemorate death but also life, so it could be a powerful omen for your personal and spiritual transformation. Pay attention to the feeling or atmosphere of the dream cemetery. Do you feel secure there or are you filled with anxiety? This will symbolise whether your mindset is helping or hindering your personal growth. Consider the question Steve Jobs famously asked himself every morning upon waking: "If today were the last day of my life, would I want to do what I am about to do today?" If the answer was no too many times in a row, Jobs knew he needed to make changes. Your dreaming mind wants you to ask yourself that very same question when you wake up with death dreams on your mind.

Dreams with a coffin or grave theme carry similar precognitive interpretations to dreams with a death or dying theme. The emphasis here is on what you need to lay to rest and what is soon to be dead and buried. If you visit a gravestone in your dream, either your own or someone else's, your dreaming mind is urging you in the coming days and beyond to keep the loving relationships with yourself and/or others alive.

Dead Body: The disturbing symbol of a dead body in a dream suggests that something in your waking life is well and truly past its sell-by date, but for some reason you are not letting it go. This could be an internal mindset if the body is your own or unknown, or it could be something external (a relationship, career, etc.) if the body is someone you know. It continues to impact and literally haunt you in your waking life. It really is high time now for you to channel your inner Elsa and let it go.

Should you see unidentified corpses in your dream, this indicates that you may soon sense that feelings you have for someone or something have died or simply run their course. If someone you care about dies in your dream, this does not foreshadow their demise, but it does suggest your relationship is about to evolve in a significant way. This is perfectly natural and healthy, as all relationships go through phases. Recall how you feel about their dream death. Whatever the reaction, communication needs to improve before the emotional distance between the two of you becomes harder to navigate.

Funeral: When the symbolism of a funeral appears in your dreams, there is a sense of finality and no going back. Your dreaming mind is firmly telling you that a phase of your life or a relationship is about to and should end. Your future well-being lies in your ability to come to terms with that and move on.

This symbolism can feel morbid, but it is pointing you in the direction of your future, urging you to let go now of the past and take the next step. It could point to the need to let go of an unhappy relationship, job, or situation or a closed mindset. Brainstorm the meaning until you get an aha moment of clarity that energises you. Dream interpretations that drain or diminish you are not the correct interpretation, and this is especially the case with any death-themed dream. Your dreaming mind uses this daunting imagery not to scare you, but to shock you into taking positive action on your own behalf.

Murder: Killing in dreams references something in your life that you consciously need to rid yourself of because it has outlived its usefulness. If you don't remove it from your life, it will negatively impact your future. If you murder someone in a dream, this is a warning of some kind of self-destructive response that could derail you. You may soon experience intense anger or frustration towards someone or something in your waking life, and when you recognise that déjà rêvé in your waking life, let the memory of this dream encourage you to vent those emotions in a safe and controlled way.

Whatever the circumstances, this kind of dream is a warning that you are close to boiling point in your waking life and you need to find a positive way to come to terms with a difficult situation or relationship. This may very well mean letting go completely in the coming days of someone or something that is no longer in your best interests.

Dreams in which you kill someone else often point to internal conflict, especially if the person you kill is someone you don't know or if you kill an animal. Brainstorm the symbolism of the person/animal you killed, because it could be pointing to a mindset that you need to kill or some aspect of yourself that is holding you back, such as low self-esteem or laziness.

In the case of someone killing you in a dream, if the person killing you is a family member, close friend, or someone you are emotionally intimate with, this suggests that some aspect of that relationship is dimming your light. This nightmare scenario is alerting you to a potential threat that someone close poses to you, and that threat will likely be emotional or psychological rather than physical, as the language of dreams is emotion. You need to work out what that threat is and find ways to manage and/or correct it for your own sake and the sake of the relationship.

If, however, you don't know who the person killing you is, or they are someone you know but are not close to, this suggests that forces outside of your control may soon derail you in some way. When/if you notice that you are feeling like a victim in the coming days, focus on what you can control, which is your response. Empowering your mindset during the day will change your dream scenarios, making killing dream scenes less likely.

Suicide: Should suicide be a theme in a dream, this suggests oncoming feelings of helplessness. If your dream features an execution, be alert in the coming days to a feeling of guilt and retribution or a sense of karma surfacing. Themes of sacrifice and martyrdom suggest you may be taken advantage of in some way in the near feature or you are going to feel like you are the scapegoat. Forewarned is forearmed.

Your Own Death: Death themes in dreams should often be welcomed, as they suggest you will soon be letting go of something that you have outgrown and there is a new dawn on your horizon. Your dreaming mind is preparing you internally for this fresh start. Reflect deeply on what you need to let go of in your life so there is space to welcome in the new. This is especially the case if you are the person dying in the dream.

Disaster

Should your dream contain any kind of accident or disaster theme, whether natural or human-made, it's an alarm to remind you to wake up and be on your guard against possible mishaps, missteps, or miscommunications, by yourself or others, in the coming days, as the path you are currently on is not optimal. Intervention may be required or things may soon get out of control or veer off course. Your dreaming mind sends you a disaster or accident dream to get you to watch your step and be more observant.

Think of disaster dreams in the same way you might think of a slip of the tongue in waking life, where the truth is unconsciously revealed. They reveal a future emotional response to a likely setback, but that setback is not predetermined. Your precognitive mind has noticed something important for your personal growth that you have not noticed in your waking life.

Whether the disaster is human-made, such as bombs or planes crashing, or natural, such as volcanoes, floods, out-of-control fires, or tidal waves, in most cases these are not premonitions of literal disasters but rather predictions of internal chaos if changes are not made fast.

A disaster dream does strongly symbolise anxiety about your future and will try to highlight for you the source of that anxiety. Often this source is a confusing mindset and/or trying to people-please or seek validation from others. Allow any disaster dream to remind you that your future well-being depends on your ability to shift your focus to get validation from the inside out rather than the outside in. This refocusing may make you feel uncertain for a while, but it is the source of all direction and meaning moving forward.

Having said that, throughout time there have been rare reports of dreams literally predicting both human-made and natural disasters, so there's no harm being cautious and doing all the necessary safety checks.

Even though disaster dreams are distressing, they should not be feared, because they are a sign that a dramatic change is on the horizon, and change is progress. If the disaster is natural, focus on what the element involved can teach you (see the Elements on page 189). If it's human-made, such as a car crash, were you the driver or the passenger? If it's the latter and you were in the backseat, who or what is driving your life? In the coming days when you feel powerless, remind yourself that you and only you should be in the driver's seat of your own life. If, however, you were driving, who or what made you lose control? Should the disaster involve groups of people, your dreaming mind may be warning you that soon you will feel disillusioned by or detached from a certain group of people or a plan of action and you may have to change your approach or your attitude towards them.

Armed with the insight above, here are some associations to help you precognitively interpret some of the most commonly reported dream disaster scenarios. You'll notice that they typically foreshadow oncoming emotional responses. When/if you experience these emotions in the coming days or recognise other elements of the dream in your waking life, be sure to pause and reflect on the synchronicity. Recall the details of your disaster dream or revisit it in your dream journal, and work out what it is trying to teach you about the best way forward or what you need to avoid or keep a watchful eye on to ensure smooth progress.

Accidents: Accidents of any kind, be they natural or human-made, in a dream are not typically precognitive in a literal sense but rather in a symbolic way. They are clearly warning you that something in your waking life is about to reach boiling point. This could be a challenging situation, relationship, or emotional tension you have yet to address. Should your dream feature acts of terrorism, your dreaming mind is warning you to make sure in the coming days that you trust only the actions and not the words of others.

Whatever the accident dream scenario, perhaps in a plane or simply tripping up, your precognitive mind is preparing you for potential danger. This does not mean that an accident is inevitable, but that you need to remind yourself in the coming days to keep your emotions in check, and just because you think or feel something does not mean it controls you.

In every accident dream, recall the nature of the accident, what you can learn from it, and how you can escape or avoid it. Are you in danger of losing control or too eager to push ahead or have you been careless? Are you a passenger or in the driving seat of the direction your life is heading in?

Vehicles in dreams always indicate the direction you are heading in. Do you need to speed up, slow down, or change direction? Be sure to rule out the literal interpretation of such a dream first and consider whether there are any safety issues with your car that you are not yet aware of.

Car accident dreams may be telling you to slow down or speed up or to take a different route and avoid a potential obstacle. This dream is all about your future direction and where you want to be headed and if your current approach is optimal. Should an accident befall you in your dream, like if your car brakes fail, be sure to check the safety features of any vehicle you are driving, especially the brakes. However, in most cases, dream accidents suggest that emotional troubles are on the horizon or there will be some kind of loss of control or rising tension if you continue your current plan of action. In short, you need to watch your step, as your current approach may be attracting crisis into your life. It could also indicate feelings of guilt about something you said or did and fear of the future implications if you are found out.

Plane crashes are often linked to a fear of failure limiting your progress at work or the risk of setting unrealistic career goals, and train crashes may relate to complications with your finances that you are not yet aware of.

Shipwreck dreams suggest that you are at risk of letting intimate relationships overwhelm you in some way, but the ship could also represent the goal you are heading towards and how a cherished and sought-after goal is at risk of dragging you down unless you change your approach and become less dependent on it for validation.

Accidents in your home in a dream, such as falling down a flight of stairs, could predict potential safety issues in your home, so do your due diligence and always put your safety and that of your loved ones first to avoid misfortune. Since homes in dreams are symbols of your personality and approach to life, it's more likely that your dreaming mind is telling you that if you want progress to be a theme in your life, you need to make changes, and some of those changes may involve breaking things down before they can fall back into place.

Breaking things in a dream portends a change of direction for you that will involve letting go of a project, idea, or relationship, but it can also be a warning to be more careful and take things slower. Perhaps you will soon feel regret for someone or something that you let slip through your fingers. Should burning feature in the dream, is your unconscious urging you to get a smoke alarm, if you don't have one already, or is it suggesting that intense emotion, either your own or that of someone you know, is about to be unleashed in your waking life?

Notice if you were injured or not in the dream, as this will suggest that you either have the resilience to cope with what life throws at you or need to protect yourself better.

Dream cuts and bruises suggest minor future letdowns unless you protect yourself better, and if you find yourself tripping and falling in your dream, this suggests there are pitfalls ahead that you need to navigate carefully. You also need to watch out in the coming days for unconscious slips of the tongue or impulsive actions. Catch yourself if/when you are about to lose control and reconnect to the message of this dream, which is urging caution and self-control.

Should an accident befall someone else in your dream, this could indicate that an aspect of yourself that the person symbolises may soon cause complications in your life unless you pay attention to it. It could also suggest anxiety about the well-being of that person or problems in their path. If you know the person very well, it could symbolise problems in your relationship looming on the horizon. Things may soon reach a crisis point between the two of you, and you need to make room for compromise.

Adventure: Should a disaster dream also have an adventure theme—for example, if you need to climb higher, run faster, duck for cover, compete, delegate, and so on—it's an indication that new challenges lie ahead, but this is nothing to fear, as they can help you learn and evolve. Any actions or activities that take place within the dream adventure point to hidden motives, and the symbolic associations you make with that action (the purpose and nature of it) are brainstorming different skills and approaches you need to experiment with moving forward in order to progress.

Apocalypse: Dreaming about the end of the world suggests that you are about to begin a period of dramatic personal change. The trigger could be a job loss or moving to another country, or perhaps a key relationship will break down or, worst-case scenario, you will lose a loved one. Or perhaps you will simply feel the need for a fresh start in some area of your life.

Whether the reason for the change is external or is a decision you make, the foundation of your life may soon be rocked to the core. There is no going back, and this is not something to fear, but rather something to get excited about. You are on a path to awakening, but to get to that enlightened state, your current worldview needs to change, as do your daily routines. You need to get right out of your comfort zone. The only way forward is to find the inner strength to start afresh. Your dream is letting you know that you have that inner courage, and it wants you to know that when you tap into it, you can survive anything.

Nuclear war dreams or dreams about stars and planets falling from the sky are also end-of-the-world scenarios warning you that you will soon experience great personal upheaval in your waking life. Whatever it is, it will rock your peace of mind. When you have this kind of dream, ask yourself how the world ends in your dream and who or what is causing it. This will help you prepare and protect yourself ahead of time. It will also reassure you that you will survive this turmoil and enter a new phase.

Choked/Strangled: Anything in a dream that relates to your ability to breathe and talk effectively is a warning sign that something in your waking life is about to stifle you or is threatening to drain the life out of you. This could be a person, the demands of your job or lifestyle, or simply boredom. If/when elements of this dream play out in your waking reality, you will recognise a similar feeling of being unable to express yourself effectively or will feel conflicted about whether it is best to speak your truth or remain silent. The way forward is to let some fresh air or new honest perspectives into your life.

Earthquake: An earthquake scenario is a strong precognitive message from your dreaming mind that an area of your waking life is about to erupt and the emotional foundation of your life will be shaken to the core.

You have important decisions to make in the coming days that will impact your holistic well-being. You can move away and avoid the impending crisis, but there is no telling if it will repeat elsewhere. Or you can protect and prepare yourself, because once the earthquake has happened and the rubble has been cleared away, reconstruction of your life can begin. You will be a stronger and wiser person for it, because you will have learned what triggered the earthquake and can therefore prevent it from repeating.

Fire: In dreams, fire indicates destruction but also passion and purification. This dream is a helpful warning sign to avoid becoming consumed by a passion. If you are burned alive in your dream, this is a terrifying scenario designed to make you remember it and take steps to protect yourself in waking life. If you make efforts in the dream to put the fire out, your dreaming mind is pointing the way forward. If you don't make any effort to put the fire out or are observing it, your dreaming mind is urging you to take a more proactive role, as things may start to unravel in your waking life in the coming days.

Floods: If a flood features in your dream, you are about to feel overwhelmed emotionally, and if you are drowning, you may feel you have no control over your emotions. They are taking you down, but your dreaming mind wants you to know that you do have control. You have created the imagery of this dream, and in the daydream state you can reenter this dream and rescript it so you see yourself coming to the surface for air. You can do the same in your waking life.

Tsunami and tidal wave dreams indicate that a seriously challenging emotional response lies ahead. This may temporarily disorient you and lead to unexpected changes in your waking life, but such dreams also offer rays of hope. There is no escaping or avoiding anymore. You are in the thick of things, and your best response moving forward is not to try to run away anymore but to accept and allow the emotions to flow, safe in the knowledge that emotions are temporary and will pass. You will survive.

Holes: Should you find yourself falling into or engulfed by an unexpected chasm, ravine, abyss, well, or hole in your dream, this suggests that risky pitfalls may lie ahead and things in your waking life are not as stable or certain as you might think they are. Be alert in the coming days to someone or something (including your own inner critic) that seems intent on dragging you down.

Human-Made Disasters: Dreams of war and other life-and-death struggles carry warnings of potential destructive behaviour to be on your guard against soon, either your own or from others, but they also indicate the potential for the righting of wrongs. Are you on the winning or the losing side in the dream, or is the outcome still in the balance? What can you learn from the tactics employed in your dream? Should you be wounded in the dream, this suggests that you may have to pay dearly for what you want to achieve, but it's also a sign that you will soon be required to make a necessary sacrifice for the greater good/peace.

Disaster dreams generally suggest that if something in your present does not change, things are about to go wrong. This could be related to work or a relationship, or perhaps a mindset that you have is leading you towards some kind of crisis. The latter is especially the case if the disaster is human-made, such as a car accident. However, in the case of terrorist attacks, your precognitive mind is also pointing your attention towards other people in your life who for some reason have yet to earn your trust.

If you find yourself making a dream emergency call, your precognitive dreaming mind is warning you that an emotional upheaval is about to strike. If the disaster occurs at home in your dream, this is all about your attitude towards yourself and what it is attracting energetically into your life. If demolition is a feature, try to recall whether you are carrying it out in the dream or someone else is, as this will help you understand whether the rising and soon-to-be-released tension within you is going to be self-inflicted or something outside of your control.

Should pollution or decay be a dream theme, this is urging you to walk away from an attitude that is not good for you now or in the future. If the dream highlights toxic waste or poison, this could refer to the contaminating beliefs of others.

Hurricane/Tornado: Air-themed dreams shine a night-light on anticipated arguments in your relationships, including your relationship with yourself. If you find yourself in an argument or disagreeing with someone in the coming days or face an inner struggle with your inner critic, recall with gratitude the heads-up this dream gave you. Know that it is up to you now whether you lose yourself in the argument or not. Your dreaming mind wants you to know that you control your emotions.

Hearing thunder in your dream is warning you of a difficult-to-control situation emerging on the horizon in your waking life. Lightning is a welcome sign of sudden inspiration in your routine or your mindset in the coming days, or perhaps it points to strong, passionate feelings about someone or something that take you and others by surprise. Storms forecast an outburst of pent-up feelings on the horizon that you need to monitor closely.

Starvation/Drought: This dream theme suggests that your emotional needs are not being met or that you will soon feel you are giving more to someone or something than you are receiving. But again, you can take comfort from this disaster dream, as in nature, droughts pass, and in life, bad times don't last forever. Keep your cool. Treat this as a lesson to help you learn and grow, and moving forward, any future crises that strike will not take you by surprise.

Volcano: These dreams generally predict an imminent release of pent-up emotions that have been hindering your progress. Hot passions could be aroused and released. This can create a cathartic shift in your energy and therefore what you attract into your life, but the dream carries with it a warning that this shift may prove to be volatile. If the volcano is extinct, this is a sign that a difficult situation is about to be resolved.

Everyday

One of the most empowering aspects of everyday items appearing in your dreams is that they offer you an opportunity to meet those things again in your waking life in an easy, safe way. For example, if you dream of a bar of soap, recall your dream again whenever you use soap during the day. In other words, consciously seek a moment of déjà rêvé and create a moment of connection between your dreaming mind and your waking mind. It's a sacred opportunity to truly and deeply reflect on the future you are currently attracting with your feelings, thoughts, and actions. Tell yourself that from now on, you will only choose the path of self-awareness, self-respect, and self-belief. You will create a memory of your future that is satisfying, and you will have loving eyes only for that future.

Dreams are your pure creativity unleashed, and you will enjoy your fair share of the weird and wild in them, but you may also find ordinary objects and situations punctuated throughout their apparent madness. You may be tempted to think this is simply your brain's way of processing familiar information, but you are making a big assumption there. Everyday things in your dreams have just as much precognitive potential packed into them as surreal ones do.

In this thread, some ordinary objects and situations are discussed, with suggestions on how to interpret them as the clear precognitions they are. They are ones I have seen crop up time and time again, but if your everyday item or thing isn't mentioned here, use the following illuminations to help you see your future world in your grain of dream sand. Should any of these objects appear with cracks, this does suggest that something routine in your life is about to unravel or crumble, but it also suggests new insights, as it is through the cracks that the light comes in.

Some Ordinary Things

Remember that the following list is just a starting point to help you think along the right precognitive lines, as the number of ordinary things that can play a cameo in your dreams is countless.

Books: Should you dream of a book or being in a bookshop or library, the precognitive message is most likely related to the search for knowledge. You may soon find yourself in a position where you need to ask for advice for a specific problem and you should heed that advice, as it will likely point you in the right direction. Just make sure that when the time comes, you also check in with your own intuition. If the dream reveals what kind of book it is, this can help you identify what area of your life you need to seek advice or gather more information about to progress in the right direction.

Box: Any item that can contain things in your dream, such as a box, cupboard, drawer, or wardrobe, points towards future feelings of security. If the container is overflowing or untidy, it implies that you will soon feel called to lighten your load in some way. If it is empty, the precognitive warning is that you will find what you are chasing soon but it won't bring you the peace of mind you hoped it would. Be aware, too, that closets and cupboards carry with them associations of secrecy or hidden aspects of yourself that are soon to be revealed to the world or need to be better managed for you to attract the success you hope for.

Cars and Car Parks: Dreams that feature cars are extremely common because we spend so much of our lives in them. They are also powerful symbols of the direction your life is heading in or could head in. Make sure you reflect deeply on their precognitive meaning and the road your dreaming mind projects you are heading down.

Cell Phone/Mobile: The obvious symbolism here is related to your communication skills, so if you dream of losing your phone, or your phone malfunctioning, or not being able to get a signal, your precognitive mind is encouraging you to work on your communication skills so when the time comes, you can effectively get your message across. This may involve you getting straight to the point. When/if in your waking life you recognise a fear of openly speaking your truth, recall this dream and let it empower you to be more direct. Texts in dreams also suggest that you will soon be offered some kind of opportunity to express yourself. Don't hesitate when the opportunity appears, as it will give you the chance to immediately resolve a situation or move forward. A variation of this dream is email errors, which are a precognitive warning of impending communication issues in your waking life. Proofread everything carefully in the coming days.

Chewing Gum: Chewing gum is a well-reported dream symbol that suggests a future experience or mindset that is appealing on the surface and will consume a lot of your time and energy, but will prove itself to be undigestible or meaningless to you over time. It offers no nutrition and you will need to spit it out. Consider also if you are heading towards a situation in your waking life where you have bitten off more than you can chew.

Cigarettes: In the coming days, be sure to protect yourself from the negativity of others. Set boundaries and don't let any negativity in. If you are smoking in the dream, from now on every time your inner critic surfaces, challenge it with relentless positivity.

Clock: The appearance of a dream clock, watch, or any other timepiece, whether it is digital or analogue, is an outstanding precognition power point. It is telling you that your life right now, and your attitude towards it, is absolutely of the essence.

If the clock is moving swiftly, it suggests you will soon feel pressured in some way. To avoid this upcoming pressure, think of ways in your waking life to make time work for you and be as prepared as you possibly can for a future challenge that may soon present itself.

If the clock is moving slowly or backwards, it is urging patience and caution in your waking life to avoid a future reckless decision. If it has stopped completely, it suggests a major roadblock ahead that you urgently need to identify and put contingency plans in place for.

Bear in mind that your dream clock could be a symbol of your ticking heart, and it may well be a sign that your life right now is ruled too much by the clock. It's a gentle reminder that the future you want to attract is created by what you are feeling, thinking, and doing in the present.

Pay attention to the actual time on the dream clock or watch and then the following day, be sure to pause and reflect for a few moments at that specific time on the future you are attracting by your current thoughts, feelings, and actions. If you cannot recall the time on your dream clock, notice how often you check the time during the day in your waking life, and whenever you do so, take a moment to honestly ask yourself if you are wasting or making the most of your precious time.

Computers: Computers are symbols of your logical thinking process, so any malfunction in your dreams of a computer, laptop, or tablet is warning you of future distortions of the truth from either others or yourself. It's the same with other dream technology malfunctions, such as a lift or cash point getting stuck when you try to use it. These dreams are profound because we like to think we are in control of technology, but this dream is saying that we do not have as much control as we think, or it could be using technology to point to an area of our life, a situation or a relationship, that we need to keep an eye on, as it may soon spiral out of control. This kind of dream can also be strongly advising you to get up-to-date with the latest technology or your future will leave you behind.

Cutlery: If you are using a knife, fork, or spoon in your dream, this is a sign that in the coming days you will need to digest or swallow some essential information. Spoons anticipate something soothing, knives suggest that you will get to the root of a problem, and forks indicate that a decision will soon need to be made. If plates appear, this indicates that ideas and projects are on course to be completed, and if you drink from a glass in your dream, you will experience a spiritual awakening or eureka moment in the coming days. However, if the glass is broken or, worse still, you are eating broken glass, you could shortly find yourself hearing cutting words from others. That's okay because your reaction when/if this happens can protect you from being deeply wounded if you make sure the cutting words are not coming from you.

Date/Day/Time: Should your precognitive mind grace you with specifics in terms of the date or day or time, this is happening for a reason. For example, you might dream it is 2:30 p.m. or that it is a different day of the week than it actually is, or in the dream a date is circled on your calendar. Whatever the details, take note and when that date/day/time comes around in your waking life, this is your déjà rêvé. Notice absolutely everything that happens around you and if there are any signposts to your future. Whether there are or not, this is a mighty power point. Something about this moment in time is significant for your future self. Make it count.

Elevator: Lifts often have a habit of malfunctioning in dreams, and this is a clear precognitive warning that you may soon feel you are not progressing as smoothly as you would like in some area of your waking life. When you notice that déjà rêvé (or every time you use a lift), it is an opportunity to pause and release any mindsets or approaches to life that no longer serve you. From now on, promise yourself that you will surround yourself with people and situations that raise, not lower, your vibration.

Garbage: If rubbish, garbage, dust, or dirt appears in your dreams, your precognitive mind is drawing your attention to emotional waste that doesn't belong to your future. You need to dispose of it now before it becomes dangerous. When/if you feel emotionally drained in the coming days, recall this dream and let it empower you to release what no longer serves you. This could be a relationship, wardrobe, project, goal, or mindset.

Household Items: The key to interpreting household items in your dreams, and indeed any everyday object, is to relate the function of the item to a situation you encounter often in your waking life. For example, if you dream of a broom and the following day you feel that you are not being appreciated enough, recalling this dream can encourage you to sweep away feelings of low self-esteem. Scissors also anticipate that you will feel called to cut something unwanted out of your life. Knots predict that you will soon be required to untangle a complex situation. Prepare yourself ahead of time. Mirrors can offer clear reflections of your future. Notice whatever you see there. Should specific furniture items appear, such as beds, chairs, and so on, the precognitive message will again be found in the purpose of the item and what it's used for. For example, beds and pillows suggest that a period of much-needed healing rest should be on your horizon, or could the well-known saying "you've made your bed, now lie in it" be offering you a precognitive warning? Remember, idioms and puns and other word associations play their part in precognitive dreamwork. Curtains and carpets carry with them associations of something important being covered up, so keep an eye out in the coming days to see if you are being kept in the dark about something or if important things are not being addressed.

Internet: Given the internet is such an everyday thing in all our lives these days, it is surprising that our precognitive minds do not send more dream images of it our way. Online dreams are not that common. Perhaps this is because the precognitive mind knows that technology is not where we will find inner peace. However, should your dreaming mind take the plunge online, notice every tiny detail and do an online search the next day to see what resonates or if you sensed the future ahead of time. If nothing speaks to you, then it is possible you may soon find yourself questioning what is fantasy and what is reality in your waking life. When/if you do, take a good, long look at your life and be honest with yourself. Then look at the people in your life and see whether their actions match their words. Are they raising you up or depleting you?

Other associations with internet-themed dreams are that you may soon be asked to join a group or to network in some way or become part of something more than your life currently offers. If this offer gives you an opportunity to open your mind, broaden your horizons, and learn new things about yourself and others, take it. Be aware that this dream always comes with the warning to not be hasty and to notice details, as one small error can cause misdirection in online coding.

Letters/Words: Should your precognitive mind send you letters or words in your dreams, either spoken or heard, or you see writing of any kind, this is visionary news. It can sometimes foreshadow communication from others, but often this predicts an incoming message from your higher or future self. Be ready for it, as it will shine a clear light on the right way ahead. Should any individual letters appear in your dream, brainstorm all possible associations. For example, the letter *A* can point you towards a new beginning, as it is the first letter of the alphabet, but it is also a musical note, a vitamin, the first letter of the months April and August (could something significant happen in either of those months?), or any word, name, place represented by that letter. An A grade is a symbol of excellence in academia, so is a high grade or recognition waiting for you on the horizon? There's no better time to make it so.

Losing/Finding Things: Try to recall what it is that you lost or found in your dream, as this will help you recognise what you may be about to lose or gain in your waking life. For example, if you lost your car in the dream, this points to a loss of direction. Lost clothes point to a loss of self-image. In general, whenever something is lost in a dream, it means you are in danger of losing sight of what truly matters to you in your waking life. Your future self needs you to reconnect to what truly matters sooner rather than later. Do some free association with the object lost in the dream, as this could point to what your dreaming mind feels you are in danger of missing out on if you continue to feel, think, and act the way you currently are. If you lose your wallet or valuables in a dream, this is related to your sense of identity. By contrast, if you find valuables, you are about to discover unlocked potential in your waking life. Make time to look forward to that.

Media: Radio, TV, and newspapers are symbols of mass communication, so your dreaming mind may use them to warn you about what others may start to say about you. Examine how the media in your dream makes you feel, as this will help you decide whether you should change your approach or method of communicating. Pay close attention to what images, people, stories, and so on appear in the dream, and be sure to follow up to see if you are literally glimpsing tomorrow's headlines. If nothing connects, then see if there is any symbolic wisdom there to shed light on your future. Be aware that it could simply be your dreaming mind letting you know that you will soon be required to express your opinion, so let this dream help you prepare, and when/if the time comes, make sure you are as eloquent as possible. If you watch a movie or read a newspaper in your dream, it could be a direct reflection of what you see for yourself in your long-term future. Watching TV or online media in a dream points to your short-term future.

Messages: Should your dream feature incoming texts or other forms of instant messages, this is an urgent message from your dreaming mind that you will soon find yourself in a position where you need to respond quickly. If you are the one doing the texting, then the next day after this dream, consider all of the messages you send to yourself every day with your thoughts. Are they optimal for your present and future self? Should your dreaming mind send you an emoji, the urgency is still there, but to move in the right direction you need to lighten up a bit in the coming days and take yourself a little less seriously.

Money: Dream money, coins, and cash are most typically about spiritual rather than literal wealth. If you give money away in your dream, it is a sign that you will shortly find yourself in a position where you need to give emotional support to others. If you are receiving money in the dream, you could find yourself receiving unexpected support from others. If you make a payment, your dreaming mind is telling you that things will likely go to plan in your waking life. If your wallet or purse appears in your dream, this relates to your future sense of self if you continue with your current mindset. Is your dream purse full or empty? If your wallet is stolen in the dream, something or someone in your life may try to take advantage of you in some way. Watch your back.

Names: There is wisdom and power in a name, so if you hear your own name or any name in a dream, the following day do your research. Some believe the hidden meaning of names teaches the name bearer the important lessons they need to learn. There is a message about your future happiness there for you. You may soon find yourself being called out. How will you answer?

Numbers: Just as there is hidden wisdom and life direction in every name, there is hidden wisdom and future direction in every number. When numbers feature in your dream, they will have both a personal and a symbolic association. So first note any personal associations you have with a specific number. Is it shining a night-light on a significant date coming up that you may be in danger of forgetting? Remember, numbers can also point to your age, your house number, your mobile number, the number of your children, or any time, day, week, year, or lucky or unlucky number for you. Any of these could become significant in the near feature, so stay tuned into them. If, however, you don't feel any personal resonance, then shift your precognitive focus to the symbolic meaning of the number. If your dream number has more than one digit, do what numerology urges you to do and reduce it to a single digit by adding all of the numbers together. For example, 34 is 3 + 4 = 7, so your visionary eye needs to turn towards the number 7. Then do your research into the universal and spiritual meaning of the number 7 and see what your precognitive mind is directing your energy towards. Somewhere in your future the meaning behind your dream number will jump right out at you. If you have already done your research, you will be more than ready for it.

Note: According to numerology every number has a vibe that attracts and emits a spiritual energy. Here is a brief introduction to the meanings of numbers:

0 = Infinity, freedom
1 = Independence, beginnings
2 = Communication, diplomacy

3 = Creativity, spontaneity
4 = Productivity, stability
5 = Unpredictable, shifting
6 = Family, compassion
7 = Intuition, philosophy
8 = Material success, luck
9 = Reconciliation, completion

Paper/Pen: These symbols indicate that an opportunity is on the horizon to completely rewrite your future. If the paper in your dream is crumpled, this might mean you will need to reject old ideas and bring in fresh ones. Should you dream of a pen, your precognitive mind is using the symbol to say that you and only you can script your future. The following day when you use a pen or find yourself using a keyboard (the modern pen), let this conscious déjà rêvé remind you that the future belongs to those who believe in, write down, and live the beauty of their dreams. You are the scriptwriter of your life and the future you are creating for yourself one dream at a time.

Shopping Mall: Any dream that features a shopping centre or shop of some kind or where you find yourself buying or selling things is a heads-up about a choice you need to make. That choice will likely require you to decide whether you want to stay true to yourself or satisfy the expectations of others. Stores in your dreams may also indicate what you are going to need in the future. If you can't find what you are looking for in the dream, this may be a sign of impending frustration that you can easily avoid with some forward planning. If you are shoplifting in the dream, you may be tempted in the coming days to break the rules in some way or take credit for what is not yours. When/if you experience that urge in waking life, pause and reflect deeply on what your future self would want you to do.

Soap: Any dream objects related to personal hygiene indicate that in the coming days you may find yourself wanting to wash away something that you said or did. Be on your guard against idle chatter and recklessly letting your guard down.

Social Media: Dreams that feature apps, social media, smartphones, and other forms of online communication typically point to how you appear to others. If you are losing likes and follows in your dream, you are in danger of feeling unappreciated and lonely unless you inject some authenticity and self-belief into your life right now. In the coming days, check yourself when you are tempted to present a false persona either online or in the real world. Recall this dream and create a conscious déjà rêvé. Notice how you feel when you recall any dream featuring social media. If you feel empty, confused, or alone in your dream, your precognitive mind is telling you that you need to look outside of social media to find a sense of identity. The need for external validation, whether it is sought online or from material things, is a recipe for an unhappy future. The only way forward is to seek that validation from within.

Sometimes social media dreams forecast that you will soon expand your network in some way or you will experience an unexpected reconnection with people from your past. It can also point to you wanting to be more in control of how others perceive you. Gaining likes in a dream suggests a surge of interest in you from others, but losing followers may actually be a better dream omen, as it suggests that you are unwilling to conform to the expectations of others and want to be true to who you are. This is a liberating and exciting future to head towards.

Tools: Tools are objects that dig, hide, and repair, and the function of the tool and what is being done with it in the dream could provide a clue to its precognitive meaning. For example, a dream spade may anticipate that you are about to come face-to-face with something you want to hide or bury. When/if you recognise that situation or emotion in your waking life, recall this dream and ask yourself if it is in your best interests to dig deeper or to leave whatever is buried to rest in peace.

Weather: Should your dream showcase a specific season, be it spring, summer, autumn, or winter, then in addition to the symbolic wisdom, your precognitive mind could simply be letting you know that when this season next comes around, unexpected opportunities for personal growth lie ahead for you. Show up for them.

Feelings

How a dream makes you feel is perhaps the strongest precognitive clue you can get about the future you are heading towards.

Dreams speak to you through the language of symbols and the emotions those symbols trigger in you. Often these emotions won't initially make any sense, because in your dreams reason and logic are nowhere. There is always a method to the madness, though, and your role upon waking is to work out what the emotion of your dream is trying to signal about what lies ahead.

One of the first things you need to identify upon waking when you recall a dream is the emotion you experienced in that dream. From that point you need to follow the emotion, as it will tell you what your future is likely to bring. If you don't like the emotion, decoding the other details of your dream can help you divert that potential future by changing your emotional response. Never forget that if you have a dream that scares you or fills you with anxiety or that you feel is a warning about impending doom, it is only highlighting a potential future to give you the upper hand, as your sense of familiarity with the situation or knowledge of the worst-case scenario could help you take action to avoid or minimise any harm or hurt. Should you have a dream about something upsetting and it does play out and in hindsight you realize there was nothing you could do to avoid misfortune happening to yourself or others, you are not to blame.

Positive Precogs

The unfortunate truth is that most of your dreams will likely feature negative feelings and scenarios rather than positive ones. This is because your precognitive mind knows that your future lies in your ability to resolve your inner conflicts and acknowledge what is hidden and repressed. It is in the disorienting darkness of your own shadow that growth happens and a beautiful future is born. When you are awake, your conscious mind subdues the voice of your shadow, but in your dreams, when your ego, reason, and linear time are fast asleep, your shadow self emerges and demands your attention.

Yes, your shadow can be disturbing, but once you become aware of it and start to work with it precognitively, it can become a highly creative force driving you towards a future rich in meaning.

Remember, your role as a dream oracle when it comes to interpreting what lies in your shadow is to choose the positive interpretation. Dreams are messages from your higher infinite self that transcends time. The mark of a precognitive dream well decoded is that it will raise your vibration and fill you with a transcendent sense of meaning and purpose and interconnection with everyone and everything. It will uplift you, not demotivate you. Your future belongs to your belief in the beauty of your dreams. The more you believe in that promise, the more your dreamscape will shift from the negative to the positive. When you start noticing this shift, your waking life and the future it is attracting will shift.

In short, good dreams mean good vibes are coming your way.

Negative Dream Feelings

If the emotion you experience in your dream is negative or conflicted, such as fear, anger, regret, sadness, anxiety, shame, jealousy, envy, and so on, your dreaming mind is issuing you a serious warning about the future that your current mindset is likely to manifest in your life. This negative emotion needs to be acknowledged and understood in your waking life now, because if it isn't, it will become a roadblock to your progress.

Listed here are some of the most common feelings experienced in dreams, with scenarios to illustrate. Be aware, though, that emotions are complex and sometimes an emotion is neither good nor bad. It simply is. Whatever that emotion means to you, it will carry clues about the nature of the future you are attracting and whether you should carry on as is or do an about-turn.

Anger: Anger follows fear as the most commonly experienced dream feeling. Any hostile or threatening feeling, image, scenario, or symbol—for example, acts of physical and/or verbal violence—in a dream or weapons and explosions represent the aggressive drive within you wanting to assert itself in some way. It could be warning you that you will soon find yourself in a position where you feel threatened or minimised and your future well-being depends on your ability to assert yourself in a calm way.

Classic anger-themed dreams often include violent symbolism. For instance, accident and catastrophe dreams are clear warnings to take remedial action now before some area of your life capsizes. Ambush scenarios are warning you that someone or something is about to control you if you don't watch out. Should you be attacked in your dream, you may soon succumb to feelings of powerlessness unless you remind yourself that you, not others, are in charge of how you feel. Should you do the attacking in the dream, your future lies in your ability to come to terms with your hidden desire for greater power and control in your waking life and to find healthy ways to manifest it.

If there is any killing/murder in your dream, it is important that you identify whether this is a part of you that your future self wants you to resolve or if you need to watch out for an attack on your integrity or character. Feelings of extreme powerlessness are on the horizon if you have disturbingly violent or rape-themed dreams. Your future lies in your ability to assert yourself when others try to force their opinions on you.

Dreams about any form of violence, crime, punishment, deception, cheating, or lying or any actions or words that are considered bad in waking life are warning you about something in your waking life that will soon reveal itself to not be in your best interests. This could be a self-critical voice within you or could be related to the words or actions of others. Recalling your dream and working to decode it can be remarkably helpful, as it can then be used to help prepare you when/if you recognise the emotion, situation, or scenario happening in real time. Forewarned is forearmed.

Any dream that involves fighting, shouting, or arguing typically points to a soon-to-manifest struggle with your shadow side or a strong disagreement with someone in your waking life. Prepare for both. They offer serious life lessons. Expect the unexpected in the coming days from both yourself and others.

Your inner demons do like to come out and play in your dreams to alert you to emotions that are being repressed but that you urgently need to face because your future happiness depends on it. Should you dream of monsters and demons or the devil, you may find yourself feeling inexplicably angry and negative in the next day or so. When/if that happens, recall your dream monster and ask it questions. What is it trying to teach you? Be aware, too, that monsters and demons are fictional creatures, so your dreaming mind could simply be telling you that you are at risk of creating monsters out of molehills.

Fear/Anxiety: Fear and its close sibling anxiety are the most commonly expressed dream feelings, and if you wake up feeling terrified and physically and emotionally overcome with panic and horror, refer also to the Nightmares dream thread (page 207). But some dreams express your inner fear in less intense ways. Their aim is to warn you about the direction that your fear is taking you in and to encourage you to acknowledge and work with your fear rather than suppress it. Here are some classic fear/anxiety dream scenarios:

- *Being Chased:* If you are being chased or running away in your dream, it indicates that you will soon feel the instinct to run away or avoid someone or something in your waking life. When you recognise that feeling, recall this dream and try to identify what is chasing you. Are you trying to avoid painful memories or running away from an expectation placed on you by others?
- *Crying:* Crying in a dream indicates that something or someone in your waking life is about to unsettle you in some way. When/if you encounter tears in your waking life, let this dream remind you that crying can be healing, didactic, and cathartic.
- *Drowning:* Drowning in a dream is a warning that something or someone, a relationship or project, is soon going to demand too much of your energy and time. When/if you find yourself feeling overwhelmed in your waking life, recall this dream and let the déjà rêvé help you come up for air and remind you that connecting to the power of your inner world can give you the space you need to breathe.
- *Intruder:* Should an intruder break into your house in a dream or you know someone is there without your permission, watch out in the coming days for someone or something in your waking life

invading your privacy. When/if that happens, protect your boundaries, say no, and avoid oversharing.

- *Paralysis:* In this dream you can't speak or move or are trapped for some reason. You may be buried alive. You may soon struggle to make a key decision in your waking life. Perhaps you feel burdened by the expectations of others or your inner critic is paralysing you. When/if you recognise this tension in your waking life, return to this dream and rescript it in your mind's eye so you see yourself escaping whatever is restricting you and break free. Confinement dreams are a strong reminder that your mindset is either your future roadblock or your liberator.
- *Teeth Falling Out:* If your teeth fall out in a dream, your precognitive mind wants you to pay extra special attention to your words in the coming days. You may say something you regret or find yourself in a position where you need to assert yourself but feel anxious about doing so. When/if this happens, recall your dream and let the déjà rêvé remind you not to be toothless. This dream can also point to concern about how you appear to others, so when/if you notice yourself fearing the judgement of others, reassure yourself that nobody can make you feel inferior without your consent.

Frustration: Should frustration be the dominant feeling in your dream, your precognitive mind is urging you to do some forward planning in your waking life. One classic dream where frustration provides the emotional backdrop is not being able to find a restroom to relieve yourself, or if you do find one, the restroom is filthy or out of service. Restrooms are symbolic of your personal needs. When/if you recognise this déjà rêvé in your waking life, it is high time to release any emotions—anger, jealousy, hate, and so on—that are holding you back or blocking your future happiness. Give yourself the self-compassion and alone time you deserve.

Frustration also features in dream scenarios such as failing or being unprepared for an exam or job interview, phones malfunctioning, being late, endless waiting, trying to complete an impossible task, not having the proper equipment, or not being able to do something everyone in the dream except you finds easy. These dreams are letting you know that challenges may lie ahead in your waking life. The way forward is to be as fully prepared as possible and to focus on impressing yourself and not others. The next time FOMO strikes in your waking life, recall any frustrating dreams and consciously rescript them to send your unconscious a clear message.

Guilt: Perhaps the most common guilt-themed dream is when you have a dream affair. Such dreams are rarely about cheating in real life, but they do point to a dawning realisation that your relationship needs are not being fully met.

If you are the guilty party in the dream, pay attention to the symbolism of the person you are having a dream affair with, as they could point to aspects of yourself that you need to integrate or heal. If you don't know the person, chances are excitement is missing from your relationship, if you are in one, or from your life, if you are not. If your partner is cheating in the dream, this is a warning that you may soon feel sidelined or cheated out of quality time in some way in your relationship. Perhaps they are preoccupied with work or a new hobby. When/if you notice this neglect happening in your waking life, recall this dream and let it encourage you to talk honestly with your partner about your feelings of insecurity.

If you are not in a relationship and you dream of having an affair or cheating, you may soon find yourself in a position where telling the truth and being honest with yourself is key to your personal and spiritual growth.

When/if you recognise in your waking life the same feelings of guilt that your dream forecasts, let this déjà rêvé remind you that thinking about doing something is not the same as actually doing it.

Should your dream feature a theme of crime, arrest, or punishment, be sure to recall those dreams if/when you feel something wrong or unfair is happening in your waking life. An opportunity for a fresh start and to right wrongs or set the record straight is on the horizon.

Insecurity: Repressing and not acknowledging any emotion in your waking life is damaging for your personal growth, so dream scenarios where you are late or miss an appointment or forget your lines on stage are warning you that feelings of insecurity or low self-esteem are about to surface.

Dreams about aliens or UFOs can point to a future surge of creativity but also to feelings of insecurity about your place in the world. The next time you feel different or struggle to conform or feel a loss of identity, recall this dream and let the memory of it encourage you to celebrate your creativity and uniqueness. Robot dreams have a similar interpretation but may be encouraging you to look ahead with more logic and less emotion, or perhaps the opposite is true. It is your robot dream. You decide.

Being late for an event is among the most commonly reported dreams and indicates you may be about to enter a period where your abilities are called into question or judged, and this may trigger self-doubt. Your dreaming mind wants you to deal with something or a situation you have been avoiding and be as well prepared as possible before you really do let yourself down.

Another common dream where insecurity is the emotion that looms large is being unprepared for an exam. This dream is suggesting that your future happiness lies in your ability to prepare as well as you can for an upcoming challenge and, whatever the outcome or judgement from others, to focus on your strengths rather than your weaknesses. Sometimes your dreaming mind may choose to replay a scene from your school or college days to send you the same precognitive wisdom.

Falling is perhaps the most common dream where the emotional theme is insecurity, given that falling is a symbol of feeling unsupported. Regard this dream as a warning to take control and be honest about your abilities. Avoid any reckless mistakes in the coming days, as pride often comes before a fall.

Should you dream of being in an out-of-control car, this is a warning to avoid plunging too quickly into a new relationship, venture, or direction out of insecurity. When/if in your waking life you find your impulses taking over, recall this very common dream scenario and make sure you are in the driver's seat of your car and not the passenger. In your mind's eye, rescript that dream so you get the car firmly under control. Your precognitive mind will take note and help you redirect and get back on track in your waking life.

Rejection-themed dreams, like where you fail a job interview or are ignored or turned away from a party, gathering, or event, offer a similar precognitive warning. Feelings of low self-esteem are highly likely to hold you back in your waking life unless you turn the tables now and dispose of them first.

Jealousy: Should jealousy or envy feature as dream feelings, this is your dreaming mind telling you that feelings of personal inadequacy are threatening to derail your plans. Try to identify what you are jealous of in the dream, as this may be the quality or attribute that you need to nurture or manage to help you manifest the future you deserve.

Loss and Sadness: Should the emotional atmosphere of your dream be one of loss or feeling lost, your precognitive mind is warning you that you may be in danger of losing something important in your waking life. In the coming days, consider what you have not been valuing enough in your life. It could also be warning you to stay alert and not miss out on an upcoming opportunity to head in a new direction.

If you wake up with feelings of sadness, your precognitive mind is telling you that the way forward is to stop burying your feelings of grief and sadness when/if they strike. Cry if you need to and ask for help and support.

If you lose someone you know or something valuable in your dream, your precognitive mind is trying to tell you to reach out to aspects of yourself that you are in danger of losing touch with. If you don't take more time to self-reflect and nurture inner peace, the future you are on course for may start to feel like a lonely one.

Dreams in which you are abandoned, left alone, saying goodbye, or lost in a maze or forest all share the theme of loss, as do dreams of losing valuables, your wallet, your car, body parts, your job, or your sense of direction. In all cases, ask yourself in the coming days what you are in danger of losing. Is it your identity? A sense of purpose? Your ability to decide? When/if you recognise that feeling in waking life, allow the déjà rêvé to take you back into that dream and rescript it so you find what you are looking for. Doing this will remind your precognitive mind that sometimes you need to be lost before you can find yourself again.

Bad Omens

No dream symbol is ever an entirely bad omen, as there are always hidden positives in every negative feeling and situation in a dream. Remember, it is in the darkness that most growth happens. But some dream symbols do offer striking warnings that the future you are currently attracting with your mindset and actions is one that you need to reconsider. Should any of the following symbols crop up in your dreams, be grateful for them. They are clear red flags that something in your waking life urgently needs to regroup for the sake of your future happiness. Heed your dream signs.

- Acid
- Avalanche
- Black Hole
- Blood
- Bomb
- Burglar
- Dirt
- Drowning
- Earthquake
- Explosion
- Falling
- Landslide
- Maggot
- Obscenity
- Parasite
- Pus
- Quicksand
- Sky Falling In
- Torture
- Violence
- Volcano
- War

- Weapon
- Wound
- Zombie

Although these toxic dream symbols are distressing, your dreaming mind has conjured them to wake you up in some way and remind you to stay alert. You are not a victim and you can play an active part in creating your own future.

Try to identify what caused you the most distress in the dream and then look out for that feeling when it echoes in your waking life. Instead of denying or repressing it, listen with compassion to what the symbol wants to share with you. Understanding that it is very likely a defence mechanism will help you find ways to manage it better, so that you can let it go with gratitude for the lesson it taught you and it will no longer manifest in your life.

Positive Feelings

Although your precognitive mind often sends you warnings, if it senses that you are busy attracting a distressing future, it can and does love to send you positive dream feelings and scenarios now and again as well. Dreams that leave you with lingering feelings of happiness are less commonly reported, but this is because your dreams are always trying to help you evolve and evolution happens most often outside your comfort zone. Should you wake up feeling exhilarated, take it as a sign that you are on the right track, and in the coming days, look for confirmation of that. Happy dreams are auspicious.

Here are some of the most common positive dreams, although there is no limit to the ways your dreaming mind can send you a hug to reassure you that your future is in your hands and your hands are leading you in the right direction.

Sweet Dreams

Celebrate dreams where you are floating, flying, playing, jumping, skating, laughing, and/or dancing, as your dreaming mind is reassuring you that better things lie ahead waiting for you to live them. Keep the faith. In the coming days, find every opportunity you can to laugh and experience gratitude, excitement, and joy. Re-create the feelings your dream was predicting for you.

Indeed, any dream where you receive recognition, wear a tiara or crown, discover something valuable, or acquire money, jewels, or other valuable assets, as well as dreams where you win the lottery or succeed in a task, pass a difficult test, are awarded a prize or medal, or see yourself winning in life and being recognised by others for your achievements, are mighty powerful and positive precognitions. Upon waking, be sure to capture them in vivid detail in your mind's eye, like a photograph, and underline them in your dream journal. Then believe completely in them or the feelings of self-worth they inspire in you, as this is the future of your dreams. Set your inner GPS and move towards it in your waking life without distraction.

If you feel warmth, see sunlight, or watch a beautiful sunrise in your dreams, or bathe in moonlight, walk in a beautiful meadow, or relax by a beautiful lake, stream, or beach, inner contentment is the forecast on the horizon. Dreams of falling in love, attending a wedding or similar happy party or celebration, being gifted a bunch of flowers, shooting an arrow, or gazing at a starry night sky also point to unconditional love coming to the fore very soon in your waking life.

Although dreams can be interpreted as wish fulfilment, most dream experts, myself included, believe that dreams report on our progress and signpost the way ahead. The following dream scenarios do just that.

Birds: The appearance of birds in your dreams is generally a positive omen, a symbol of incoming joy and freedom as well as your aspirations growing their own wings.

Butterflies: Creativity, joy, romance, and transformation are on the horizon for you if butterflies grace you with a dream cameo. This is a deeply spiritual and reassuring dream. Cherish it, and in the coming days and weeks, recall it often. It will bring you strength when you need it from the inside out. Dreaming of a rainbow is similar in its joyful implications for your future. Butterfly dreams also suggest that you are about to experience a higher awareness. Should you dream of a caterpillar, this is also a positive sign, but it does suggest that a complete transformation or metamorphosis must occur before you realise your full potential.

Climbing: Any kind of climbing image in your dreams, whether it is stairs, a ladder, or a hill or mountain, suggests that challenges lie ahead but you can overcome them if you look up and take one careful step at a time.

Fame: A dream of being famous or meeting famous people suggests that you will soon be recognised by your peers in some way, but it can also be a reminder to make sure you are being credited for your work or abilities. If you find yourself being overlooked in waking life, recall this dream and double down on boosting self-belief.

Flying: One of the most thrilling dreams you can have also belongs in the Actions thread (page 96). You suddenly discover the ability to fly without wings. It is almost always an exhilarating experience and feels entirely natural. It suggests that you will soon celebrate a sense of achievement or experience great satisfaction. This can relate to a leap forward in your personal life or your career or relationships. It forecasts a feeling of great liberation. The only caveat is to note how you are flying. Is it with ease or is it a struggle? If the former, your positive attitude is the only way forward. If it is a struggle, work on your self-belief. It will take you far.

Should you discover other superhero powers in your dreams, the interpretation is similar, whether those abilities be X-ray vision, invisibility, super strength, telepathy, and so on. There is hidden power within you waiting to be unlocked. The next time you feel challenged in your waking life, recall this special dream and connect to your inner superhero.

Running: This is a positive sign for your future, as running is a symbol of speed, momentum, and direction. Notice, though, how you are running and whether you are running with joy or trying to escape from something or someone.

Treasure: In this type of dream, you find something valuable: a secret treasure, precious jewellery, a stash of cash, an ancient artefact, or a secret room in your house. Every exciting, beautiful discovery is a sign that you will soon uncover valuable information about yourself or a situation, project, or relationship.

Walking: Walking is a dream symbol of discoveries you are going to make shortly. This dream bodes well for your future, as it depicts you relying on your own steam to get where you want to go. You are judging your pace well and living your life on your own terms. If you are walking through mud or broken glass, this will have the opposite implication. Crossing a bridge is an auspicious sign, as it indicates an upcoming leap of faith.

Whales: Should a whale or a dolphin appear in your dreams, you are about to see things in your waking life as they really are. You will soon get to the heart of the matter and acquire transcendent knowledge. It is going to be life-changing. Knowledge is power, but with all great power comes great responsibility. Whales are associated more with spiritual transformation, and dolphins with an optimistic mindset changing everything for the better.

Other Auspicious Dream Symbols

The following dream symbols tend to predict that the best is yet to come, so if you recall any of them or any other dream symbol that makes your heart sing when you recall it upon waking, let it fill you with a sense of calm optimism.

In China and Tibet, dreams that are believed to portend good fortune are known as auspicious dreams. These include dreams of holy people, clear lakes, receiving gifts, climbing a tree, eating fruit, a sandy beach, gentle rain, elephants, pandas, being kissed and/or hugged, and receiving flowers. Other strongly positive symbols include feathers, dragons, mermaids, angels, unicorns, centaurs, the phoenix, and other mystical symbols of magical possibility, as well as all of the universal symbols referenced in the Positive Feelings thread and your own personal good luck signs.

Should popular good luck superstitions appear as symbols in your dreams, such as finding a four-leaf clover, a rabbit's foot, the new moon, picking up a penny, horseshoes, and so on, take this as the auspicious sign that it is. If your dream shows you living your best life and doing things you love, again take this as a serious vote of confidence in your future. If you can't relate to the happy feeling and content of your dream, take it as a sign that if you inject a massive dose of positivity and gratitude into your life, your future can be mended.

From now on whenever you wake up with a smile on your face and fond memories of a dream, your first instinct should be to celebrate the unconscious shift you have pre-lived in your dream. If your unconscious is ready for good things, trust that good things really are coming your way.

Senses and Sounds

You may sometimes wake up remembering a dream that felt highly sensual. You recall hearing the action in your dream, tasting your dream wind, smelling the breeze, and so on. The dream felt so real that you may take a few minutes to question whether your night vision really happened.

Should you have a dream where the clarity is vivid and intensively real, congratulations! Your precognition is using this visceral tactic to ensure you recall the dream but also to remind you that what you dream is what you unconsciously attract and what you are in the process of becoming.

As with every dream experience, your feeling reaction to the sensual experience of your dream is key. Dreams are overwhelmingly visual memories, so it is not surprising that sight is the most common sense to be vividly recalled. It's a precognitive statement that if you don't have vision, you can't see the way ahead. Treat everything you see in your dream as a symbol of some aspect of your inner world rising to point you in the direction of learning, growing, and healing and of a happier future.

The second most common sense to be recalled in dreams is sound, and people who have been blind from birth tend to have dreams that are primarily auditory. This is a precognitive reminder in the coming days to listen more than you talk. Sounds in dreams, as in waking life, carry important information and can give rise to specific feelings. For example, a bell sound indicates greater urgency than the sound of birds singing. A knocking sound is calling out for you to answer it. Gunfire is associated with violence.

Should you hear music in your dream and the sound is melodic, this is a deeply auspicious sign, as listening to harmony in your dream suggests that you will soon feel deeply connected to the flow of life and your creative spirit. Look out for that eureka moment in your waking life. If the music in your dream sounds jarring, it carries a warning to protect your ears and yourself from harmful gossip in the coming days. Should you be playing a musical instrument in the dream, research all of the symbolic implications of that instrument to see how they can guide you forward in your waking life. For example, a piano can suggest a period of incoming harmony or can indicate that a more black-and-white approach to life will soon be required. Music can inspire and motivate. Singing is a symbol of self-expression as well as self-belief. May you all sing in your dreams.

If you hear your name being called in your dream, this is your future self. It is speaking to you loud and clear, trying to wake up your unconscious mind to your innate ability to attract and create the future of your dreams. Listen to it. Take note of any voices, conversations, or sounds in your dreams, as your precognitive mind is drawing your attention to them and the future they are leading you towards.

Speaking in dreams is your unconscious mind talking to your conscious mind or aspects of yourself that need a talking to. Should you encounter difficulty in hearing or speaking in your dream, there is something you need to know but it's buried in your unconscious. Often it is a fear of what others think that is blocking your chances of success. Imagine yourself speaking to this fear (or other block) clearly and allowing it to tell you what you need to know to communicate freely in your waking life.

Smell, taste, and touch are less common dream memories, but if you do recall them, see what personal associations they trigger and work forward from there. Is the scent, taste, or touch a positive or a negative experience in the dream for you? Treat these as precognitive signs and decode their implications for your future in the same way as for the visions you see in your dreams.

Last but by no means least, uber-realistic dreams are often a precursor to lucid dreaming—knowing you are dreaming when you are dreaming. Should you experience a lucid dream, don't wake yourself up with excitement. You have been offered a sensational opportunity to rescript your unconscious and what it is attracting into your waking life in the dreaming state. Stay calm, please, and carry on dreaming your way.

Food

Given that food is familiar and essential for your survival, it's not surprising that your dreaming mind uses the potent symbolism of food to send you precognitive messages that are not just important but *essential* for your future well-being. Ignore them now at your peril.

According to Freudians, dream food suggests a sexual appetite, but most dream analysts, myself included, follow Jung's directive that dream food indicates the qualities you need to experience (or avoid) for your future personal growth. Your dreaming mind is highlighting areas of potential hunger you need to pay attention to right now before personal malnourishment occurs in the future.

Whenever the symbolism of food and drink appears in dreams, in most cases it refers not to physical hunger or thirst but to other needs. For example, it becomes a metaphor for what information or experience you need to absorb or avoid for your emotional, mental, or spiritual nourishment as an individual. Should you choke on food in a dream, you may soon find yourself in a position where there is something you need to say but can't. If someone is choking you in the dream, you may soon feel forced to swallow your words.

Should cooking or an oven feature in a dream, this is a metaphor for something in your waking life, be it a relationship or a project, that will require a recipe—in other words, careful planning and preparation—if it is to develop or succeed in the future. A microwave in a dream warns against the temptation to take a dangerous shortcut, and an air fryer points to an upcoming pivotal meeting or discussion that might throw everything up in the air. Should dieting feature, this could be a warning to limit your emotional involvement in something or someone in the coming days, or it could be a sign that you need to make sure right now that you are not going to be starved of emotional or mental support in some area of your waking life.

The opposite is true if you dream of overindulging, as it could be warning against taking on too much or self-destructive habits or being dragged down by something or someone soon. If you are hungry or starving in your dream, your precognitive mind is making it clear that if you don't prioritise your needs now, you may soon feel that you are missing out on all of the important things in life.

Should you find yourself eating, biting, sucking, or chewing in your dream, this indicates that you will very soon be required to absorb a lot of new information. Notice what you are eating and whether you are enjoying it, as this will help you be more prepared for the new insights that lie ahead. Be aware that this dream symbol can also anticipate potential biting comments or something that bites or hurts you.

The type of food you are eating in the dream is very significant, as it suggests what you need to absorb in the coming days to whet your appetite for life again. But everything depends on how you feel while you are eating it in the dream, because if you don't enjoy it, this indicates what you need to actively avoid absorbing because of the potential damage to your future well-being.

Dream Dishes

Listed below you will find specific foods that often crop up in dreams, along with suggested precognitive interpretations.

When decoding dream food precognitively, be sure to let your personal food preferences dictate the meaning before exploring the more common/generic references to your waking desires and appetites. For example, if you don't eat meat but find yourself eating meat in a dream, this refers to a challenging situation on the horizon that will feel unpleasant at the time but will also teach you something valuable. You need to get out of your comfort zone, because all progress is to be found outside of it. But if you are a meat eater, it may suggest that you will very soon get to the heart of the matter or receive essential and much anticipated information.

Bread: Your basic needs in life and emotional necessities will increasingly become your focus in the coming days. Double down on your practical and emotional self-care and make sure you don't get distracted and neglect the value of things money can't buy in your waking life.

Breakfast: You may soon begin a new project that will give you a new lease on life. Notice the quality of the food in your dream, as this will help you understand how you are going to feel about this new beginning.

Butter: Soon you will be offered the opportunity to appreciate life's simple pleasures. Seize it, as it will offer you a priceless opportunity to focus on self-care.

Cake: The precognitive theme here is the transformative power of sharing and delegating. Soon you will find yourself in a position where you need to decide whether to go it alone or to share, ask for help, and learn from others. When it comes time to make that decision, recall your cake dream and how you felt about it, as that will help you decide whether going solo or collaborating is the way ahead. The dream may also be suggesting that an unexpected treat is heading your way. Should a pie feature in your dream, it will have a similar interpretation as a metaphor for getting your fair share or piece of the pie.

Cheese: Potential profit and satisfying gain are waiting for you in your future if your focus is on "less is more." In other words, don't be excessive or try to do everything at once. Take small and steady steps every day towards your end goal.

Chocolate: Pleasure is on the horizon for you, but it is temporary. To avoid feeling guilt soon, you are advised to exercise restraint and know when to step away or let go.

Cookies/Biscuits: You will soon find yourself in a position where you will start to experience the benefits or rewards of something you have been patiently working on. Savour that moment and let it spur you on to even greater success.

Dessert/Sweets/Ice Cream: A time of indulgence and reward lies ahead, perhaps because you are about to complete a project or celebrate a milestone in your life. Whatever it is, you will soon feel ready to have your say or make your mark on the world. When you feel that moment happening, don't hesitate—trust your gut and go for it. Timing is everything.

Drink: The association here is with feelings of longing and thirst for something you do not yet have but need to seek out for your future happiness. In your waking life, you need to pay closer attention to your emotional needs and what exactly you are absorbing into your life daily (what you are taking in emotionally).

Notice what the dream drink is and whether you are drinking it and how you feel about drinking it. If you don't enjoy it, this suggests that what you think you need isn't good news and you need to try a different approach. If the drink is coffee, this suggests the need for more intellectual stimulation in your future life, and if it is tea, you need to spend more time with loved ones. If the drink is water, this is emotional nourishment. If it is lemonade, you may soon need to transform something challenging into something sweet. If it is milk, you need to focus on ways to bring more comfort, warmth, and security into your daily life. If it is alcohol or your dream places you in a bar setting, in the coming days you may find yourself longing for more relaxation time or for less inhibition in your waking life, as wine reveals the truth. Should your dream feature someone who is drunk or you being drunk, then watch out for future distortions of the truth. When/if that moment arrives, avoid oversharing, and moving forward, choose who you share your truth with wisely.

Eggs: This symbol is all about the magic of new beginnings and your creative potential soon to be unleashed. A gain of some kind, be it financial or in self-confidence, is out there waiting for you to claim it in your potential future. If the eggs in your dream are rotten, however, it is important that you don't let a current situation take a turn for the worse.

Fish: If a fish features in your dream, your precognitive dreaming mind is drawing your attention powerfully to the importance of seeking spiritual nourishment in the coming days. Be aware, too, of the word association here of "fishy," as it could indicate that you may soon feel suspicious of or be questioning something or someone in your waking life. Stay alert.

Frozen Food: Your future happiness and fulfilment depend on your ability to thaw any hidden emotion and recognise that you need to get in touch with the precognitive wisdom of your feelings. Listen to your gut wisdom.

Fruit: A time of significant personal growth is on the horizon for you, and the nature of the fruit in your dream will point you in the right direction. Be sure to follow your personal associations and also explore the rich and ancient symbolism of specific fruits in history, medicine, and religion as potential clues to help you move forward positively. There may be sexual associations, because fruit is typically sweet, soft, and juicy, suggesting that you may soon enjoy a new feeling of vitality either through a relationship or through feelings of inner empowerment. Helping others see their own potential so they can help themselves is another potential precognitive message here. In the coming days, if you find yourself in a position where you can offer help or advice, take it. It will bring you a feeling of deep satisfaction. By contrast, if the dream fruit is rotten, it suggests that your instinct may be to walk away. You may want to reconsider that, as helping others can be a potent opportunity for your own personal growth. Having said that, if your own needs have not been met, the first person you need to help is yourself, and this dream is urging you to do so immediately, because rotten fruit is toxic.

Legumes: If legumes feature in your dream, watch out for small problems heading your way that could put your energy and time at risk. Think ahead as much as you can, as forewarned is forearmed.

Lunch/Dinner/Supper: With this dream symbolism, you may be taking some much-needed time out from your daily routine in the coming days, and when you do so, recall your dream meal and feel revitalised by the conscious déjà rêvé. Let it reconnect you to your soul. If you are eating your dream meal with others, this may point towards sharing your experience with others soon. Notice whether you are serving the food or being served, as this will indicate whether you will be the person reaching out or others will reach out to you. If you are eating your meal alone, you may soon find yourself in a position where someone or something in your life lets you down or disappears. On the plus side, you will regain a sense of independence.

Meat: With meat featuring in your dream, you will soon be getting right to the heart of the matter of something that has been troubling you recently. When you do so, don't allow minor details or alternative facts to cloud your judgement. The way forward for you is with a clear-eyed focus on the essentials or basics of an issue. If you know what kind of meat is in your dream—for example, chicken, lamb, beef, or ham—be sure to brainstorm both your personal and common associations, as they will help bring even greater clarity to a situation that appears complicated but is in fact very simple. For example, if you dream of chicken, could this suggest chickening out of something?

Nuts and Seeds: These are symbols of hidden wisdom within you waiting to be discovered and cracked open by you in the future. The future you are attracting and the answers you are seeking are already within you.

Oil: With this dream symbol, you will soon find yourself in a position where you can smooth over a difficult situation in some way to keep everything going or everyone happy. When/if you find yourself in that situation, your dreaming mind wants you to ask yourself if keeping the peace is the way forward or if you need to get things out in the open.

Pasta: The appearance of any kind of pasta in a dream suggests that in the coming days you may need to economise or save your time or energy. When/if that time comes, understand that this is a necessary sacrifice for your long-term satisfaction.

Pepper: With this dream symbol, watch out for a minor irritation coming to the surface soon. When you notice it, don't deny it, as it will help you understand an issue in your waking life better. Alternatively, you may soon find yourself offered the opportunity to inject some variety or spice into your life. Take it.

Pizza: When pizza features in your dream, a welcome dose of fun and laughter and abundance is waiting for you in the short term. Enjoy it when/if it comes and let it remind you that your present mindset is constantly creating and attracting your future.

Potato: The precognitive message of a potato in a dream is to ensure that laziness or overindulgence does not cloud your perspective soon. You may also need to get back to basics.

Rice: With this dream symbol, a promising development lies ahead for you that brings great responsibility and hard work but also the potential to bring you much satisfaction. If, however, the rice is mixed with dirt, make sure you weigh the pros and cons very carefully when you are asked to take on new commitments.

Salt: With salt featuring in your dream, you will soon experience an increased zest for life. Savour it. You may also soon find yourself in a position where honesty is the clear way forward to improve a situation or relationship.

Sandwich: A sandwich in your dream indicates that in the coming days you may find that you are being provoked in some way or feel confined by a situation, relationship, or belief. The way ahead is to listen carefully to your intuition, and if you are doing two things at once, make sure the compromises being made do not drag you down.

Soup: Soup is a symbol of caring in a dream. When you recognise your loving compassion at work in the days that follow this dream, make sure you also nourish and empower yourself.

Spices and Herbs: With this symbolism, your precognitive dreaming mind is urging you to consider a different perspective when it comes to a personal situation or relationship in the days ahead. Open your mind to new ideas, as this is where you will experience great personal growth. Many herbs and spices have ancient spiritual and medicinal associations and strong associations with holistic health and well-being, so enjoy brainstorming and free-associating to help you see the way ahead more clearly.

Sugar/Sweets: This symbolism is a clear reminder from your dreaming mind that a positive mindset attracts a positive future, but it's a gentle warning, too, to make sure that you avoid overindulging and that your future is cleared of toxic positivity. Negative feelings should not be repressed or denied but rather understood and learned from. You tend to evolve outside your comfort zone. That is why every time you wake up from a dream feeling anxious, you need to switch over to feeling excitement, as disturbing dreams are often a sign that you are about to learn and grow—and learning and growing are what give life its purpose.

Vegetables: With vegetables featuring in your dream, in the coming days it is more important than ever for your future well-being that you actively do things that may not be easy or great fun but are good for your long-term holistic well-being. The way ahead is to double down on making healthy choices in your diet and exercise plan. When a specific vegetable appears in a dream, focus on your personal associations with it first and then brainstorm the symbolic meanings, as there is a wealth of historical, spiritual, and medicinal significance associated with specific vegetables to explore. Be aware, too, of word associations here, such as a couch potato.

Restaurants

Dining in a dream restaurant is significant because it suggests that the beliefs you are assimilating into your life and the quality of the dining out experience will speak volumes about the future direction of your life if you continue with the same mindset. Is the atmosphere positive or shabby? Are you dining alone or in a group? Is the experience leisurely or rushed? All of this will give you strong indications, as will your level of enjoyment and satisfaction. If you don't feel comfortable and nourished in your dream restaurant, you have the power to make changes in your present to avoid an unfulfilling future.

Should you be presented with a menu, it indicates the power of your personal choices. Your future well-being will depend on the decisions you make in the coming days. Make sure those decisions are well-informed and carefully tailored to your emotional needs.

Houses

Should a house or home enter your dreamscape, this is not about the actual building but about aspects of your personality that are going to make themselves known to you in the coming days. Your mindset is transformed into a building or structure to help you understand what aspects of your personality have already been built and are going to help or hinder your progress moving forward.

According to Jungian dream analysis, dream homes represent mansions of the soul and all aspects of who you are in body, mind, heart, and spirit. In essence, perhaps more than any other symbol, dream homes tell you everything about you and your approach to life and whether it is optimal for your future well-being or not.

To interpret this dream precognitively, recall the type of home and what condition it is in. Drink in all of the details, from the colour scheme to the furniture layout to the house design. If the house is in disrepair, the warning from your precognitive mind could not be clearer: In the coming days, you need to focus on inner repair work. Your dreaming mind is offering you a preview of how you feel about yourself and the kind of future this mindset is leading you towards. Do you feel comfortable and safe in your dream home or out of place? If the latter, it's time to do some inner DIY.

The outside of the home in a dream anticipates how others are going to react to you, and the inside of the home is where your heart or true feelings are going to settle. Each room in the house reflects different aspects of your personality and whether they are going to be challenged in the future or not. For instance, the attic represents memories or things you have stored away in your unconscious because you think you don't need them, but perhaps you do need to revisit them. Bedrooms represent what is deeply personal to you, bathrooms your instincts, and the basement your unconscious and the things you think you have buried but are going to surface. The kitchen represents how you nourish yourself, the library your mind, the roof how you protect yourself, the bathroom what you need to cleanse yourself of, and the living area your need to give and share love with others. Stairs represent connections between the different aspects of your personality and whether you are going to be taking steps forwards or backwards towards your life goals.

Open doors or gates in a dream home are a clear sign that an opportunity will soon present itself to you that will feel like a breath of fresh air. Roofs and walls are symbols of boundary setting, and windows symbolise your future point of view. Should you find yourself locked out of your dream home, your task in the coming days is to figure out how to unlock your self-awareness. Hallways and corridors point to an incoming transition period in your life that is necessary to help you progress. Notice the direction in which you are walking in the corridor in your dream. If there are lots of doors, you need to be more discerning and think deeply about the choices you will soon make. If you are pacing backwards and forwards in the corridor or the hall doesn't appear to have a clear exit route, this forecasts indecision in the coming days that could stop you in your tracks or send you on energy-wasting dead ends unless you stop and find your calm centre and the sense of direction it will bring you.

If your dream house has a well-kept garden, this indicates that seeds are being sown in your waking life that have the potential to bring future joy, but take note of the condition of that garden. If weeds are choking it, this suggests that your own well-being has been neglected and you need to do some inner work. A backyard symbolises the need to let go of the past before welcoming the future. Similarly, if housework features in your dream, this suggests that the way to progress in the coming days is to clarify your motives and feelings. If you dream of a home that isn't familiar, you may very soon find yourself in a position where you are called to make a radical change in your personal life. How will you answer that call?

To precognitively interpret any aspect of a home, remember to always ask yourself what that part of the house is used for and how you feel about it. If the house was unfamiliar to you, you might want to spend a few moments in that part of the house or drawing your dream house in your waking life to see what precognitive insights this conscious déjà rêvé inspires in you. Chances are it will remind you that keeping your house clean and clutter-free is just as important as keeping your mind clear and negativity-free.

House Dream Scenarios

Childhood Home: A well-reported dream is returning to your childhood home. The house you grew up in is a symbol of your upbringing and basic beliefs, and your dreaming mind may use it to get a precognitive message to you. This does not necessarily mean you are stuck in the past, but it does mean that you will soon find yourself in a situation where whatever shaped your personality in your childhood will come to the fore and potentially be challenged and upended. Are you repeating patterns from your childhood that are no longer relevant? Is it time to cut the ties that bind? Can this dream help you relate lessons you learned in your past to the future you are attracting? If the childhood home is changed in your dream, this represents the growth or change that needs to happen for you to move forward.

Damage to Home: Any kind of damage to a house, home, or place of residence in a dream is a warning from your dreaming mind to make extra sure in the coming days that you protect your boundaries. Pay close attention to who or what you are letting into your life and whether it is in your own best interests or you are being taken advantage of and your privacy is being disrespected in some way. This may be a person or a situation, but it may also apply to negative self-talk that has the potential to get out of hand if left unchecked. Consider also the possibility that you may soon feel taken advantage of in some way or that someone will take the credit you deserve. This applies to dreams about burglaries, robbers, or intruders in your home, too. Another potential interpretation here is that some aspect of yourself is trying to break through to you and make its presence felt, and the way forward is not to ignore it but to capture it.

Should your dream home fall down or be set on fire, this portends radical change upcoming in your waking life. That change could be related to your work or relationships or to your worldview. Don't be daunted by this upcoming shift, but instead get excited about it and what it will reveal to you. Should you find yourself buying or selling a property in your dream, this can predict an upcoming house move, but more likely it indicates that a big decision is on the horizon for you in some area of your waking life. Just as you would when buying a house, don't act on impulse. Instead, take your time, carefully weigh the pros and cons, and get advice from trusted sources before deciding.

Haunted House: This dream symbol alerts you to potential unfinished business related to relatives or repressed memories making their presence felt in your life in the coming days.

Secret or Unused Room: One of the most commonly reported home-related dream themes is finding a secret or unused room in your house that you didn't know existed. Your precognitive dreaming mind is telling you through this metaphor that there is hidden creative potential within you and you need to find the courage in the coming days to unlock it.

Opportunities for personal growth are on the horizon, but for some reason you are either not aware of them or not embracing them. Let this dream encourage you to get curious and start noticing what is going on around and within you.

Key to your understanding of this dream is what you discover in the room, as this may point you towards the aspect of yourself or your life that needs to be discovered. If you find nothing in the secret room, then you need to ensure in your waking life that you understand both your strengths and your weaknesses. Bear in mind that a secret dark room can also be a sign that you need to come to terms with your shadow side.

Trailer: If you dream of a trailer or a very small home that feels restrictive, then a closed mind is something you need to guard against in the coming days. It will not serve you well.

Buildings

Any dream building can be interpreted in a similar way to a dream home as a preview of what aspect of your inner world or construction of your personality is soon going to demand your attention in some way.

If a building appears in your dream, decide what aspect of yourself it represents. Consider the purpose and function of the building, as that will give you a clear indication of the precognitive message. For example, a castle indicates the need to put up barriers or protect yourself from negativity, either your own or from other people, as castles were originally built to protect those inside from their enemies. This symbol may also reference the past either as a source of inspiration and guidance moving forward or as something you need to leave behind to move forward. Tomb and cemetery dreams typically point to aspects of yourself that have long been buried. Your task is to decide if you need to mourn and let them go or revive them.

The nature of the building in the dream will always point the way ahead. Hospitals are all about healing yourself and others, while offices are about work but also about restriction. Churches are about your conscience and what it is telling you, libraries are about information gathering, courts are about justice, and prison is about karma. Hotels are about escaping or taking time out from your daily routine, factories are about productivity and conformity, and farms are about getting back to life's basics. Lighthouses offer safety and warn about rocky areas to avoid in your future, towers represent self-reliance and the potential for arrogance, and so on.

Weigh the positive and negative aspects related to your dream buildings to help you understand what is likely to manifest in some way for you in the coming days. But in all cases, be aware that your personal feelings and connections must take centre stage in all precognitive interpretations of dream houses and buildings. Those personal feelings are manifesting all your tomorrows.

Life Stages

In recent years, the hashtag #dreambabies has consistently topped online dream searches, suggesting a collective desire to acknowledge the part within us that is creative, loving, and spontaneous but also deeply vulnerable and in urgent need of guidance and protection. This dream thread will explore the precognitive interpretation of baby-themed dreams as well as other ages and stages of life that can appear in your dreams.

Dream Babies

Baby: Notice what your dream baby looks like, as this will be super revealing. It will symbolise the part of your life that is changing and how the future is likely to treat this new development. Is it human? Is it an animal? Is it a monster? Is it someone you already know? Is it an object? Is it twins or more, suggesting multiple upcoming new beginnings and fresh starts?

Brainstorm your associations with your dream baby, as that will point towards the potential future outcome of a project, plan, situation, relationship, or mindset you are currently creating with your thoughts, feelings, and actions and whether you need to make changes. Above all, notice how you feel about your dream baby, as again this will point to a future mindset that will either help or hinder your progress. If you don't like what you have conceived in your dream, now is your chance to make changes.

Babies in dreams, as in waking life, need constant attention and care, and whenever they appear in your dreams, the message that your dreaming mind is screaming at you is clear. If you want something in your waking life to survive, you need to take extra loving care of it, not just in the short term but in the long term as well. Your inner baby will be content only if you give it unconditional love and emotional support not just now and again but all the time.

Should you hurt or harm your dream baby, this is a clear warning from your dreaming mind that your future contentment depends on your dedicated ability to take better care of yourself. If your dream baby is not your own, this could suggest that you soon will feel responsible for someone else's well-being or project. When/if you recognise that feeling of responsibility in your waking life, let this dream urge you to prioritise your own self-care too. You can't offer someone else a drink from an empty cup. Fill your own cup first. Fostering and adoption dreams have a similar interpretation.

If your dream includes a baptism or christening or your dream baby is named, this is a sign that soon you will be revealing to the world an exciting new idea or reinvention. When/if that revelation happens, your life will be turned upside down.

Birth: Although parents who are already pregnant, or hoping to be, do sometimes recall baby-related dream themes upon waking, clearly foreshadowing the actual birth and all the joys and anxieties of becoming a future parent, your precognitive mind will often conjure up birth-related dream themes for other future-forward reasons.

If you are not consciously trying to start a family, your dreaming self is signalling a future filled with beginnings. This dream can signal a new relationship, ability, project, or attitude. Whatever is coming up, it will bring a period of tremendous change.

Alternatively, birth-related dreams may be a sign that the baby within you is in the driving seat of your waking life and creating the future you are attracting. Since a baby can't survive without being taken care of, this dream is urging you to give more attention to the needy aspect of your personality. In your waking life, you likely have no idea that the baby within you is crying loudly for attention, as you have learned to suppress or ignore it over the years, but this dream indicates that, for your future well-being, you really can't repress it anymore.

This baby is the creative, spontaneous, joyful part of you longing to be reborn, but it is also deeply vulnerable and dependent. Your future now lies in how you respond to the demanding cries from your inner baby. Do you continue to ignore or deny your inner baby and seek nurturing from others, or do you look within and nurture it with unconditional love?

With this dream it is extremely important that you look within. Doing so will help you avoid a potential future where your validation and survival become overly dependent on external factors, such as the approval of others or money, career, popularity, etc. If you can course correct now and start to become the source of your own nourishment, this dream is a strong indication that good times are ahead for you.

A common theme in baby dreams is a baby born with an adult head, which is a powerful symbol suggesting that you are too focused on gaining intellectual or theoretical knowledge that lacks emotional depth and life experience.

Be aware that this dream theme could also suggest a creative idea or brainchild that you are eager to give birth to. This dream symbol is all about fresh starts, but it can also suggest the need to be patient and take small steps in the right direction. Birth-related dream themes tend to occur when a serious change is about to happen in your waking life. In preparation for that imminent new phase, your dreaming mind is urging you to prepare and protect yourself now ahead of time.

According to Jung, birth dreams signal the start of a period of deep personal growth. They represent your journey towards a sense of self or wholeness or individuation. If you are to thrive, you must let go of the past and any mindsets that no longer serve you. It is high time to trust completely that good and new things are coming your way.

In essence, birth-related dreams strongly urge you to take extra loving and consistent care of your inner baby, whether that be an idea, a project, or a neglected part of you in need of new life and protection. Prioritise self-care and boundary setting in your waking life, and in due course you will wake up each morning feeling reborn.

Conception and Pregnancy: If you dream that you have conceived or are pregnant, rule out the literal interpretation first. Your dreaming mind often knows things about your body that you don't.

If you are not actually pregnant, notice how you feel when you recall a pregnancy-related dream. These feelings will likely foreshadow feelings you may experience should this dream come true in a literal sense one day, offering you an opportunity to prepare yourself. However, it is far more likely that this dream is suggesting that soon you are going to have a eureka moment or a revelation will change absolutely everything. Nothing in your life will feel quite the same again. Watch out for this aha moment or gut instinct in your waking life, and don't second-guess yourself when it happens. Trust yourself.

Should birth control feature as a dream theme, this indicates that the theme of personal responsibility will soon loom large in your waking life.

Labour: Dreaming about actually giving birth is common for expectant parents to help them feel more prepared for all possibilities in the future so the experience does not feel unfamiliar. But if you are not pregnant, it suggests that something startling is about to enter your life and will throw everything up in the air. Notice whether the delivery in your dream was problem-free or hard, as this will indicate the likely path towards making this new idea a reality. If it was traumatic or the baby did not arrive at all, it is possible that you are headed in the wrong direction. This dream is urging you to reassess or try another approach.

Miscarriage: You will likely wake up feeling extremely anxious if you have a problem pregnancy dream involving a miscarriage, abortion, or stillbirth or a loss-related image such as an empty rocking chair, pram, or cot. If you are pregnant, it may well feel like a nightmare. You are always advised to check with your health care provider to confirm that all is progressing well with your unborn baby, but rest assured that in most cases this dream is simply playing out your unconscious fears for cathartic reasons to help you feel more relaxed when the happy event happens. Also, problem pregnancy dreams typically refer to an idea or plan you conceived, and they are warning you that you need to pay vigilant attention to the practical details now or there are going to be deadly roadblocks to its smooth progress in the future.

Perhaps someone else will take credit for the idea, or perhaps, if miscarriage is the theme, your dreaming mind is sensing an imminent miscarriage of justice in your waking life that you need to be aware of. Or more likely, does your current mindset need to die to ensure your future success? These are the kinds of intimate questions that birth-related dreams require you to ask of yourself.

If the baby in your dream is stillborn, this means that something you have been working on or are currently involved with, be it a relationship or a project, lacks the spark of life, and if energy isn't injected into it soon, it will fail or die. Alternatively, it could mean that you need to breathe new life into your hidden talents now rather than in the future, when it might be too late to do anything with them. Reflect deeply and trust your personal response, as your intuition will know what your dreaming mind is trying to tell you.

Childhood Dreams

Although dreams of childhood appear to be about the past, they always point to your future as a rule of thumb. They are telling you what you need to remember about yourself now to move forward. They can also signal a growing desire to escape responsibility and be more spontaneous.

Dreaming of a child, whether that child be you or a child you know or an unknown child, may represent your authentic self or the part of you that is impressionable.

This type of dream can warn you to be on your guard against childish or immature behaviour in the coming days, either your own or that of someone you know. It could also reflect some aspect of your life that is about to fully grab your attention. If the child is a boy, you may soon feel the need to be more adventurous, and if the child is a girl, your intuition will be speaking to you clearly over the next few days.

Should your dream feature children, notice any feelings of vulnerability and/or dependency or a desire to follow the crowd in your waking life over the next day or so. When you notice it, remind yourself that the power of choice is always yours.

Abandoned or Lost Child: If you dream of losing a child or being unable to find them or you are the child who is abandoned in the dream, this anticipates a feeling of being unwanted. Should you recognise that moment in your waking life in the next day or so, consider it a reminder that the only person who can make you feel unwanted is yourself. Believe in yourself more. Tell yourself that you have your own back. This dream theme could also be a reminder to focus on what truly matters, and in the coming days if you notice yourself prioritising work over your children or loved ones or neglecting the importance of your work-life balance, recall this dream.

Finally, if you are not a parent but hope to be one day, dreaming about children may simply be your precognitive dreaming mind time travelling into your future to offer you an opportunity to meet your unborn children ahead of time.

Childhood Scenes: Your beliefs are typically shaped during childhood, so your precognitive mind may take you back to a place or scene from your childhood to give you a heads-up that important lessons you learned or didn't manage to learn are coming up again to test you in your waking life. For example, if you dream of your first day at school, this dream is anticipating that you will soon find yourself in a situation where you need to make your mark in some way.

Should toys feature in your dream, you will soon experience a burst of creativity, or if you didn't enjoy playing with the toys in the dream, you may soon feel a need to put away childish things and take greater responsibility. Dolls, when you recall them in dreams, often represent the projection of your emotions onto someone or something else, so if you notice yourself doing that in the coming days, take a step back to reflect. Is this about them or all about you?

The precognitive interpretation of a playground scene rests on how you feel about the group of children you are playing with. If you feel elated, then in the coming days people you live or work with will raise your vibration. But if you feel alone in the playground, you may soon experience a sense of distance from a group of people or you may notice how immature they are.

Teenage

Should you dream of being a teenager, the future-forward implication is that you may soon experience a desire to experiment with or be warned about immature behaviour. If you are a teenager, one of the most common dreams is burying a dead body, and from a precognitive perspective, this points to a growing desire to rid yourself of things you consider childish or unacceptable to others. It is also not uncommon to dream about the death of your parents or carers, and when this happens, your dreaming mind is preparing you for the birth of a more adult relationship with your parents. Dreams of meeting a celebrity predict a future period of admiration and acceptance by others.

Adulthood

Should you dream of being in your twenties or thirties and this is not your actual age, this dream points towards the importance of stepping out on your own in the future. It's related to independence and the fears and uncertainties that accompany that. It is common for people in their twenties or thirties to have imposter syndrome dreams, such as forgetting your lines on stage, not being prepared for an exam, missing a plane or train, or losing your tickets. These dreams all point to the importance of preparation and paying attention to the details.

Midlife

Should you dream of being middle-aged and you are not actually in midlife, your dreaming mind is pointing towards a growing sense of responsibility and a desire to make your mark on the world but also to a period of seriously questioning your life choices. If you are in midlife, one of the most reported dreams involves cars and driving. You may find yourself in a car that is spinning out of control—a reminder to reflect on the direction you are heading in.

You may also not remember where you parked your car in your dream. This anticipates feelings of confusion in the coming days, where you feel you have followed the rules but it hasn't brought you fulfilment. When/if you recognise that sense of confusion in your waking life, tune into your instinct or intuition for answers rather than into the expectations of others. A forgotten baby is another typical midlife dream. This anticipates a rediscovery of hidden potential or the need to revisit something unfinished. Dreams of natural disasters, which indicate a growing feeling that life is out of control, are a power-point reminder to focus on what is in your control, your reaction or perspective, when it comes to attracting future success.

Mature Years

If you are not in your mature years and you dream of yourself as an elderly person or your dreams feature old people or themes, you may soon discover the wisdom and maturity that age and experience can bring. When/if in the coming days you feel that time is running out or getting older bothers you, such dreams can also remind you that time is what you decide it is. You can't halt time. All you can do is flow gracefully with it. When/if you experience anxiety about ageing in your waking life, reread part 1 of this book, shift your perspective, and remind yourself that time can always be on your side. Age is just a number, and no one who is truly wise wishes to be younger.

If you are enjoying your mature years, you may experience more dreams of departed loved ones to help you prepare for and remove the fear of what is inevitable. Dreams of poor health could anticipate future health concerns, so always take them as a prompt to double down on your self-care and visit your doctor for regular health and well-being checkups. You may also experience dreams of finding hidden treasure. Your precognitive mind is telling you that your future lies within you and accepting who you are from the inside out is the way forward. Your perceived weaknesses can transform into strengths.

Another common dream in later life is getting lost or losing valuables, most typically your wallet or purse or credit cards or phone. You may also find yourself somewhere unfamiliar in the dream, asking for and getting the wrong directions. These dreams foreshadow potential feelings of irrelevance in your waking life. When/if you recognise them in the coming days, let those dreams remind you to reframe irrelevance as feelings of affirmation and to interpret misdirection from others as an incentive to rely more on your own intuition than on the advice of others, however well-meaning that advice may appear.

Metaphysical

When your precognitive mind chooses to speak directly to you in out-of-time and space themes that bear little or no resemblance to your waking reality, it is doing so under the assumption that you have within you the ability to look deep beneath the surface of your waking life—the material world—for hidden meaning. You just need to believe in your inner visionary, and the keys to your future happiness are yours. Your future is not unknown if you regard what is unknown in these dreams, or the sudden shifts and changes of plan that these kinds of dreams predict, as an opportunity for you to progress.

Elements

Your precognitive mind will often send you dreams that feature themes related to earth, air, fire, or water because these are the four elements of the material world and they bring with them a wealth of metaphysical and symbolic precognitive implications for you to reflect on.

Earth-related images typically relate to physical well-being and forecast the importance of reliability, patience, discipline, and being more grounded. If you are lying on the earth (or the ground or floor) in your dream, perhaps you need to be more realistic. If the ground gives way, you may soon feel disconnected from reality. It is also a reminder that the best-laid plans for mice and humans can sometimes flounder due to forces outside our control. If you are buried underground in the dream, watch out in the coming days for someone trying to smother or control you—and that someone could be your own self-limiting mindset.

Air is the element associated with communication and the intellect. If the air is foggy in your dream, be prepared for miscommunication in the coming days. Make sure you double-check everything. Struggling to breathe in a dream anticipates limited thinking holding you back in some way. Make sure the limited thinking is not your own.

Fire themes and symbols such as volcanoes, fires, candles, smoke, and so on in your dreams point to both creative and destructive forces within you ready to erupt in your waking life. When/if they do, make sure they are a source of warmth and light and not devastation.

Water is the most likely dream element to appear in your dreams because water is a symbol of emotion and your dreams speak in the emotional language of symbols. A dream will use the symbol of water and its constant ebb and flow to predict how your future will feel or flow if your current mindset doesn't change.

If you have been having a challenging time recently, the appearance of water in a dream is often a sign of more positive things ahead. You are about to enter a new phase, because water in your dreams, in whatever form it takes, is a symbol of much-needed refreshment and healing and fresh starts. This is the case even if you dream of a storm or tsunami, as all weather is temporary. It will pass.

Pay attention to how clear the water is and, if you are swimming or sailing in your dream or observing the water, how calm or chaotic the water is. Dirty water suggests that a lack of honesty with yourself and an overreliance on the opinions of others may soon loom large in your waking life. Showers and baths in a dream are encouraging you to purge or cleanse yourself of negative thinking in the coming days. Swimming/sailing is a positive omen if you are moving calmly and joyfully through the water in your dream, but the opposite is true if you are going against the current or struggling to stay afloat. If you are drowning in your dream, this is a sign that your emotions are in danger of taking over. Reenter this dream in the daydreaming state and rescript it so you either come up for air or discover the ability to breathe underwater.

If you dream of swimming in a swimming pool, ask yourself why you are limiting yourself to the confines of a swimming pool when there are infinite seas and oceans for you to discover in both your waking life and your dream life. This is a classic "frog in a well" precognitive dream scenario. The frog can choose to jump out of the well at any time and see a whole new world beyond the dark walls that it has grown accustomed to.

Fantasy

There is no judgement—moral or otherwise—in your dreams, and fantasy is unrestricted. Should your precognitive mind conjure up fantastical scenarios in your dreams, it is a sign that your future is being powerfully shaped by your unconscious. Fantasy dreams can foreshadow potential problems and solutions and show you what aspects of yourself can help or hinder your future progress. In other words, like all dreams, fantasy dreams just want you to evolve.

Fairy tale characters appearing in dreams should be interpreted in the same way as in waking life. They're all about learning and growing as you journey through life. The same applies to fictional, mythical, and magical characters in books and movies appearing in your dreams. A night-light is shining on qualities they symbolise that you need to face in your near future and be prepared to nurture or manage. For example, if you dream of a mermaid, your future self is urging you to find a balance between your unconscious (fish) mind and your conscious (human) mind. If you dream of a dragon, you will need to inject some fire and passion into your life in the coming days.

If you dream of monsters and demons, these indicate aspects of yourself that are conflicted and have the potential to derail you in the future unless you take time to understand them. These kinds of dreams tend to happen just before a major life change or to warn you against deciding on something that you may soon regret. The opposite is the case if you dream of beings of light, as these are reassuring you that your inner beauty will light the correct way ahead for you in the coming days.

Above all, fantasy dreams are a reminder that your future potential is hidden within you, and if you believe in yourself and your ability to face and learn from your fears, it will always guide you forward.

Mystical Arts

Dreams that feature the zodiac, tarot, alchemy, feng shui, palmistry, crystal work, spell work, or any other ancient mystical art could be urging you to learn more about and experiment with the personal and spiritual growth self-help tool featured in your dreams in the coming days. It might offer you deeper insight into the direction your life is heading in. You have nothing to lose and everything to gain. Should your dream feature mediums and/or psychics, in most cases the dream is urging you to connect with the inner psychic within.

Space

Should you dream of floating in space or the sun, moon, stars, or planets feature in your dreams, your precognitive mind is on overdrive. It is telling you that your future lies in your ability to boldly seek out new and unexplored horizons. You need to let go of fear and self-imposed limitations. Go beyond what you thought and felt before. The future is all yours. You just need to believe it is.

If you see Earth from space in your dream, this can suggest you will soon feel on top of the world, but it could also point to some kind of disconnection from waking reality that could derail you if you don't become aware of it in time. Let this dream be your heads-up.

The sun is a symbol of upcoming warmth and joy. The moon shines a night-light on your intuition in the coming days. Pay attention to the moon phase in your dream, as a new moon is about intentions, a waxing moon about actions, a full moon about celebration, and a waning moon about reflection. Shooting stars represent an incoming eureka moment. Look forward to that. Stars also express the possibility of success and opportunity on your horizon if you believe in them enough. Should planets feature in your dreams, research their symbolic associations. If the planet in your dream is unknown or you meet aliens, this could suggest potential feelings of being an outsider, but it is more likely pointing to a future filled with unfamiliar experiences. Instead of fearing them, embrace them. The best is yet to come.

Using a telescope (or spectacles or an eyeglass) in your dream suggests the need to focus on something. Avoid turning a blind eye. It is also a beautiful symbol of seeing into your future through the vision of your dreams.

Spirituality

Dreams are spiritually transcendent experiences. They remind us that there is an unseen and inexplicable part of us that can exist outside of space and time, a mysterious part of us that is infinite. According to some schools of thought, every dream recalled is a memory of reconnecting with your soul, the part of you that may survive bodily death.

Should religious or spiritual figures appear in your dreams, if you are a person of faith, your precognitive mind may simply be using their symbolism to remind you that your future happiness depends on your spiritual values. If you are not religious, the precognitive implication can be found in the personal associations you have with these figures. Why has your precognitive dreaming mind conjured them up for you? What can they teach you about the optimal future path for you? Do your research and see what insights come. Perhaps the simple but empowering message is to approach your life in the coming days with more humility, commitment, and sacred reverence for the gift of your life.

In general, spiritual dream themes are foreshadowing the importance of nonmaterial values for your future happiness or the need for your focus to shift in this direction for your future happiness. Your dreaming mind is trying to help you connect to what truly matters in your life now and for all time.

Priests, gurus, nuns, monks, yogis, and religious leaders, as well as shamans and wise elders, in your dreams all foreshadow spiritual progress. Crosses, ceremonies, and rites such as baptism are spiritual signposts. Whatever the spiritual scenario, it is a reminder that your future happiness lies in your ability to look within and connect to a part of you that is way ahead of any time. Spiritual dreams are also a reminder/warning that the decisions you make both today and tomorrow can create either a hell or a heaven for you in the future.

Supernatural

Paranormal dream themes mirror highly creative aspects of yourself that your dreaming mind wants you to discover and then incorporate into your future. It knows that your future happiness lies in your ability to suspend your disbelief and trust your infinite creativity.

Ghosts and spirits in your dreams may be pointing to unresolved events from your past becoming roadblocks in the future unless you face and resolve them now. If you dream of a departed loved one, this is your dreaming mind reassuring you that death ends a life and not a relationship and your future self can and will form a new relationship with that departed loved one in spirit.

Dreams about wizards, fairies, and other supernatural beings are telling you that issues that are currently troubling you can potentially be solved with an out-of-the-box perspective or by trusting in your sixth sense or things that others can't see with their physical eyes. Vampires, zombies, and other forces of undead darkness in your dreams are warning you that something or someone in your waking life may soon feel draining unless you prioritise self-care and start to establish clear boundaries.

Time

Dreams manifest outside of linear and material time, but on occasion they will send you familiar images related to linear time or the passing of time, such as a watch or the sun setting, to remind you that the future you attract is being created by you in every moment with every heartbeat.

Should you become conscious of linear time in your dream, then the following day or days, be sure to connect when you are awake to the moment in time that your dream foreshadowed to see what revelations come. Consider in that moment of conscious déjà rêvé what kind of future your current mindset is attracting your way. Recall how you felt in the dream. For instance, if it was clear to you that it was evening or the sun was setting, did you feel calm or anxious? If the latter, this suggests you may not be making the best use of your time, and uncertainty about your direction is manifesting an uncertain future.

If a specific time or a clock (see page 146) is highlighted, what a priceless gift this is from your precognition! Consider your personal associations with this symbol first, as well as common ones. For instance, mornings predict new beginnings, afternoons a period of incoming productivity, evenings reflection, and nights liberation. Always pay close attention to your emotion in the dream and your feelings in waking life when you recall and reflect upon that dream, as you have glimpsed a potential future, assuming you continue along your current path. Your feelings will let you know if this path is the right or wrong one.

Watches, clocks, calendars, timepieces, sundials, or any reference to marking time or a deadline in your dreams, or images of rapid ageing and the appearance of wise elders in your dreams, are all deeply precious and empowering precognitive dream markers. They bring with them an urgent precognitive message/warning.

Time is for everyone and belongs to no one. Your future is in every one of your dreams by night and in your hands by day. Make the most of every precious moment gifted to you, because time is the only gift you can't get a refund on.

Transformation

Dreams with transformation themes point to the only constant in life and, by extension, your future, and that is change. In almost all cases, these dreams shine a night-light on something or someone in your waking life that needs to be released so you can let your future in.

These dreams may feature combinations that are surreal or impossible in waking reality, such as animals with human body parts or objects changing into people. There may also be a rapid, inexplicable shift from summer to winter or night to day or people you know aging rapidly in the dream. You may find yourself suddenly changing into something, like a chair, or into someone else, like your schoolteacher, in these dreams.

These kinds of irrational shapeshifter dreams predict radical change coming soon in your waking life, and your precognitive mind is helping you pave the way for that change from the inside out.

Your dreaming mind never tires of finding creative ways to present the theme of transformation to you. The key to understanding the precognitive implication is your emotional response, as this response is what the dream is most likely to foreshadow. Do the changes being foreshadowed fill you with excitement or fear? Joy or sorrow? Do they feel natural or unnatural? When/if you recognise this emotional déjà rêvé in your waking life, it is a reminder that life is all about beginnings and endings, loss and gain. The secret to manifesting a fulfilling future is your ability to choose whether it becomes a positive or a negative transformation.

Nature

Nature themes and symbols in your dreams refer to what is instinctive or natural about you, what has not been shaped by others or consciously created by you. In these dreams, your true nature or essence is expressing itself. Such dreams always point towards the growing importance of focusing on what feels authentic in yourself and your life. The way forward is to get closer to your natural self and harness what comes naturally to you or is second nature. Always bear in mind that perhaps the simple and most obvious precognitive interpretation of a dream featuring nature or the natural world is that your future self wants you to spend more mindful and reflective time in the greatest school on Earth: nature.

Here are some common nature dream scenarios.

Caves: Caves anticipate a period of exploration of your inner world, or are you in danger of caving in soon in some area of your life? Remember how much the dreaming mind loves puns. Should you find yourself barefoot in your dream in a natural scene, there could not be a more powerful warning from your precognitive mind to make sure you stay grounded in the future. Use your common sense in the coming days.

Crystals/Precious Stones: Should crystals or gemstones feature in your dreams, this is a powerful precognitive sign, as they point to what is unique about you and your potential for personal transformation. Alchemy is the ancient art of transforming metal into gold, but for dream analysts, this is a symbol of the ability to find harmony or balance between the conscious and unconscious parts of yourself. It is turning your focus from the external or material world to the internal world. If you do notice a rock or stone in your dream, pay attention. If you tune into the symbolic wisdom of that rock or stone in your waking life, your future can change for the better.

Crystals are associated with healing, and there is the potent symbolism of looking into a crystal ball to see your future. What does your dream crystal tell you about your future? The colour and condition of the crystal will reveal illumination, as will the ancient healing and spiritual qualities associated with the crystal. For instance, amethyst is intuition, carnelian is courage, jade is wisdom, rose quartz is compassion, and so on. Do your research.

If a precious stone appears in your dreams, try to figure out what that stone means to you personally. That is the essential precognitive wisdom that may appear in your life or that you may soon need to draw on. If nothing jumps out at you, consider the precognitive wisdom of the colour of the gemstone (see the Colour and Shape thread on page 127) and its associations. For example, diamonds are powerful symbols of integrity, but there is also the association with greed. Should you notice those kinds of feelings surfacing in your waking life in the coming days, let the memory of this dream help you reset and choose the right path. Bear in mind, too, that each astrological sign has a birthstone to represent it, so delve into the associations hidden there as well.

Should you notice jewellery in your dreamscape, this is a sign that you are about to enjoy a leap in self-esteem and find yourself in a position to share or reveal precious parts of yourself to others and receive their admiration. In other words, you will soon feel rather pleased with yourself. If the jewellery is lost or stolen, this may have the opposite precognitive meaning. Much depends on how you feel in the dream.

Fields: Green fields in a dream champion your right to free speech and indicate areas of potential growth in your future. Countryside scenes also spotlight green pastures and new horizons waiting out there for you.

Flowers: Should flowers surface in your dreamscape, the reassuring precognitive message will lie in the language of that flower, as since ancient times, flowers have been symbols of the spiritual self, a.k.a. your inner beauty, joy, and love. They likely signal the optimal path for your future self to take and your capacity for unconditional love. Follow their advice.

The condition of the flower in your dream will speak volumes about your inner life and what you need to work on for your future well-being. Are the flowers fresh or wilting?

If the flowers in your dream are cultivated, this points to the need to control your emotions better, whereas wildflowers symbolise spontaneity. Flowers that are being planted or blossoming symbolise the flowering of new intentions and the soon-to-be-realised start of a potentially rewarding project, relationship, or direction in your life. If the flowers in your dream are dead, a negative mindset in the future may create disappointment. Hidden thorns in a bunch of flowers ask you to pay greater attention to tiny details. If something appears too good to be true in your waking life in the coming days, it probably is.

Notice the colours and shapes of your dream flowers and read the insights about their symbolism in the Colour and Shape thread (page 127). Be sure to consider their traditional associations. For example, daisies are friendship, roses are passion, daffodils are beginnings, dandelions are friendship, lilies are endings, orchids are vitality, poppies are rebirth, sunflowers are your inner light, tulips are fertility, and so on. Many flowers also have medicinal qualities, and the precognitive message could be in their name as well. For example, if you dream of a forget-me-not, is there some important date or anniversary in the coming days that you need to remember?

Should you receive a bunch of flowers in your dream, something or someone will soon pay you a compliment. If you are picking or walking among flowers, you are becoming your own best friend and are on the right track. If you see a lotus or a flower growing in the most unlikely place, this is telling you that no matter how tough things get in the coming times, you will overcome any challenge. Take heart from the fragile beauty of this dream.

Bear in mind that certain flowers have associations with specific countries and/or cultures, such as the cherry blossom, which is associated with Japan. As my personal story about my cherry blossom dreams in the introduction proved, brainstorm all possible associations, as you never know what they might predict about your potential future and where they might lead you.

Forests/Woods: These dream symbols typically suggest mystery and the unknown but also showcase your wild sense of adventure exploring them. Should you dream of being lost in a forest, this predicts uncertainty and confusion in the near future. When/if you encounter those feelings in your waking life, use this déjà rêvé to rescript the dream so you find the way out of your dream forest, and then in your waking life, be sure to reconnect with what truly matters to you.

Grass/Leaves/Plants: These all indicate that hope lies ahead, but pay attention to the freshness and colour and vibrancy of the grass, leaves, and plants.

Metal: The appearance of metal in a dream indicates that great strength of will may be required of you in the coming days. Brainstorm all of the qualities and associations with that metal, and in the coming days, see how they can help you make better decisions in your waking life. For example, gold suggests that something precious may soon be discovered in your waking life, but be aware of the saying "all that glitters is not gold."

Mountains: Mountains predict a challenge or struggle ahead, but they also offer the promise of savouring the view at the peak and all the satisfaction and fulfilment that comes with it. Valleys indicate that a much-needed period of reflection lies ahead, and caves point to the need for secrecy or the importance of not oversharing.

Mud: Mud may slow or drag you down, so this dream is urging you to prepare ahead of time for potential frustrating setbacks so you can move swiftly through them. Weeds have a similar interpretation but most likely indicate a potential self-destructive mindset or toxic relationship to guard against.

Rivers/Lakes/Streams/Oceans/Seas: These are a reminder that life is a constant flow and change is inevitable. In the days ahead, when/if you feel stuck in your waking life, let this dream memory help you understand that time just carries on and everything, including negative feelings and situations, will pass.

Rocks: Should a rocky landscape feature in your dream, this suggests that a period of stability and security lies ahead. Depending on how the dream makes you feel, you may soon find yourself in a situation where you need to stand firm, like a rock, even when others try to persuade you otherwise. Be aware that rocks in a dream are also associated with stubbornness that you may soon need to guard against in yourself or others.

Seasons: The seasons are potent and enduring dream symbols of natural life stages. Spring is associated with birth, summer with childhood, autumn with adulthood, and winter with old age.

Should you become aware of it being a specific month in your dream, brainstorm all possible associations with that month, including the traditional ones. For example, January is all about the fresh starts. Don't neglect to consider the astrological signs linked to each month and the symbolism there too. Take your own personal associations into account. When that month comes around in real time, be sure to revisit this dream and its precognitive wisdom in your mind. Your dream referenced this specific month for a reason, as something will come to pass in that month that will offer you an opportunity to learn and grow—and learning and growing are what give our lives meaning.

If spring is a feature of your dream, the precognitive interpretation is that there are new perspectives and insights ahead. Summer themes highlight the importance of planning ahead for relaxation, as well as windows for creativity. Autumn is all about the importance of forgiveness and letting go to harvest a vibrant future, and if the symbolism of falling leaves appears in your dream, this is showing you just how beautiful letting go can be. Bear in mind that sometimes the most important person we need to forgive is ourselves. Winter signals the need for contemplation and applying the lessons from your past to your future.

Trees: Trees are universally regarded as cosmic symbols of the self in the process of growth. The tree of life or world tree is an ancient archetypal symbol revered by people of many cultures and belief systems.

Notice the condition of the tree and the colour and type, as they all carry with them symbolic messaging about your potential growth or where your inner life is heading. The branches of a tree can indicate future abilities. The roots symbolise your unconscious mind, your family background, and the place you started from and from which you have grown. The trunk represents your conscious choices and how you direct your energy. The bark is the image you present to the world, while the leaves are the constantly growing and changing parts of you. The top or height of the tree represents your aspirations and ambition and where that is likely to take you or if you perhaps need to reach a little higher. In essence, it is possible to see all of the parts of a tree as a depiction of your internal reality and the energies, both inherited and natural, that either push you forward or drag you back.

Should you find yourself walking among trees, your dreaming mind wants you to focus in the coming days on reconnecting with your inner world. How did your walk in the woods make you feel? If you are lost in a sea of dream trees, perhaps this suggests you may soon forget what your goals are. Make sure you don't lose sight of the forest for the trees. If you are climbing a tree in your dream, the glorious symbolism is clear: In the coming days, you need to draw on your inner strength to help you overcome any challenges and/or anxiety you encounter.

Brainstorm both personal and traditional, medicinal, and cultural associations if your dream reveals what species of tree it is. You may find in the coming days that applying the symbolic wisdom of that tree species to a challenging situation in your waking life offers you the optimal way forward. Many trees are credited with specific qualities, powers, and sacred messages. For example, ash is a symbol of optimism, birch of honesty, elm of caution, oak of strength, and so on.

The Weather

Due to the changeability of the weather and the fact that in our waking lives we hear or listen to weather forecasts all the time, a weather dream is a strong sign from your unconscious that a change in mood or circumstances is going to happen in your future or is required to help you move forward. Sunny weather dreams suggest that happy times may be coming your way. However, your dreaming mind, in its wisdom, may also use the metaphor of a sunny day or a gentle, calming breeze to remind you of the importance of shifting your mindset to one of optimism and inner balance and away from negativity. If you have been feeling gloomy and dream of blue skies, you can expect a change of heart soon. Plan for it.

Your ability to manage your emotions rather than allowing your emotions to manage you is the central precognitive message of weather-themed dreams. In the coming days, whenever you notice anxiety getting on top of you in your waking life, refer to the emotional weather reports and warnings in your previous dreams. This is your reminder that finding inner calm is the best and only way forward.

The dream's predictive message is underlined if you experienced extreme weather conditions or if the weather was contrary, such as a winter forest scene with sunflowers growing there or snow falling on a sunny beach. As a rule of thumb, sunny scenes in dreams are typically metaphors for upcoming optimism and happiness, whereas winter scenes with snow and ice suggest emotions that are blocked or frozen in time. Stormy clouds and rain may indicate potential arguments and tension lingering out there on the horizon.

Dreams of natural disasters strongly indicate intense emotions that, unless they are dealt with, will create increasing layers of tension and erupt soon. Sometimes these kinds of dreams can also indicate a future external event that is unexpected and totally outside of your control. The only thing you can do to prepare for the certainty of the unexpected is to learn to focus more on what you can control: your mindset and keeping your head cool when everyone around you is losing theirs. Indeed, terrifying weather dreams are positive, because they are a reminder that perhaps it is not a situation in your waking life that is going to be the issue that drags you down, but rather it is your anxious mindset or unnecessary worry that could attract bad things your way.

Although your dreams can feature a wide variety of weather conditions, here are some of the most likely. Learning how to interpret these precognitively will help you decode all other possibilities that may emerge in your dreamscape as the emotional forecasts they are.

Breeze: This is a refreshing dream symbol of sudden inspiration in your very near future, as breezes have symbolic associations with spirit or the life force. It could also be your dreaming mind's way of hinting that the way forward for you is to be more of a free spirit, or to pull yourself together and shift your perspective towards creativity rather than routine.

Fog: Any kind of fog, mist, or smog in a dream scenario is a symbol of confusion on the horizon in some area of your waking life. When/if you encounter that confusion in your day-to-day routine, it is very important that you don't let emotions cloud your judgement and that you rely on your common sense to clear a hazy perspective. If the fog lifts or light breaks through in the dream, let positive expectations carry you forward.

Frost: These dreams have a similar interpretation to snow dreams (see below), but as frost is a precursor to snow, the emotional shutdown foreshadowed is less fully developed. It could also indicate meeting someone in the coming days who behaves coldly towards you in some way or an unexpected frosty response to something or someone. When you recognise that frosty response in your waking life, know that the best approach is to try to understand the emotional reasons behind it rather than the superficial ones.

Ice: Your dreaming mind is using this image to alert you to an area of your life that may soon freeze over. You need to decide if you should stick around and break the ice or look forward to something or something warmer entering your life.

Rain: Since water is so strongly linked to emotions in the dreamworld, the key to interpreting the appearance of rain in a dream is how you feel about it. Does it refresh you or drench you? If it's the latter, then it's possible you will soon feel overwhelmed by your emotions in some way or by the emotions of someone else. Forewarned is forearmed. If, however, you feel euphoric about the rain in your dream, it indicates that in the near future your heart will feel ready to live, learn, love, and laugh fully again.

In most cases, rain in dreams is a healing omen. Keep that in mind if you find yourself weeping in the coming days. If your dream rain turns to hail, however, this suggests that you may be the target of negative gossip or that your own self-talk is your own worst enemy. Guard against both in the coming days.

Should the rain lead to a flood in the dream, this could be a symbol of a fresh start ahead and a washing away or release of the past or what has been dragging you down emotionally to the point of overwhelm. As with anything in life, be aware that there can also be a negative interpretation, in this case the risk of intense involvement with someone or something in your life that might sweep you away emotionally if you don't prioritise finding inner calm. This may require you to avoid identifying your happiness with that of others. Finally, just as floods always eventually subside in waking life, this dream is also telling you that your feelings of overwhelm will lessen in intensity. It will pass.

Sky: This is a clear symbol of a future mindset that is going to either help or hinder your progress. Is the sky dark or bright? Is it blue, red, or grey? And what do you see watching over you from above there? The colour and shapes of any clouds will be significant, suggesting that brighter times and rays of hope lie ahead, or can you expect a bout of oncoming gloom?

Clouds equate to future thoughts, so if your dream features changing cloud shapes, this foreshadows an incoming change of mind. Is there a looming problem that you are burying your head in the sand about or refusing to acknowledge because your head is in the clouds? Don't forget to reflect on the expressions "having a cloud hanging over you" or "living under a cloud," as it could forecast that someone or something is about to make you feel apprehensive in some way.

Be aware of forecasting superstitions when interpreting your weather dreams precognitively, for example, "Red sky at night, shepherd's delight" and "Red sky at morning, shepherd's warning," as your dreaming mind may be using them to speak to you. Should a rainbow appear in your dreams, celebrate! It is without doubt a message of great hope and suggests that you are on the right road and need to keep following it in the coming days. Enlightenment is signposted ahead.

A rainbow is a spiritual symbol of the bridge or connection between the divine and the earth, so if a rainbow appears in your dreams, it is more important than ever that you make the choice now to feel radically optimistic about your future. Peace, redemption, and inspiration are waiting around the corner for you. Notice and appreciate them fully.

Snow: Should snow feature in your dream, this forecasts an impending interaction or experience that may feel cold and impersonal. You will need to decide whether shutting down your emotional response is truly the best way forward or is a self-defence mechanism that will falter in the long term. Much will depend on whether you are playing in and enjoying the snow in the dream, suggesting that the coldness will melt, or if the snow is slowing your progress, pointing towards an impending sense of emotional overwhelm (as in "snowed under") that needs to be addressed sooner rather than later. Pay attention if the snow in your dreams is covering everything up so you can't see what lies beneath. This, along with the appearance of ice in your dream, could suggest a closed-minded approach. If you want your future to feel warm, energising, and inviting, you need to open your mind to new perspectives.

Storm: A storm in a dream is a sign of an impending lack of control or pent-up feelings that are about to be released, either your own or those of someone you are intimate with. Either way, you are about to reach a crisis point in some area of your life, and this may trigger strong feelings of uncertainty.

Notice whether the wind in your dreams pushes you forward or stops you in your tracks, as this suggests a future situation by which you will feel either carried away or frustrated. When you experience that déjà rêvé moment in your waking life, ask yourself whether you should go with the flow and bide your time until the crisis passes.

The more extreme the storm in your dream—for example, a hurricane or tornado—the more extreme the emotional reaction you are likely to experience. Your precognitive mind is using this imagery to remind you that even though many things are out of your control in your waking life, you always have control over your response. The eye of the storm is a calm spot, so the best thing you can do to prepare and protect yourself against the oncoming winds of change is to face the challenge head-on and stay calm and centred.

Should your dream feature a whirlwind, some area of your life will soon change forever. This doesn't have to be a bad thing, as sometimes in order for things to fall into place, they have to be thrown into the air first. And change is how we learn, grow, and evolve.

Bear in mind, too, that those storms, like the emotional eruptions they symbolise, eventually blow out and every storm carries with it brainstorming potential (remember how much your precognitive dreaming mind loves puns). You may be about to unleash stunning creativity on the world, and this is especially the case if your dream storm includes bolts of lightning. Great clarity may suddenly strike in your waking life, so be prepared for it. Lightning in a dream may also symbolise the voice of your conscience and a powerful desire to do the right thing.

Alternatively, be aware that storm dreams can also indicate that you may soon feel imposed upon by an authority figure or that someone will offer you unhelpful counsel. If you feared for the safety of others in your dream storm, your dreaming mind is urging you to reflect more deeply on the impact of your words and actions on others in the coming days.

Pay attention to the details of the dream and what the storm destroyed, as they may all offer advice on what you can do right now and in the coming days to prepare/protect yourself. If you were swept away by the storm in the dream, this suggests you may soon feel that things in your waking life are outside of your control. The way ahead, when you experience that déjà rêvé, is to once again focus on what you and only you can control, which is your mindset.

Sunshine: Should you find yourself basking in glorious sunshine in your dream, this reflects a growing sense of energy and optimism within you that will lead to happy times. If you don't currently feel that sense of positivity, your dreaming mind is showing you that there is a glow and a fire within you. You need to warm up to all you have to be grateful for in your waking life. Someone or something is going to make you question yourself soon, and if this happens, be sure to reference the sunshine in your dream and renew your faith in yourself. You are more than worthy. Should you find it hard to feel positive, your dreaming mind is sending you this dream to motivate and encourage you, to let you know that within you there is always an invincible summer, even if it feels like a bleak winter on the outside.

Should you experience sunburn or feel scorched in your dream, this is a warning to avoid overexposure in the days ahead to someone or something in your waking life that is temporarily intoxicating but not good for you in the long term.

Temperature: If you sense extreme heat or cold in your dream, the most obvious thing to do first is to check that your bedroom isn't too hot or too cold. The right temperature for sleeping is important for quality sleep and dreaming. If that's not an issue, feeling or noticing heat in your dream could be a warning about impending tension or danger or someone in your life whom you consider hot or unsettling in some way. This dream is warning you to prepare yourself and to remove or distance yourself from a situation or relationship that is overpowering or all-consuming. Should humidity feature in the dream, watch out in the coming days if you feel oppressed or drained of energy in some way and take steps to protect your energy ahead of time. However, if you feel refreshed by the warmth in the dream, this suggests that feelings of contentment are on the way. The opposite is true if you feel cold or are shivering in the dream, as this could be warning you that you may soon find yourself acting ruthlessly or that you will feel compelled to remove the emotion from a situation.

Should your dream feature winter scenes but you don't notice the cold, take this as a sign that whatever challenges lie ahead, you have the resources to overcome them. If, however, you feel cold when it is warm outside in your dream, this may forecast a need in the future to stay impartial. Whatever the reason, when/if you recognise the mindset from your weather dream forecast playing out in your waking life, be sure that any decisions you make are empowering you and making you feel warm from the inside out.

Nightmares

Whether you meet monsters, are buried alive, are attacked by wild animals, or experience other typical nightmare scenarios unfold behind your eyes, the feeling uniting them all is one of dread. You wake up knowing you are a decent kind of person but wondering why on earth you would conjure up such horror, such gore, such violence, in your mind. You may also worry that this dream is a sign of impending bad luck and misfortune, a bad omen.

Stress, poor diet, alcohol, and certain medications can all increase the risk of ghoulish images moonlighting in your dreams, but even if none of these apply, you will still experience the odd nightmare, or perhaps more. Nightmares tend to be more frequent in childhood, with up to 50 percent of children reporting them on a regular basis, but one in two adults report having them on occasion, with approximately 5 percent reporting them on a frequent basis.[48]

Nightmares shake you up physically, mentally, and emotionally and force you to confront your inner demons, a.k.a. your shadow, or aspects of yourself that have been hidden, repressed, denied, misjudged, or mishandled for too long. The longer you have buried or ignored an issue, the

48. Fisher, Lereya, et al., "Childhood Parasomnias and Psychotic Experiences at Age 12 Years in a United Kingdom Birth Cohort."

more disturbing the nightmare will be. You may experience an intensity of emotion in the nightmare that you rarely experience in your waking life.

Chances are your dreaming mind has tried to send you the same warning with gentler dream scenarios, but you have not reflected or acted on them. It then has no choice but to send you a nightmare, because it knows the shock value will compel you to think about the reason behind it. In most cases, the nightmare is a clear and present warning from your precognitive mind that unless you change a situation or mindset in your waking life, you are going to face a seriously difficult time in the coming days.

Nightmares offer you a striking and memorable opportunity to acknowledge and process your dark side and transform it into inner strength. Nightmares are gifts for your self-awareness, which matters greatly, as self-awareness is the beginning of all wisdom.

Nightmares often point to toxic mindsets or situations in our waking lives that we urgently need to face rather than run away from. That is all the nightmare wants. It wants you to enter into a dialogue with it to understand what it is trying to tell you. Most of the time, negative mindsets, such as anger, self-criticism, and so on, originally developed with good intentions, typically in childhood, to protect us in some way. We felt vulnerable, so we built up defences we thought would help us survive. However, as adults, we don't need those mindsets to protect us anymore. It is time to understand why we clung to them at the time, thank them, and then let them go. In most cases when a self-destructive impulse has been acknowledged and understood, it loses its power. The more it is denied, however, the stronger its hold becomes. It might help to think of a nightmare in the same way we think of a fever as a positive sign that the body is trying to self-heal and sweat out infection-causing toxins.

Be aware, too, that sometimes what we have been repressing and denying isn't toxic at all but is essential to our personal and spiritual growth. This is called the "golden shadow." For instance, if a child has been told to speak only when spoken to, they may have buried their assertiveness in their shadow. To thrive as an adult, they must find the courage within to exhume that shadow.

Whether the shadow is golden or not, it is important to acknowledge and respect all aspects of ourselves, even those we may find unsavoury.

Just as night needs day and day needs night to be whole, we need both light and dark for our journey to wholeness. Just because you feel something negative or dream something toxic does not mean you are negative or toxic. It simply means these are aspects of yourself that you need to acknowledge and learn and grow from. True strength of character is not being relentlessly positive, so-called toxic positivity, but is knowing you have the capacity for darkness within you but making the choice to seek the light and do the right thing for your own well-being and the well-being of others.

Interestingly, when you are dreaming, although the emotional limbic system is active, which is why you feel so much during dreams, the stress hormone associated with the fight-or-flight physical response, giving you a physical adrenaline response when you are awake during moments of crisis so you can protect yourself, is not activated. This means your dream allows you to role-play and cathartically feel all sorts of terrifying worst-case scenarios without causing any physical harm to yourself or anyone else. Then when you wake up in the morning, the nightmare has become a memory. Your brain can't tell the difference between dreaming and waking and will believe you have experienced your worst fears and lived to tell the tale. There is confidence-boosting power to be gained from that reminder from your inner therapist that you are braver and more capable than you think you are.

In essence, think of any frightening dream you recall as a strengthening or training exercise prepping you for an upcoming challenge so you are prepared to face it. However, if your dreams are often (rather than sporadically) disturbing, terrifying, or violent and are damaging the quality of your sleep and your life, you should consider seeing a therapist to discuss them.

From a precognitive dreamwork perspective, nightmares are priceless gifts showcasing a potential future that your current mindset—what you are feeling, thinking, and doing with your life—is attracting your way. Chances are you are not going to like how this future memory makes you feel, which is exactly the purpose of the nightmare. It is using disturbing imagery to get you not just to think about which part of yourself is threatening to derail your happiness but also to make changes now before it is too late. If you do have a nightmare, treasure it. Your precognitive mind is refusing to be silenced. It is speaking to you with urgency about the future you are currently manifesting and offering you an opportunity to reset. There is no choice for you now. You must wake up and do something different.

Night Terrors

Night terrors are not the same as nightmares. Night terrors occur in non-REM sleep, not in REM sleep, when most dreams happen. They typically occur in the first few hours of sleep when the person wakes up screaming in terror and sometimes sees things with their eyes open. Night terrors are most common in childhood but can occur in adulthood and are associated with a sleep disorder. Should anyone you know experience them, help them calm down and go back to sleep. The night terror is unlikely to recur the same night, but if night terrors are frequent, be sure to consult your doctor. A hallmark of night terrors is that the person does not typically remember what happened the next morning, in contrast to a nightmare, where dream recall is astonishingly clear.

Recurring Dreams

Recurring dreams can involve nightmare themes and symbols, such as drowning, falling, or sinking in quicksand, but often the scenarios are less alarming, like being late or forgetting lines on stage.

If you recognise a recurring dream theme in your dream journal, focus your dreamwork on that, because your dreaming mind is using the power of repetition to get a point across that you have yet to understand in your waking life. As soon as you do understand the message of that dream and adjust accordingly in your waking life, whether that be with practical or mindset changes, the recurring dream will stop. It will likely be replaced by another theme, but the rule of thumb is that if scenarios keep repeating, your dreaming mind is using tough love by sending you similar scenarios repeatedly until you deal with the problem that is triggering it in your waking life. For example, if you keep on dreaming about being late, the message could be to be more prepared in your waking life. Be aware that recurring dreams can also relate to past traumas that you need to come to terms and make peace with.

Sleep Paralysis

As is the case with night terrors, so-called incubus/succubus demon attacks, where a person feels a crushing weight on their chest and sometimes sees demons, hags, or aliens on top of them, are not nightmares. They are likely a symptom of sleep paralysis, where your body falls asleep to protect you from acting out your dream. Sleep paralysis happens every single night when we fall asleep naturally. Most of us are not aware it happens, but sometimes we do become aware of it and can feel trapped in our body.

Common Nightmares

The following nightmare scenarios and optimal ways to interpret them precognitively are the most common or frequently reported, but be aware that nightmares are deeply personal. If you have a morbid fear or phobia of something that would appear totally innocent and harmless in someone else's dreams, the appearance of that symbol in your dreams will have nightmarish connotations. For instance, globophobia is an extreme, overwhelming, and irrational fear of balloons. This phobia often includes extreme fear, anxiety, or panic at the thought, sight, sound, touch, or smell of balloons. If you suffer from globophobia, a children's birthday party dream scene with balloons jumping out at you would be your nightmare.

Blood: Seeing blood in a dream, either your own or that of someone or something else, always feels alarming when you recall it upon waking. Your precognitive mind is urgently using this evocative symbol to warn you to protect your energy (blood is your life force) in the coming days and to make sure the energy you're giving out is returned. Are you putting too much time and energy into someone or something? If you don't start replenishing your own resources right now, you are in danger of bleeding out and feeling utterly depleted somewhere down the road.

Chased: Being chased in a dream is a potent symbol of running away from or avoiding your fears and problems. There is some situation, relationship, issue, or mindset in your waking life that you are not willing to confront and that you need to face for your personal growth and to attract the future you deserve. Think about who or what is chasing you in the dream, as this will help you identify what may soon chase you in your waking life. If it is a wild animal or anything menacing or sinister, try to identify what aspect of your personality this symbolises.

You could be refusing to face the threat because you fear it too much or don't think you can handle it. The looming threat is most likely to your own self-esteem. Your precognitive mind is telling you that this is not the best approach now or in your future. Stop running when you next feel tempted to do so in your waking life, because if you don't, the future forecast does not bode well for you. When you do encounter an intense emotion in the coming days, use the memory of this dream to redirect it in a positive and satisfying way.

Death: When the symbol of death appears in your dreams, it does not refer to your physical death or the death of those you care about but to some area of your life that is about to end, and when it does, your life will change forever. This nightmare is trying to help you let go of the old so you can welcome in a whole new world, either in your own life or in your relationship with someone else if the dream features their death. As a rule of thumb, when someone dies in your dreams, if you are close to that person in waking life, it will point to something about to change in your relationship with them. If you don't know them that well or at all in your waking life, it will point to an aspect of yourself that is like that dream person and is about to change. Focus here on the beginning or fresh start that death nightmares are forecasting, because whenever something dies, something new is always born.

Drowning nightmares portend emotional overwhelm, as water in dreams is a symbol of your emotional life. You are at serious risk of losing yourself in something or someone unless you learn how to breathe underwater, a.k.a. stop trying to be everything for everyone and start taking better care of yourself. Watch out for nightmares with fire themes, too, as they suggest that there is a threat on the horizon or a great deal of personal risk in some area of your life. Manage your emotions and expectations to minimise that risk.

Falling: There is a misguided belief out there that if you dream of falling and hit the ground, you or someone you know will soon die. This is an entirely incorrect and misguided belief. Ditch it right now. In all of my decades of being a dream researcher and writer, not one person who has shared their falling dreams with me—and that's a lot of people, as falling dreams often top the charts as the most common dream globally—has ever died or reported a death following that dream.

Having said that, if you dream of slipping over or falling from a great height in your dream and have the sensation of rapid descent, it is a clear precognitive sign that you may soon feel unsupported in some area of your waking life and that things may start to head in the wrong direction if you don't make immediate changes or start looking up. Try to identify what area of your life is at risk of capsizing. Your dreaming mind is warning you that the bottom is in sight if you don't instantly redirect your thoughts, feelings, and actions in some way.

Should things fall apart or crash on you in a dream—for example, the roof falls in, rocks fall from the sky, or you fall into a hole—the forecast ahead suggests a feeling of being out of control or that your self-esteem is in danger of eroding.

Monsters: Should your nightmares feature monsters, zombies, and/or other ghoulish images, this could not be a more gripping representation of what will become of emotions that you have been repressing or hiding if you don't find a way to acknowledge and manage them. The future lies in your ability to come to terms with whatever it is that is inwardly intimidating you. The unknown loses its fear once it is identified and understood. It could also predict a situation where your boundaries are not respected and your feelings are not considered. This nightmare could also warn against hyperbole or exaggeration being a threat in the coming days.

Zombie dreams are increasingly common, and they portend a feeling or situation in your near future where the life or energy has been sucked out. When/if you notice that déjà rêvé happening in your daily life, remember your zombie nightmare and remind yourself that zombies are terrifying because they are brain-dead, literally dead bodies walking. Your future well-being lies in what you decide to feed your mind.

Murder: Should murder be a nightmare feature in your dreamwork, the precognitive theme is of a change. Murder is death, and the implication with death is always change, but the difference with murder is that this change is forced or nonnegotiable. There appears to be no choice.

If your dream features murder or killing, take note. If you are doing the killing, try to identify what parts of yourself this is pointing towards and what you need to kill off. What aspect of yourself or your life do you feel you have no control over or is there an unwanted intrusion into? Your precognitive mind is showcasing something in your future that is going to feel outside of your control. Prepare for it now, don't take unnecessary risks, and understand that whatever it is, it will feel like a test of your resolve. Overcoming that challenge will set you on the right path to manifest the success you deserve.

If someone else is doing the nightmare killing or you are the victim, this may foreshadow feelings of guilt in the coming days about something you said or did.

Punished: From time to time, your dreaming mind may use the theme of punishment to warn you about saying or doing something you will regret. In this nightmare, you may find yourself being executed, beaten, lynched, tortured, or punished in a way that is disproportionate to any crime committed. In the coming days, be on your guard against any thoughtless words or actions. Think before you speak and act. Most important of all, keep your eyes open, because mistakes can often be avoided if you pay close attention to important details. The ultimate punishment nightmare scenario may depict scenes of hell, which is a red-hot warning from your precognitive mind to always act with integrity.

Trapped: In contrast to death-themed nightmares, which forecast impending change or the need for it in your future, the equally common nightmare theme of being trapped in some way, like being buried alive, sinking in mud, in prison/jail, unable to speak or scream, and so on, suggests that you will soon find yourself in a situation that you need to escape from. You can avoid that potential confinement by making changes now in your situation and/or mindset. Similarly, if you dream of being paralysed or a part of your body being paralysed, this again is a precognitive symbol of something in your future that is not progressing and that urgently needs to be addressed before it stops you completely in your tracks. If you don't recognise the signs and reset, you may soon feel helpless or lack confidence or something may not work out as you'd hoped.

World Ending: Dreams of an apocalypse or the end of the world can warn of imminent danger, but they can also forecast more expansive endings and beginnings or change on the horizon that isn't going to affect just one aspect of your life but all aspects of it. This nightmare is suggesting that the way forward is to start creating and exploring a whole new world for yourself. It is never too late to start afresh. You have the resources within you to survive both now and in the future. What you need is to believe in those inner resources.

People

When people feature in your precognitive dreams, both people you know and those you don't know, it is important to understand that this dream isn't about them. It is all about you, as they represent a quality within you that may come to the fore in the coming days. In other words, whether they are a boss, a friend, a colleague, your hairdresser, and so on, these dream people are aspects of your own personality that you are about to get up close and personal with in your waking life.

Sometimes when people you know from your past appear in your dreams, your precognitive mind is reminding you of the person you were when you knew them. It is warning you not to repeat old patterns of behaviour. The definition of stupidity is to do the same thing repeatedly and expect a different outcome. Precognitive dreamers are not stupid people.

Ask yourself what aspect of yourself that might be. It will likely be a potential that is currently hidden but that your precognitive self knows will soon need to be in the spotlight. This is especially the case if you dream of meeting celebrities. If your dream people are deviant or faceless strangers, your dreaming mind is giving you a warning about shadow aspects of yourself that are about to be unleashed.

The key to understanding dreams about people you don't know is what those people say and do in the dream and how the dream makes you feel rather than who they are. For example, people bumping into you in a crowd or on a busy street may suggest oncoming frustration about intrusions into your private life or boundary crossing by others.

A simple technique is to ask yourself what one word describes your opinion of the person in your dream, if you know them, and if you don't know them, ask yourself what role they are taking on in the dream. They are in your dream because they represent something symbolically about you or about qualities that you admire or envy in others.

In addition to their symbolic associations with aspects of your personality that you need to integrate, people in dreams may be archetypal figures that belong to the collective unconsciousness. If this is the case, the interpretation would be more universal and generic rather than individual. Your precognitive mind will sometimes conjure up these figures to warn you about something that is about to happen in your waking life and to offer guidance. The key to understanding this guidance is your instinctive reaction to them and whether you feel comforted and inspired or threatened and minimised by them. If it's the latter, you can avoid that future confrontation by changing your mindset and, if need be, your actions in the present.

The only exception to the "all about you" guideline for decoding people in your dreams is if the people who appear are family members, loved ones, or people you are intimate with on a regular basis. When this is the case, the dream could be more about something that is going to happen in their lives or in your relationship with them. For deeper insight into how to precognitively decode these dream images, refer to the Relationships thread (page 224).

Listed here are some of the common people symbols to appear in dreams.

Archetypes: Every time a person or character appears in your dream, whether you know that person in your waking life or not, it is potentially an archetype. Many of the people in your dreams may well be undercover archetypes at work. The term *archetype* has a lengthy history, but according to Jung, archetypes are universal instinctive tendencies and behaviour patterns that are innate to us all. They belong to a kind of psychic storehouse or collective human memory that Jung called the collective unconscious.

Everyone can connect to this psychic storehouse and its archetypes, and one of the most powerful and transformative ways to do that is through dreamwork. This is because in dreamwork we connect directly to the collective unconscious. The archetypal dream images we meet there are all aspects of ourselves that we need to understand better and that can offer us wisdom and insight and guide us towards a fulfilling future.

We tend to dream more about archetypes during times of dramatic change in our lives and whenever we feel anxious and most in need of direction. They represent basic and common human instincts and qualities that can help or hinder us. You will likely be familiar with archetypal images such as the hero, the villain, and so on, as they feature strongly in fairy tales, ancient myths, and legends, as well as in books and films, in particular superhero movies.

However, one way to know for sure if you have dreamt of an archetype is if you have a super strong or intense emotional reaction to it upon waking. Pay extra close attention to that emotional response, as it is your compass moving forward. Think about what the archetype is trying to teach you about your future and what area of self-development it is pointing you towards. Understanding exactly how and why it triggers you can help you become more self-aware and able to make better decisions moving forward.

Then stay alert over the course of the next few days. Notice whenever you experience a similar intense reaction to a person, situation, or experience in your waking life. This conscious déjà rêvé is a precognitive signpost for you and an opportunity for you to reconsider your life and the future it is constantly attracting.

There is no limit to the number of archetypes you can potentially meet in your dreams, as they can manifest in virtually any dream symbol, image, character, or theme, but according to Jung, archetypes are all aspects of the following four personality constructs: the persona, anima/animus, self, and shadow. Integrating or becoming aware of and understanding these four constructs operating within you all the time is the royal road to a future of wholeness and inner harmony.

The *persona* is the part of you or the personality that you present to others. It is how others perceive you and is therefore the mask or face others see, and it may or may not be the authentic or real you.

The persona is usually a dream theme rather than a character. It is most obvious when you find yourself in a dream wearing a mask or the focus is on what you are wearing or not wearing. For example, if you feel uncomfortable about your dream clothing or lack of it, this is a precognitive warning that you need to change the way you are presenting yourself to others because a false persona will soon lead to inner conflict and/or exposure.

The *anima* is the unconscious nurturing aspect present within us all, and the *animus* is the unconscious powerful aspect within us all. An important step in personal growth is to find harmony between both of these aspects of ourselves, regardless of our biological sex and the traditional gender expectations that culture and society can often impose on us.

Be aware that the anima and animus will typically comply with ancient gender stereotypes in your dreams. For example, the anima may appear as a maiden, priestess, witch, or mother figure, and the animus may appear as a prince, soldier, priest, or father figure. Sometimes the anima and animus can appear collectively as a coven of witches or a court of law and so on.

If a character or person in your dreams arouses deep feelings of yearning and attraction, then your dreaming mind is telling you that in the coming days you are going to be triggered in some way by gender expectations, or you will seek or see in another person or situation what you need to discover within yourself first. When/if that yearning or attraction happens in your waking life, the way ahead is to look within yourself. Find greater balance, love, and harmony between your own inner anima and animus first before seeking it outside yourself.

Perhaps the most significant archetype of all is the *self*, but in dreamspeak it is the *higher self*, or the aspect of you that is spiritual and longs to help you evolve. The most likely way for you to see it in your dreams is in a baby or childhood dream; however, it can also appear as an animal or a wise old person, priest or priestess, queen or king, or other mythical images, as well as symbols such as a cross, maze, or mandala.

Should you wake up with an intense reaction to a specific dream symbol or character, this is a surefire sign that you are about to enter a period of rapid personal and spiritual growth. Prepare yourself for something wildly unexpected and progressive in the days ahead.

Should you encounter that archetypal symbol in your waking life, for example, you see it in a film or somehow notice it in your daily life, pause and reflect. This is your precognitive sign. What you choose to do from this moment on matters greatly for your personal and spiritual growth.

Finally, the *shadow* archetype is the part of you that you feel ashamed of or that you feel is unacceptable in some way, so you have learned to repress or deny it. It is primal and survival-oriented and points to things about you that you feel uncomfortable admitting to. One way to detect your shadow is to think about what you despise the most in your waking life or what quality in others triggers you the most, such as arrogance or cowardice. Therein lies your shadow self!

Typical dream symbols/themes of the shadow include monsters, murderers, snakes, spiders, demons, thieves, strangers, wild animals, blood, the devil, shadows, and so on. The shadow loves to take centre stage in nightmares. It can also appear in the form of a trickster or clown that appears friendly but is anything but, or any dream character, theme, or symbol that makes you feel deeply uncomfortable.

If you wake up from a dream feeling shocked, humiliated, fearful, or repulsed, chances are you have encountered an aspect of your own shadow in the dream state.

Just as day cannot exist without night, there is a shadow side within us all, a darkness and a light. Both need each other to exist. The way forward is not to repress your shadow when it surfaces but to acknowledge and understand it, because in the darkness is where growth and all hope for your future lies. Most of the time our shadow simply wants to be noticed and acknowledged. It is neither good nor bad. It is simply what is unacknowledged within us.

Shadow-themed dreams are urging you to face your fears and understand what your shadow is trying to teach you about yourself. True strength of character is not denying or repressing aspects of yourself that you find unappealing (which just leads to unhappiness), but is knowing what lies within you. If what you discover is toxic, inner strength is choosing not to indulge it and doing the right thing instead. Sometimes when you investigate, you find that what you thought was negative isn't negative at all, but a golden shadow. For example, someone who was told as a child not to speak up for themselves may have buried their assertiveness in their shadow side. Reconnecting with that assertiveness in adulthood through dreamwork can be utterly transformative.

In essence, the appearance of the shadow in your dreams is a message that you are about to be seriously tested both personally and spiritually in your waking life, but this testing is a transformative gift. Your shadow side may well soon express itself powerfully in your waking life. Instead of being blindsided by its appearance, your precognitive mind has sent you an alert in your dreams so you can fully prepare ahead of time and avoid any loss of self-control or belief in yourself.

Talk to your inner shadow, understand it, and show it compassion. It may have formed with good intentions in your childhood to protect you in some way from being hurt when you depended on others for your survival, but you don't need that protection now that you are an adult and can validate yourself. It has no power over you now or in your future unless you allow it to have that power.

Authority Figures: The appearance of an authority figure in your dreams, such as your boss or your teacher, points to aspects of your personality that are responsible and assertive. You will soon be required to stand up for yourself big time. Pay attention to how this authority figure acts in your dream and whether they are respected, as this will suggest how in charge of yourself you are right now and what you need to reconsider when you are called to take the lead. If the behaviour of the boss in your dream was toxic and made you feel uncomfortable, this could also be a clear precognitive warning to avoid being too overbearing in the coming days.

The appearance of a doctor or medical professional in a dream points to your ability to take care of yourself emotionally when your authority and/or competence is challenged in waking life. It could also suggest how you are going to deal with pain or trauma. Similarly, police or law officials in your dream represent the part of you that protects your boundaries when challenged, chooses the positive and not the negative, and in general has your own best interests and what you know to be right at heart. They can also be your conscience if, in the coming days, you feel guilty or conflicted about someone or something you have done. When you recognise this response, ask yourself if you need to forgive yourself, exercise restraint, or own up to your behavior and let justice or karma take its course.

Celebrities: Should a celebrity, actor, or famous person in history, past or present, feature in your dreams, the precognitive message lies in what the person is best known for. This could be their gifts, their personality, their behaviour, or the way they project themselves to others. Let your dreaming mind know how seriously you are taking it and consciously create your déjà rêvé by researching this person. Notice if any feelings of synchronicity arise when you uncover information about them that you didn't already know and follow its guidance. Is there something about this person's life or behaviour or how they handled a crisis that resonates with you?

Should the famous person of your dreams be someone with a negative reputation or impact on history, don't let that faze you. Your precognitive mind is sending you a warning that soon you will face a clear choice between doing the right thing or not. Learn the lessons from history, as the definition of stupidity and evil is to repeat the same mistakes without learning or to lose your moral compass in the pursuit of fame and financial reward.

In general, when celebrities appear in your dreams, the precognitive sign is that you may soon find yourself the centre of attention or that you will notice a desire within yourself for more recognition. There is nothing wrong with that, as everyone deserves to shine. Just don't allow your desire for applause to eclipse your own feelings of self-worth or descend into self-importance. If you dream of a famous actor or being an actor yourself, you may soon find yourself embracing a new role in life. Are you the lead actor or a supporting act? How do these roles make you feel? If you don't like how this future-forward vision makes you feel, this is your opportunity to reset the direction your mindset is pushing you towards.

Classmates: Dreams about former classmates, whether you have kept in touch with them or not or knew them for a day or for years, are among the most commonly reported dreams for a reason. During childhood you are deeply impressionable, and the people you encounter then make a deep impression on your precognitive mind. Your dreaming mind may return to your past classmates and use them as templates or symbols to warn or guide you.

When a former classmate crops up in your dreams, the first question to ask yourself is what immediately springs to mind when you think of them and what role did they play in your life? Then in your waking life pay close attention when something about that classmate resonates with a certain situation. This is your moment to either expel this aspect of yourself from your life or embrace it. Be aware that your old classmate may also be encouraging you to reflect not on them but on who you were when you knew them. Do you need to let that state of mind go or bring some of it back to your future? It is your dream and your future. You choose.

Crowds and Groups: This dream image points to future interactions that are going to be significant because your peer group is about to pressure you in some way. This is all about your social ability and whether you can or should stand out from the crowd. Your fiercely individualistic precognitive mind is rooting for you not to become a reed blown in the wind.

Friends: Dreams in which friends suddenly turn on you are a strong precognitive warning against future self-destructive behaviour. However, depending on how close you are with your friend, be aware that this could be warning you that one of your friends is about to cross boundaries or is becoming overly dependent on you in some way. The time may soon come for you to have an honest discussion with them about the nature of your relationship and how helpful or not it is in your life.

Person Asking for Money in the Street: These dream people warn of an impending loss or loneliness unless there is a change of mindset in the present. If the person begging asks you for something in the dream, this will give you a big clue. What are you starving yourself of? If the person asking for money in your dream does not appear to be in distress or starving but rather is content in their role, your dreaming mind is telling you that you are on the right path.

Spiritual Figures: The appearance of any religious or spiritual figure, whether famous, such as Buddha, Jesus, or Muhammad, or anonymous, such as a guru, monk, priest, or nun, points you in the direction of your own conscience. In the coming days you may well encounter a moral dilemma, and your dreaming mind, rather than directing you to a specific religious or faith system for answers, is directing you to consult your own inner guru or moral compass and/or the advice of someone you trust. Important decisions await you, but whether you seek support or not from a role model, the best way forward is to keep your focus away from material success and reward and direct it to higher values, the things in life that are truly priceless.

Strangers: Should the people in your dreams be unknown or a stranger, try to determine the person's gender, as this may help you interpret them as archetypes or shadow parts of your personality that are going to need your attention in the future in order for you to find a sense of inner peace and balance.

If you aren't sure if your dream strangers are archetypal in their symbolism, they will still represent an aspect of your personality that you have yet to consciously understand and acknowledge. The more outlandish or bizarre your dream strangers appear, the more urgent it is for you to begin a dialogue with them sooner rather than later.

How your dream strangers look and behave will give you a clue as to what to look out for. Should the stranger appear sinister, it is important to note how they try to dominate the action in the dream. Then in your waking life when you recognise a similar self-destructive feeling within you, don't try to avoid it, but take time out to understand it. Most of the time negative impulses simply want to be noticed and understood. They often develop with good intentions to protect you in some way. Let them know you understand that and have compassion and gratitude for them, but you don't need them anymore and it is time to let them go.

You: When you dream about yourself, notice what you are doing in the dream and how you feel about doing it. Also notice if you are in the action or if you are observing yourself, as this will give you a heads-up about the best approach for your future self in the coming days. You need to either get more involved or take an observational stance.

Here is a reminder that whether you appear as yourself in your own dream or not, it truly is all about you. Your future self, how you are likely to relate to yourself and others, and your attributes and anxieties are reflected to you in a hall of timeless dream mirrors.

Seize on your dream people images as opportunities both to understand yourself better and to predict what roles your future self needs to take on or expel. Use those dreams also to help you predict whether conformity or conflict lies ahead and to ensure you always keep your focus on what you can control and not on what you can't.

Relationships

Facial recognition in dreams is like facial recognition in our waking lives, suggesting yet another powerful link between our dreams and waking reality. Should faces you recognise pop up in your dreams, your precognitive mind is projecting that either your relationship with that person is about to change in some significant way or there is soon going to be, or needs to be, some shift in understanding the aspect of your own personality that person symbolises to you. As a gentle rule of thumb, if that person is a partner or close loved one you live with, the precognitive dream will foreshadow changes in your relationship dynamic with them.

If you don't know the people who appear in your dreams, or you do know them but not well or you don't interact with them daily, then the dream is predicting that you will soon be getting up close and personal with the aspect of your own personality that they symbolise to you. This aspect of your personality may be one you need to discover, understand, or manage better so that it will either help or hinder your evolution. The details and feelings of the dream will clarify which is the case. If you wake up feeling energised, chances are this is an aspect of yourself that can help you evolve. If you wake up feeling dissatisfied, the opposite is true.

Listed here are some of the most likely people you will meet in your dreams and their future-forward implications. Each entry includes advice on decoding the precognitive meaning of these common sex and erotic dreams.

Family: When it comes to dreams of family members, the precognitive interpretation will depend not on how much you love or admire them but on how regularly you interact with them or how much their presence impacts your waking life. For example, you may have left home several years ago and keep a loving relationship going with your parents, perhaps contacting them a few times a month. If that is the case, then should your mother or father appear in your dreams, this will point you towards the need to mother or father yourself. However, if you live at home and communicate or work with your parents daily, then dreams about your parents will likely predict where that relationship is headed if the current relationship dynamics continue. Bear all this in mind when interpreting the appearance of family members in your precognitive dreams. Be aware, too, that your precognitive dreaming mind may use family member images to reveal and confirm hidden conflicts that are going to be roadblocks to your progress in the future.

Should you dream about your daughter or son, this dream could simply be telling you that the future of your relationship with them lies in your ability to see their point of view. Alternatively, the appearance of your children in your dreams could also point to future changes in your relationship with them, most typically the importance of letting go when the time comes so they can grow their own wings. Dreaming of your daughter and/or son could also point to something you are responsible for that will need your continued nurturing in the future.

The rule of thumb with any family member to grace your dream is to first consider how much interaction you have with them and how much impact they have on your daily life. How do you feel about them in your waking life? If their influence is strong, then this dream scenario will be pointing to a predicted shift in that relationship and foreshadowing whether that shift will enhance or hinder the relationship. If it's the latter, the dream is offering you a golden opportunity to get one step ahead of things. If you are not in regular contact with the family member, this dream is foreshadowing aspects of yourself that the person represents that will soon surface. How you handle or manage them will be vital to your personal and spiritual growth.

Bear in mind that it is within your family that you get a sense of belonging, so if you wake up from a family dream feeling safe and calm, you are well on your way home to healing parts of yourself that need to be healed. Should you wake up feeling anxious, then your future well-being lies in establishing what aspects of yourself need healing.

Dreaming that you are orphaned, fostered, or abandoned suggests you may soon feel rejected or misunderstood in some area of your life. If you don't give yourself unconditional love right now and surround yourself with people who raise you up rather than drag you down, those feelings may manifest as a crippling loss of self-confidence. Your future always lies in your ability to heal the parts of yourself that are hidden and unloved in your dreams.

Father: This is an archetypal symbol of authority, discipline, law, and financial know-how and competence, so whenever your own father or father figures appear in your dreams, your precognitive mind is foreshadowing the importance of following the guidance of a positive role model or seeking expert advice when it comes to finances, law, or life planning. It could also indicate the importance in the coming days of being a role model of discipline, justice, and authority for yourself.

Grandparents: It is often said that parents don't know how good a job they have done raising their children until their children have children of their own, so should grandparents feature in your dreams, this is foreshadowing the wisdom that has been handed down to you. In the coming days, that wisdom either will be challenged or will help set you on the right path.

Alternatively, this dream may be predicting the appearance of a wise person or be encouraging you to seek out the guidance of a wise elder. This is also the likely interpretation if you dream of your ancestors, but with the implication that the answers and the future you seek may lie in ancestral healing work and fully understanding and resolving the cultural and family dynamics you inherited.

Mother: Gaining independence from your mother is the first great step towards individuation, so pay close attention whenever your mother features in your dreams, as your precognitive mind will likely be using that symbol to showcase where your journey towards gaining inner independence is heading if you continue with your current mindset.

The dream may also be shining a night-light on the mother archetype within you and letting you know that very soon you will encounter issues in your waking life where the key to your psychological growth will lie in your ability to nurture, comfort, support, and love yourself unconditionally. If the mother figure in your dreams looks healthy and calm, this is a positive omen.

Parents/Carers: From our parents we learn both positive and negative relationship patterns and attitudes towards ourselves and others. We then carry those patterns into our waking lives, where they unconsciously attract our future relationships and impact our chances of happiness. This is why the appearance of your parents in dreams carries great precognitive power.

In your early years, your survival depended on the level of care given to you by your parents/carers. You were completely dependent on them. When you become an adult, you are no longer dependent on them for your survival, but memories of that early dependency remain with you on both a conscious and an unconscious level. Your precognitive mind will then use images of your parents to forecast where your journey towards independence and self-reliance is likely to end up if you decide to strike out or not on your own.

Whatever your personal circumstances, your dreaming mind will repeatedly conjure up dream scenarios involving your parents to encourage you to break free from parental control and establish your own identity. For example, if you kill or bury your parents in your dreams, this may feel alarming, but it is a healthy indication of you on your way to creating an independent future. Recurring dreams about parents suggest that your future needs to be one where you are more independent of them.

Should in-laws and stepfamilies appear in your dreams, the precognitive interpretation will be like that of blood relations and will depend on your level of familiarity/closeness to them in waking life.

Siblings: If you are not in regular contact with your sibling(s), dreams about them forecast aspects of yourself that are soon going to demand your attention in some way. Because they are close to you in age and life experience, siblings can often represent your shadow. You may unconsciously be projecting your own unresolved issues onto them, and your precognitive mind is sending you a dream foreshadowing the implications of this projection on your future.

Love and Sex

Whatever the dream theme, your precognitive mind will always be nudging you in the direction of the most transformative and healing love of all: self-love. Your future happiness literally depends on it, hence your dreaming mind's obsession with it. Because relationships often take centre stage in your waking life and your waking and dream lives are interconnected, both reflect, comment on, and foreshadow each other. The dreaming mind seizes on the theme of love and relationships to underline the importance of nurturing a strong relationship with yourself.

Don't be surprised if, during periods of your life, you find yourself having dream affairs, reuniting with an ex, discovering that your partner is cheating, kissing and falling in love with a stranger, and so on. You may wake up wondering why on earth you had this sensual dream that felt so real when you were in it. What does this mean for your future? If you are in a relationship, are you or your partner destined to have an affair? Or if you are single, is a passionate relationship on the horizon?

First, relax. You are not alone. Dreams themed around love and sex are exceedingly common. We all have them, a lot of the time, the reason being not just because of the central role relationships play in our lives but also because human beings are curious beings. In the dream state, we can safely explore intimate relationships without hurting anyone. Thank your dreaming mind—your inner nocturnal therapist—for offering you this virtual relationship training playground!

The next step is to understand the precognitive implications of your erotic dreams. They often appear incomprehensible, but dig deep enough and the symbols you find will suggest a likely potential future if you continue to feel, think, and act as you currently are. Remember that what your mindset attracts is the future you tend to see. With every relationship-themed dream, your night vision is showing you what urgently needs to shift within you to attract love in the future.

Despite the Freudian school of dream interpretation, which suggests that all dreams are wish fulfilment about unfulfilled sexual desires, most modern dream interpreters believe that any sex dream scenario is symbolic and not literal. It is pointing you towards what your future self needs for personal and spiritual growth and wholeness.

Night after night, sex and love dreams are telling you that all the magic, adventure, and love you are seeking in your waking life is already right there within you. Your future self is longing for you to notice, understand, and unconditionally fall in love with that potential first in your dreams and then in your waking life.

Here are some the most commonly reported sex and love dream scenarios. Be aware that every dream is personal to the dreamer, and these are the most likely precognitive interpretations that may or may not be relevant to your unique situation. However, these dream forecasts can help you think along the right lines, so the next time you wake up from a passionate dream affair, you have a head start in understanding what it is trying to tell you about the future of your relationships with yourself and others.

Cheating Partner: You may be in a loving relationship and have a dream about your partner cheating. It is not a prediction, but it does suggest that your partner may soon become overly preoccupied with work or another outside interest and you may find yourself feeling a little neglected. This interpretation also applies if you are the person having an affair in the dream. Perhaps you are the one who isn't giving your relationship the attention it deserves. When/if you notice feelings of emotional neglect in your waking life concerning your relationship, consider it a gentle warning. Seize on the déjà rêvé as an opportunity to book some quality time together and rekindle the passion and sense of adventure your relationship needs to thrive.

Crazy Pairings: If you find yourself dreaming about being in an intimate relationship with an animal or object, this forecasts potential problems with communication and self-understanding in your close relationships that you need to work on. Animal sex dreams do not mean you are weird but suggest that you may soon find yourself in a position where you need to choose between social conventions and your emotional and sexual needs.

The same applies to disturbing and graphic depictions of sex in your dreams. They do not predict sexual assault or deviance. Your dreaming mind is simply offering you an opportunity to indulge in ways that will harm no one, and again, in most cases the interpretation is symbolic and nonsexual. In the coming days, notice when you are not treating yourself or others with respect or personal boundaries are being crossed, and use the memory of your sex dream and how it made you feel to make positive changes.

Divorce/Separation: If you have this dream and are married or in a relationship, it does not portend actual divorce or separation, but it does suggest that some kind of lack of communication or emotional breakdown may be on the horizon. When that happens in your waking life, let your memory of this dream remind you that the future is not yet written and you can always rescript it in the present by changing your mindset. Be aware that divorce and separation dreams may be using your partner as a symbol of something else you are wedded to, such as work, or a perspective that you need to distance yourself from. Your dreaming mind is saying that you may soon find yourself questioning why you are giving your energy to something that no longer works for you.

Erotica: Arousing sex dreams do not forecast the physical act. They shine a night-light on cravings for deeper emotional connection and intimacy that you are likely to experience in the coming days. This can be the urge to merge with others, but more likely it's about an increasing need for greater self-awareness and uniting conflicting aspects within you.

The identity of your sex partner in the dream will give you the keys to what aspects of yourself need to be opened or integrated for your future well-being. You don't want to sleep with them, whoever they are, but there is something about them that your future self wants you to learn and grow from. If you find the person repulsive, this is urging you in the coming days to address aspects of yourself that you feel uncomfortable with. Bear in mind, too, that these kinds of dreams can forecast that a new perspective or sense of excitement is about to manifest in your life. Look forward to it.

If oral/anal sex is a theme in your dream, carefully watch how you communicate with others you are intimate with in the coming days. What you are about to tell them will speak directly to their heart. Should masturbation feature, this is warning against future self-involvement or, depending on how the dream makes you feel, is forecasting a growing sense of self-satisfaction and independence. Orgasm dreams have a similar interpretation to dreams of self-pleasure. Be aware that during REM sleep, blood tends to rush to the genitals, whether you have an erotic dream or not. This is a physical reminder that your dream life is forever arousing and guiding you from the inside out.

Should you encounter a sex worker in your dreams, watch out in the coming days for feelings that you have sold out in some way. When/if you recognise those feelings, let the memory of the dream encounter remind you that you have the power of choice here. You don't have to cheapen yourself.

Ex: If an ex reappears in your dreams and you make out with them, it is not a sign that you want to or will go back to them. It is a sign that you may need to inject some of the passion you felt for them into your life and relationship moving forward, or that you will soon need to apply the lessons you learned from that relationship to a current relationship. They are an ex for a reason.

Think about the first word or feeling that comes to mind when you reflect on your ex from your dream. This will help you understand what quality your dreaming mind wants you to face within yourself or notice appearing in your life in the coming days. Is it something you either need to integrate into your own personality or need to release because it is hindering your progress?

Dream affairs reflect the aspects of yourself that your future self wants you to feel passionate about. In your dreams you really are having an affair with yourself. Other people in your dreams symbolise aspects of your own personality.

The feeling this type of dream inspires is often simply one of excitement and adventure. If this is the case, your dreaming mind wants you to bring that sense of adventure into your own life in the coming days but not by having an affair. Vary your routine a bit, laugh more, do something different, or book a holiday. Don't look to others to bring a sense of magic your way. Spice up your own life.

Having an Affair: If you dream of having a relationship/affair and you are not currently in a relationship, this dream isn't necessarily forecasting the likelihood of you having a relationship in your waking life, but it is a positive sign that you are heading in the right direction, because it is telling you that your relationship future rests in nurturing the relationship with yourself and opening your mind to new perspectives. Get that key relationship right and your future chances of attracting others who love you for all the right reasons will dramatically increase, as like energy seeks like energy.

Having an Affair with Someone You Know: This person may or may not be someone you fancy. Either way, they are appearing in your dreams for a reason, and that reason isn't necessarily romantic.

Having an Affair with a Celebrity: Celebrities dominate the media these days, so don't be surprised if you find yourself dreaming of having an affair with a celebrity, and an unlikely one too. Think about what association comes to mind when you think about that celebrity. It is that association that carries the hidden meaning. For example, if you dream of a reality TV star, your precognitive mind is letting you know that you will soon find yourself the centre of attention. When that happens in your waking life, allow the memory of your dream to empower your personal growth or warn you against hubris.

Having an Affair with a Stranger: If you dream of falling in love or having an affair with a stranger—someone you have never met—your dreaming mind is forecasting an opportunity soon that will encourage you to step outside your comfort zone. This is not necessarily about relationships, but about seeking out different perspectives. In the coming days, let the memory of this dream encourage you to challenge yourself when your instinct is to settle or close your mind.

Bear in mind that making love to a dream stranger can also suggest that you may soon find yourself in a position where you need to question whether you are being honest with yourself or not. If/when that happens, work on your self-belief and consider what you may be cheating yourself or others of, especially when it comes to your relationships. Dreams about unreciprocated love or being ignored by a crush have a similar interpretation.

Incest Dreams: Unless there is actual buried trauma, you have nothing to be concerned about if you dream of incest. Just make sure in the coming days that you pay extra close attention to and nurture your inner parent, inner sibling, or whatever relative appeared in your dream. Be aware, too, that you may be craving greater emotional intimacy with the target of your dreams. Perhaps they have insight to share with you that will be significant for your future. Talk to them not about your dream, but about your relationship with them and how important it is to you.

Marriage/Wedding: This dream does not forecast a literal marriage, but it does forecast a union or commitment of some kind in your near future. This precognitive interpretation applies to all engagement and wedding themes, symbols, and stories that may feature in your dreams. Your dreaming mind is telling you to expect nothing but the best for your future and to talk to your future self every day with love and enduring commitment. Pay attention to the bride and groom in the dream, as these symbols will predict what aspects of yourself you need to learn from or integrate to feel fulfilled in your waking life. If you find your dream wedding partner unattractive, consider what aspects of yourself that you dislike that they might represent. Your dreaming mind is telling you that if you don't better understand and have compassion for these aspects, they may become future roadblocks to your happiness.

At a very deep level, this type of dream may anticipate a union of reason and intuition, logic and emotion, within yourself in your waking life. Whenever that happens, you will get goose bumps, and those goose bumps are a sign that your precognition is awakening.

Be aware that dreams that highlight intimate relationships are showing you how your relationship with your own heart is going to impact your future happiness. You will see aspects of yourself played out in other people. Your precognitive mind is alerting you to aspects of yourself that you need to fall in love with, merge with, or cultivate in the coming days to grow in self-awareness and self-love and become a happier person. Your future self is dreaming of a loving union with all of them.

Someone Falling in Love with You: When you wake up from a dream in which someone falls in love with you, consider how this surreal affection from someone else made you feel. If it made you feel good, then in the future you need to focus on the quality rather than the quantity of your close relationships. Allow your memory of this dream to empower you to set boundaries and seek out people who raise you up rather than drain you. If this dream made you feel insecure about the dream affection, the precognitive message is loud and clear: your future well-being depends on nurturing a loving relationship with yourself.

Your precognitive mind is using the most emotive symbolism of all—love—to urge you to fall in love with yourself sooner rather than later. Without self-love, it is difficult to have fulfilling relationships in your waking life, so your precognitive mind resorts to all sorts of relationship dream scenarios to try to get this message across. Should one of those scenarios involve a totally inappropriate pairing, like if you marry a car in your dream, you are being warned that there may soon be a serious lack of understanding in one of your close relationships.

Are your current relationships dragging you down? Are you longing for a deep connection with others but failing to understand that relationships risk becoming toxic or codependent if you don't feel deeply in love and connected to yourself first? You can't give to others what you can't give to yourself.

Should you find yourself in a dream searching for a place to be intimate but feeling frustrated, this points towards future roadblocks to healthy communication with yourself and others you are close to. Forewarned is forearmed.

School

School and workplace dreams have much in common, as they are all places of learning and ambition but also anxiety and the need to impress or get validation from others. Should a workplace, colleagues, peers, coworkers, or your boss appear in your dream, always look for links with school dream scenarios. You spend much of your time at work, so your dreaming mind is using it as a metaphor to give you a similar precognitive warning. Are you about to lose your sense of identity in your work? When/if you notice that happening in your waking life, stop and take stock. It is time to seriously rethink, as nobody on their death or dream bed should ever regret not spending more time in the office. Should you dream that you are preforming a repetitive and impossible-to-complete task at work, perhaps in a zombie-like state, the urgent warning from your precognitive mind could not be clearer.

Typically, school dreams and their close sibling, work-themed dreams, forecast how well you feel you are going to perform, as rightly or wrongly many of us link our self-esteem to our competence at work. It's all about your learning process, how others perceive you, and your relationship with authority.

Whenever places of learning appear in your dreams, be it a school, classroom, nursery, college, lecture hall, or university, the forecast from your dreaming mind is that you are about to (or need to) learn something of great value in your waking life. Or a lesson you learned at school in the past or an event you experienced at work may soon become extremely relevant again in your waking life. The way to move forward now is to apply the lessons you learned from that past event or experience.

Back to Night School

Examination: Should you have the common dream of arriving late for an exam or not being able to find the exam room or classroom, or if you do finally get there but it's pointless because you can't follow what is going on, listen closely to this heads-up from your dreaming mind. In your waking life, do all you can to be as prepared as possible for a future event that you may feel anxious about. Preparation is key. Alternatively, this dream is suggesting that you will soon feel tested in some way, and again it is helping you prepare for that test by showcasing the worst-case scenario so that you have mentally been there in the dream and can take steps to avoid it in your waking life.

Believe it or not, failure dreams are not predicting disappointment but are trying to help you avoid it. They are very common dreams for people who suffer from imposter syndrome. In most cases, people who suffer from imposter syndrome don't fail or make mistakes. They don't allow themselves to. But the dreaming mind, in its infinite wisdom, knows that failure is the only way to learn and grow, so it takes them there in their dreams, knowing they won't allow themselves to go there in their waking lives.

Locker: Dreaming you are at school and have forgotten the combination to your locker or some similar embarrassing scenario is a sign that you may soon find yourself feeling like you don't fit in or are being inauthentic. The locker symbolises your sense of identity, as it is where your personal items would be kept.

In the coming days when you notice feelings of embarrassment rising within you, check in with this commonly reported dream. It is trying to tell you that there may be things in your school locker that symbolise authentic parts of yourself, or even the real you, that you feel cut off from. You need to find ways to reconnect to them in the future. This dream does not forecast social inadequacy or isolation in your waking life, but is encouraging you to stop trying so darn hard to fit in. Focus your unique energy on self-understanding instead.

Occupations: Should a specific occupation that is not your own feature in a dream, your dreaming mind is using this symbol not to give you career change advice (although there is no harm in ruling that out!) but to shine a night-light on the abilities you need to foster or work on within yourself in the coming days to increase your chances of success. For example, if you dream of a scientist, perhaps you need to be more logical. If you dream of a doctor, maybe you need to look after yourself better. If you dream of a salesperson, perhaps you need to be more assertive, or if you dream of being a writer, maybe you need to work on your communication skills, and so on.

Should your dream feature you being interviewed for a job or your work performance being judged in some way, for example, you are auditioning for a show or are giving a presentation, your dreaming mind is forecasting that you will soon find yourself in a position where you will be observed or evaluated. When/if that happens in your waking life, keep your cool. Recall this dream and rescript it so that you ace your audition, delight the dream interviewer, audience, or adjudicator, and impress not just others but most importantly yourself. Convince your unconscious that this is the case and your waking mind will follow its lead.

Schooling: If your dream puts you back at school, the key to interpreting it precognitively is to recall how you felt about your own school days. If you didn't enjoy school, your precognitive mind is warning you that similar feelings of uncertainty are incoming. You may soon find yourself in a situation where you feel like an outsider or anxious about your value or abilities or restricted in some way. When/if you recognise that trapped or claustrophobic feeling in your waking life, recall your school-themed night vision and think about how you can rescript the dream to feel more secure. Then apply that positive and proactive approach to your waking life. Remind yourself that your perspective is crucial, regardless of what judgements others make about you. If, on the other hand, you loved school, then returning to school in your dreams forecasts a steep but exciting learning curve on the horizon. You are going to be offered the opportunity soon to learn and grow. Don't hesitate. Seize it.

School dreams do often suggest that an opportunity to learn something crucial that can help you jump ahead is soon to materialise. The meaning and purpose of our lives is found in learning and the growth it triggers within us. Your job is to keep your eyes and mind open so you don't miss out. You were a child at school, so the dream is telling you that the way to ensure you don't miss out is to bring a sense of childlike curiosity and spontaneity to an upcoming challenge you may face.

Be aware that school-themed dreams may also shine a night-light not just on incoming opportunities to learn but also on your need to fit in and how much it is derailing your chances of success. This is especially the case if your school-themed dreams involve frustrating scenarios, such as being expelled, failing an assignment, going to the wrong classroom, not being able to open your locker, and so on.

Teacher: In dreams, teachers are points of guidance and wisdom, so heed what they are saying to you, as you may be able to apply that guidance and wisdom to your own life in the coming days. In many cases, these dreams don't actually relate to other people coming to your rescue, but to your own inner wisdom already knowing the answers to your questions before you ask them in real time.

University: College and university-themed dreams have a similar precognitive interpretation to school and classroom-themed ones but with more emphasis on the need to think independently in your ongoing acquisition of knowledge. Dreams of graduating indicate that a liberating phase is about to begin in your life. When/if you experience this moment of renewal in your waking life, be sure to celebrate it, because you have worked hard and deserve it.

Work: Dreams themed around work have a similar precognitive implication to school-related dreams, given school is our first job, so to speak, or the place where we are expected to make our mark or prove ourselves to others.

Should work-related themes and scenarios feature in your dreams, your precognitive mind is warning you that you will soon feel a strong need to impress others in the workplace or you will reach a point where work has become overwhelming and overtaken your identity. This is especially the case if you dream of arriving late at work, performing mindless tasks at work, or disappointing yourself and others in some career-related way.

When/if you notice that "work is all-consuming" feeling wash over you in your waking life, treat it as a priceless moment in time for you to consider whether you work to live or live to work. If it's the latter, your dreaming mind is urging you to change your mindset and the direction your life is heading in.

Settings

Think of the setting (landscape, place, location, backdrop) where the action takes place in your dreams as a metaphor for a situation or, more likely, an emotional reaction that is close to manifesting in your waking life. However suggestive the other symbols are in your dream, interpreting them within the context of their setting will significantly boost your ability to use your dreams to sense the direction your future is heading in and the most likely destination. Just as location is perhaps the most important consideration when you are buying property, it is just as decisive a factor in all your precognitive dreamwork.

Where you are in your dream or where the action centres is where you will find yourself at some point in the future if you continue to think, feel, and act as you currently are. If you are uncertain about what the future holds for you in your waking life and want to know if you are heading in the right direction, your dreamscape will offer clarity. We are all trying to get to a place in our lives, both externally and internally, where we feel fulfilled. Your dream settings can let you know how near or far your current mindset or situation will get you to your destination.

Become conscious that your dream settings will also showcase the things in life that you may soon start to take for granted but that matter greatly. Try to assign a feeling and a function to the dream setting, and when/if in your waking life you encounter a situation, experience, or emotion that compares, use that priceless déjà rêvé as an opportunity to express gratitude for what you have and a reminder to focus on what you want in your life, not what you don't want. What you focus on is the future you tend to attract.

A helpful tip when interpreting dream settings is to imagine you are a movie director or novelist. When filming or writing your story, you would carefully consider the setting, because it would convey deeper meanings.

Ask yourself if the setting in your dream is familiar or recurring. Both suggest a lesson waiting to be learned. If the dream setting is unfamiliar to you, you need an out-of-the-box perspective to carry you forward. Don't forget to pay attention to the lighting in the dream. Dark places in general represent confusion but also the opportunity for growth. Light indicates greater clarity. Consider the weather in your dream, as it will reflect your feelings about the future emotional landscape that the dream is showcasing.

Take note of your own position and the position of other symbols in the dream setting, scenario, location, or situation, as this could be a highly significant guide towards what will help or hinder you moving forward. If you are looking down in the dream, you will need to rise above and see the bigger picture. If you are next to the action or adjacent to it, this suggests that you need to get more involved and focus on the details. If you are looking back, you will soon need to let go of what no longer serves you. If you are upside down, you may soon need to throw everything up in the air to see how things land. If things are in the distance in your dream, this is your future waiting to be born.

Here are some of the most common dream settings repeatedly sent to me for evaluation, but as with every dream thread in this section, it is simply impossible to list all of the infinite possibilities your dreaming mind can conjure up to speak to you about the future you are busy manifesting. If you can't find your specific dream setting here, try looking for it in related threads, such as Nature (page 195).

Dreamscapes

Abroad or Unknown (Unfamiliar) Location: With this dream setting, your precognitive mind is anticipating that a completely new or previously unknown situation, relationship, or perspective is coming your way. Anticipate and expect it.

Airport/Train Station/Docks: These are all places where you depart and arrive, and your dreaming mind could be showcasing a fresh start or opportunity for you in the coming days. It could symbolise an inner journey to parts of yourself that you didn't even know existed and are about to discover. If the airport in your dream is deserted, this is a sign that your plans may soon unexpectedly change. Be prepared for any possibility.

Battlefield: Should conflict, soldiers, the military, war, or battlefield imagery appear in your dream, this is warning you either of upcoming conflict or disagreement in your external world or of some inner dispute that has the potential to turn volatile. This is an opportunity to hold peace talks before there are casualties, and if that doesn't work, to fight for what is right. Should concentration camps feature in your dream, this is suggesting that your best way forward is to agree to disagree with others and to appreciate what is unique about you and everyone who crosses your path.

Car Park: If you find yourself in a dream car park, your precognitive mind is foreshadowing a period of inactivity in the coming days. Patience will be required. If you are lost in the car park and can't find your car, the precognitive interpretation is different, as it suggests that if you want to move forward in your waking life, you need to find a sense of direction. The upside of car park dreams is that they are temporary places, so when/if you notice that you are feeling stuck or inactive in your waking life, recall this dreamscape, as it will remind you that this will pass.

Casino: Your future success lies in your ability to take a calculated risk and then to relax about the future outcome and simply enjoy the game of life. The precognitive implications of this dream very much depend on how you feel about being in a casino.

Castle: If you are in a castle in your dream, this suggests you are about to be honoured or recognised in some grand way in your waking life. If you are outside the castle and trying to get in, there may be challenges for you ahead. Overcome them to gain a sense of accomplishment. Be aware that fortresses also carry with them themes of protection and self-defence.

Cave: Depending on the details of this dream, it anticipates deeper and deeper self-discovery. Even though few of us have explored caves, they are a well-reported dream symbol, because they are a metaphor for retreat, reflection, and self-knowledge. Dreams within dreams also have this precognitive implication. This is when you are dreaming about dreaming.

You are going deeper than before. Underground dreams have a similar precognitive interpretation but with the suggestion that the journey will be less spontaneous and more conscious. Should tunnels appear in your dream, this is another call from your precognitive mind letting you know that your future happiness lies in your ability to look within, explore your unconscious, and, most important of all, see the light at the end of each tunnel you are in.

Church: With this dream symbol, questions about what is sacred and deeply meaningful to you will become more relevant than ever in the coming days. Think about what your values are when/if those questions surface in your waking life.

City: Urban landscapes in dreams are precognitive signs of how others are likely to perceive you in the future if you continue with your current mindset and approach. These dreamscapes are also strongly linked to work and career, so notice what is being signposted to you about the optimal direction.

Corner: With this dream symbol, you may soon experience a feeling of being trapped or cornered by a dilemma. When/if you find yourself in a situation where you feel like you're between a rock and a hard place in the coming days, recall this dream and let it remind you that corners are for turning. Turning right suggests a more logical approach and the right thing to do, while turning left favours a creative approach. Be aware, too, of things that need to be left behind or of feeling left out.

Countryside: This symbolises the forces of nature within you that are about to erupt or that you need to get in touch with to increase your chances of happiness and success in the future. Mountains, gorges, ditches, slopes, and so on all suggest challenges waiting for you on the horizon, but despite the uncertainty, these challenges are all opportunities for you to see your future as an exciting adventure.

Courtroom: A courtroom in your dream is potentially a warning that you may soon be held to account for something you said or did or that you will need to reflect on your attitude toward authority. As with all of your precognitive dreams, forewarned is forearmed.

Desert: This symbol is perhaps a precognitive warning that the sands of time may soon run out for you in some area of your life. It can also suggest that everything may soon shift.

Forest: A forest is a symbol of being tested in the coming days but also a promise that whatever happens, you will emerge wiser from the experience. Jungles are wilder versions of forests and woods, suggesting that your future success lies in your ability to face and understand untamed parts of yourself.

Gatherings: Should your dream feature gatherings of people that you either observe or participate in, this anticipates a likely emotional reaction soon to other people in your life. The People thread (page 215) will offer more insight, but key to the precognitive interpretation will be the function, atmosphere, and feeling of the gathering, as well as the people attending. Celebrations, parties, graduations, and award ceremonies predict that feelings of satisfaction are close to being realised in your waking life. You may soon move up a level. The opposite is true if the dream showcases an atmosphere of conflict, confusion, or tension. This predicts feelings of uncertainty if you continue to base your happiness on the validation of other people. Should someone you know in waking life behave totally out of character in your dream, your precognitive mind is warning you to be vigilant in the coming days and to notice when the words of others do not match their actions.

If you are super close to the people in your dream gathering, for example, partners or family members, this dream points towards a potential emotional confrontation within that relationship. If you don't know the people in your dream gathering, the future-forward focus is on potential inner shifts.

Crowds in dreams predict a future social encounter or public judgement/response of some kind. Notice how your dream crowd makes you feel. Suffocated? Lost? A sense of belonging or unity? Use this dream to help you plan and decide whether a little conformity or a hint of rebellion is the best way forward.

Hospital: This dream symbol is a clear precognitive warning not of actual physical illness but that some area of your life is about to head in an unhealthy direction and it can be prevented with self-healing.

Hotel: When a hotel features in your dream, some area of your life is not going to satisfy you in the long term. Enjoy what you can now, but know that you will soon be required to check out, hopefully with lessons learned.

Positioning: In general, the dream setting—where the action or story of your dream happens—offers you a powerful clue to your emotional response, whether helpful or hindersome, to a potential future situation or experience or mindset. Consider your personal associations with the setting before exploring the universal ones. For example, a park is about relaxation and fun, but if you had an argument in a park recently with a loved one, it might not have this lighthearted emotional association.

Prison: Should a prison scenario feature in your dream, this is a sign that you may soon feel trapped or stuck in some area of your life and this will be caused not by yourself, but by things that are outside of your control. When/if you recognise this feeling in your waking life, recall your prison dream and let the conscious déjà rêvé remind you to focus on what you can control, which is your reaction. Let your mindset liberate you.

Restaurant: This dream symbol points you towards what your future self craves or will need to acquire for your emotional fulfilment. See also the Food thread (page 169).

Restroom: The second most common dream setting after classrooms is public restrooms, and the symbolism is clear. You will soon find yourself in a position where you can no longer hold in or contain something that needs to be expressed or released. That's why the restroom is typically a public one, as this dream is foreshadowing the importance of sharing the load with others or asking for help. See also the Body thread (page 114).

School/Classroom: This dream symbolism most typically foreshadows issues and pressures related to your work, because in many ways going to school is your first job or role. It can also point towards social expectations. When you encounter these tensions in your waking life, recall your school dreamscape and apply the lessons that you learned or should have learned while you were at school. See also the Birth entry (page 182).

Seaside/Beach: In precognitive dreamwork, a seaside or beach anticipates a new dimension of experience. You are on the shore, but the water suggests creativity, freedom, and new horizons. In my research I have found that whenever this symbol features in a person's dreams, it is a clear sign that the worst is behind them and good things—and a much-needed dose of hope—are on the way. If there are footprints in the sand on your dream beach, it is a reminder that you are being guided from above and are never alone.

Theme Park: It is often said that life is a roller coaster. Your future is going to be a mixture of highs and lows, ups and downs. Sometimes things may spin out of control. The key to interpreting a roller coaster dream, and whether it predicts a future high or low, is how you feel. If you feel exhilarated in the dream, this suggests that wonderful opportunities lie ahead. If you are anxious and fearful in your theme park dream, the way forward is to remind yourself that progress is never made inside of your comfort zone.

Wedding: This symbol is a precognitive sign of a serious commitment you are about to make either to someone or something, such as a relationship or a job, or to yourself, such as committing to exercise more or recall your dreams every day. How you feel about your dream wedding will give you all the information you need about the chances of this commitment succeeding.

Travel

In some rare cases your dreaming mind can predict a literal change of location or an upcoming journey, but it is most likely using the metaphor of travel to forecast future challenges in your ongoing journey of self-discovery.

It's all about where you are likely to head in your waking life or where you will go if you continue with your current approach and mindset.

In all cases, transport-related imagery is underlining the importance of moving forward in your life, not standing still. Identify where the journey began (your intentions) and where you are heading (your future vision). If you don't know, this does suggest that unclear goals have the potential to derail your future chances of success.

Notice if you are traveling alone or in a group and what delays or misdirections happen along the way, as this will offer illumination about the optimal way ahead. The pace at which you are travelling indicates whether the potential future that this dream is forecasting will manifest sooner rather than later. The surroundings you view along the way, as well as any obstacles you encounter or rest stops, add to the bigger picture when you interpret the dream.

Your mode of transport in the dream suggests what is driving you forward and how it is going to help or hinder your progress. Are you walking, running, flying, climbing (see the Actions thread on page 96), or travelling in a vehicle?

Here are some of the most common dream travel symbols and scenarios, along with their precognitive implications.

Bike: If you are cycling or see a bicycle in your dream, finding balance is going to be the key to your future happiness. You will soon find yourself in a position where the only way forward is to make a compromise and find harmony between opposing forces, such as work and family or mind and body.

Should you ride or see a motorcycle, your dreaming mind is telling you that you may soon feel a strong desire to strike out on your own. When/if you recognise that feeling in your waking life, don't let it go to your head. Recall the wisdom of your dream. Maintain your balance and keep your eyes on the road ahead.

Boat: This dream symbol indicates an upcoming exploration of your emotional life. Again, notice the details. If the boat in your dream is sinking, you may soon find yourself questioning whether you should stay in a certain relationship or mindset or take a risk and abandon ship. Indeed, if anything sinks or shrinks in your dream, it can suggest that something may soon drag you down. Should docks or harbours feature, this is a sign of incoming security, but it is also a reminder that a ship is safe in a harbour but it is not where it is meant to be.

Bus: Bus dreams have a similar interpretation to train-themed dreams, but there is less of a sense of urgency and speed. You can cruise along for now, but at some point you will need to make a decision about whether you want to remain a passenger on the bus, get into the driver's seat, or leave at the next stop.

Car: The most commonly reported dream vehicle is a car, which isn't surprising, as cars are the most common form of transport. Dreams about out-of-control cars often feature in lists of the top ten most common dreams. The precognitive warning here is clear. You may soon feel as if your life or some area of your life is out of your control or like your drive is veering off course. Take this as a sign that you and only you can course correct, even if it is just a shift in perspective. Should your dream feature a crash, this suggests that something in your waking life is about to get messy, come to a full stop, or reach a crisis point.

Should you have a car dream, consider what destination your inner Satnav is directing you to and whether it is where you want to go or you need to recalibrate. Consider, too, the make or type of car and brainstorm the associations you have with that type of car. Should the car be a truck, do you need to lighten your load in the days ahead? If it is a taxi, do you need to seek expert guidance to stay on track?

Caravan (RV): Should an RV manifest in your dream, perhaps the best way forward for you is to take an unconventional approach. Should vans, lorries, or trucks feature, this is warning you about taking on too many heavy burdens in the coming days. Lighten your load.

Directions: Should you notice paths or roads or other routes in your transport dream, these are common symbols of the direction that your life could head in if you decide to follow them. Pay attention to every detail.

Life is often compared to a journey, and in your dreamscape, every path, road, or direction you head in matters and will predict your chances of success moving forward. Is the road you want to follow in your dream clear and straight or bumpy and windy? Were there shadows ahead in the dream, suggesting perhaps that a negative mindset may be the chief roadblock or that your vision of the future is unclear?

Notice how you feel on your travels, as this is very significant. If you are not excited about the journey ahead, why are you setting off in the first place? In the coming days when/if you find yourself in a position where you need to make a quick decision, revisit this dream in your mind. Let the intuitive associations you make with it help you take the right path.

If you dream that you are going on holiday, your precognitive mind is suggesting that your future happiness rests on your ability to fulfil your needs and make sure you enjoy what you are doing. If you travel alone and/or to an island, the forecast for you ahead is an independent one rather than a lonely one.

Luggage: Any luggage you carry with you on your dream journey is typically associated with emotional issues that have the potential to seriously weigh you down if you don't find ways to ease or share the load in your waking life. Should you have this dream, you may soon find yourself questioning what is and is not essential for your emotional well-being. Let this déjà rêvé encourage you to let go of what is holding you back. A very common dream is arriving on holiday without luggage, with the wrong luggage, or with essential items missing. This suggests that you may soon feel you lack the resources or ability to begin a new phase in your life. Should you notice yourself feeling like you haven't got what it takes, remind yourself that the strength is within you. Double down on your self-belief.

Missing, Wrong, or Running Late for Transport: Should you miss a train or plane in your dream, your precognitive mind is informing you that your future happiness hangs on your ability to stop waiting for external validation—from others, your bank balance, career, popularity, appearance, and so on—to complete you. The only way to find meaning in your life is to seek inner fulfillment first, from the inside out.

Dreams where you miss your plane or train are also urging you to examine the dream carefully so that in the future you can avoid that frustrating feeling of missing out. Look closely to see if there was something you could have done in the dream to make sure you were on time. See if there was an action or a shift in mindset that would have made all the difference. Then when you have something important coming up in your waking life, be as prepared for it as you possibly can.

Should you dream of taking the wrong bus, train, or plane, your dreaming mind is warning you against making any hasty decisions in the days ahead. Should you suddenly find yourself being asked to drive a train or fly a plane because the driver or pilot has gone missing for some reason, your precognitive mind is telling you that you will soon find yourself in a position of authority where others rely on you. Don't doubt yourself. Your inner psychic is telling you through this dream that you are ready.

Movement: Movements in dreams, either those you make or those you observe, forecast change on the horizon in your waking life and your ability to adapt to that change. Notice how effortlessly your movements flow, as positive change is typically indicated by dreams where there are no impediments to your actions. If you are trapped, blocked, or paralysed in the dream, this is warning you to look out for potential sources of anxiety or roadblocks presented by others hindering your progress in the future. If you are hiding in the dream, this foreshadows a tendency to avoid confrontation and encourages you to ask yourself what you don't want to be found out about. If you feel dragged down in your dream, someone or something in your waking life will soon feel like an albatross around your neck. Be aware that this draining influence could be a mindset or a preoccupation with the material world.

The way you and the other people move in waking life can speak volumes to body language experts, and it is the same in dreams. Should you recall a particular posture or movement in your dream, for example, skipping, jumping, and so on, re-create it safely in your waking life and notice what inspirations this conscious déjà rêvé inspires in you. Tune into the symbolic meanings with specific movements. For example, skipping is positivity, jumping is a leap of faith, and running is urgency. Changing direction is new perspectives, sitting is observational and passive, standing is being proactive, and so on. Pay attention to how you feel about the movements and body language in your dream and if they are appropriate to the scenario. Then, in the coming days, notice when a similar feeling arrives and assess whether your response is appropriate or if you need to either take a step back or stand up more for yourself.

Think of travel symbols and movement themes recurring in your dreams as precognitive postcards constantly giving you updates on the never-ending journey of your life and the happiest direction for you to head in.

Plane: Should airplanes feature in your dreams, this suggests you will soon feel the need to broaden your mind with new experiences. In many cases plane dreams relate to work or career goals, as we often have high hopes for ourselves there. If you have this dream, consider all of the details, and if there is a crash or it's a bumpy ride, don't let it dampen your expectations or increase your fear of a letdown. Your precognitive mind is showing you that the sky is the limit. Aim higher.

Stops: Dreams where you travel from one place to another or visit another country forecast a soon-to-be-experienced urge to move on or an impending change in some aspect of your life. The dream symbols and your feelings about them will give you clues to the progress that needs to be made before you can successfully take off. If you find yourself dreaming of an airport, bus stop, taxi rank, port, harbour, bridge, crossroads, roundabout, or any form of queuing, this indicates that an opportunity to redirect lies ahead that you don't want to miss out on. Prepare yourself ahead of time.

Train: If you are on a tube or train or see one in your dream, then you will soon find yourself in a situation where you must decide whether to people-please, conform, and do what is expected of you or do what feels more authentic to you. Trains can warn of potential dependency on others in the coming days or an inflexible approach that needs to be reconsidered. The metaphor of a train points to a predetermined outcome, but as you surely know by now, your future is not predestined. You always can change it through your current mindset and actions. If you truly believe something is possible, your chances of arriving there on schedule increase dramatically.

Vehicles: The vehicle in your dreams comments on your ability to reach your goals or get to where you want in your waking life. Notice how fast or slow you are moving in your dream, where you are heading, who is with you, and, most important of all, who is doing the driving. If you are not the driver, this isn't optimal, because your dreaming mind uses the metaphor of vehicles to symbolise your drive or vibes and the direction your life is heading in. If you are not driving the vehicle in your dream, pay close attention to who or what is and the implications that your passenger approach in this dream is going to have on your future chances of happiness and success.

The mode of transport in a dream matters too. Pay attention to whether you are the only one on that route or it is crowded. If it's the latter, this foreshadows a turning point in the coming days where you must decide whether you want to continue to follow the crowd or strike out independently. When/if that happens, return to this dream and how you felt in it and let your intuition guide you.

UFOS: Should your dream feature a spaceship, rocket, or UFO, this forecasts a radical new perspective or experience waiting out there for you that will utterly transform your life. You can increase the chances of it manifesting by believing fully in your own infinite worth.

Conclusion

Just as a mind that has been stretched by a new experience can never go back to its old dimensions, so can a soul that has been empowered by a precognitive experience never go back to its subservience to linear time. It has seen its infinite nature and value. It has tasted the illumination of timelessness. To quote poet Alfred Tennyson, it has "dipt into the future far as human eye could see; Saw the Vision of the world and all the wonder that would be."[49]

In essence, once you savour precognition with your eyes wide shut, nothing will ever look, feel, or be the same again for you. Your big dreams have transformed you into a true visionary. You now know for sure that what you think is what you create and what you feel is what you attract, but what you dream is what you become.

You will know without a shadow of doubt that the future you are looking for—and forward to—is forever looking back at you in your dreams.

Dreaming of Your Future has, moment by moment, dream by dream, challenged you to repeatedly suspend your disbelief and stretch your mind to bring your future right into your present. Considering this, it is only fitting that the final pages offer you yet another future-forward shift.

There is a school of philosophical thought that suggests that this life—your waking reality—is the dream. Precognitive dreaming does blur the

---

49. Poetry Foundation, "Locksley Hall" by Lord Tennyson.

boundaries between reality and the world of the dream. It is often said that the older we get, the more life begins to feel like a dream. It becomes easier to lose track of time and for memories of the past, present, and future to somehow merge. Daydreaming is inner peace, and everyday life takes on a surreal quality.

You may well find that your precognitive dreamwork brings with it a sense of wholeness and peace that may have been lacking before. This inner shift happens because your precognitive dreams remind you that this material life is not all there is. They take you to an invisible place outside of time where symbols speak directly to your soul and everything you thought you knew about life and how it works is turned upside down. This is the place where all true vision is born.

Even if you don't think you are visionary, your dreams show you that you can always transcend time. Your night vision reminds you how stunningly creative, infinite, and deep you are. The answers to your questions and the future you are seeking are already within you waiting to be remembered and understood.

Perhaps the world of dreams is who you truly are, where you meet your most authentic self. Perhaps when you fall asleep and see with your night vision, you are simply reconnecting with your essence and visiting the only reality. If this is all starting to sound rather heady and far-out, remember that there is scientific backing for it, as there is with all of the illuminations shared in this book. According to science, what you see as solid matter is 99 percent empty space, suggesting that your attachment to and confidence and belief in what you see as reality could be misplaced![50]

Is your waking reality an illusion? Is it all a dream within a dream, depending on your perspective? Is letting go of attachment to the material world as the only reality the way forward?

Who knows?

It's always going to be your decision, your perspective, your dream time. Only you can choose what you truly believe, think, feel, see, and dream.

---

50 Sundermier, "99.9999999% of Your Body Is Empty Space."

Dream Again

In addition to using this book to sense your future, you can use it as inspiration to help you better understand and value your waking life. You can use it every night and every day to dream and live bigger.

Ask yourself this: If a recent experience appeared in a dream, how would you have decoded it precognitively? Could you have recognised the potential future being signposted in plain sight?

Why not interpret everyone and everything you encounter in your waking life as if it were a precognitive dream symbol, rich in future-forward meaning? Use the profound knowledge you have gained here to look deep beneath the surface of everything and everyone, not just in your dreams but in your waking life too. Measure your progress by the number of times you smile during the day and think to yourself, *Yes, my life is indeed stranger than a dream!*

If you can experience the miracle of your life as a waking dream, if you can understand that your thoughts have absolutely no reality nor power over you unless you give them reality and power, if you can understand that in every dream and in every moment you are choosing and creating the future you are attracting, then you are awakening psychically and spiritually.

I, Dream

In your own dream time, you are reborn as the timeless being having a human experience that you are, have always been, and always will be. Liberated from the confines of linear time, the past, present, and future are now one within you.

René Descartes's famous quote "I think, therefore I am," has transformed infinitely and blissfully into "I dream, therefore I am." Your future now belongs to your belief in your precognitive power and your decision to live the beauty of your dreams.

Appendix

The Science of Precognition

There are many related terms—premonition, extrasensory perception, intuition, sixth sense, and so on—but precognition is typically the catch-all word scientists use to describe an inexplicable knowing about the future that later proves to be correct.

Research into intuition, and how we unconsciously make decisions about our future without knowing why, is currently booming.[51] It is increasingly regarded as a supernormal power by scientists and psychologists.[52]

Several respected studies have confirmed that intuitive decisions are reached faster and are subjectively better than those landed on by rational means.[53] As far as precognitive dreams are concerned, studies where a person was invited into a lab for several nights and asked to dream about a target experience that was decided upon only the next day, after the dreamer had recorded their dreams, have also produced promising results.[54]

Promising results have also been produced in studies on physiological predictive changes that occur before unpredictable and random events

51. Robson, "Intuition: When Is It Right to Trust Your Gut Instincts?"; Beidel, "More Than a Feeling: ONR Investigates 'Spidey Sense' for Sailors and Marines."

52. Lufityanto, Donkin, and Pearson, "Measuring Intuition."

53. Kutsch, "Can We Rely on Our Intuition?"

54. Callaghan, "Precognitive Dreaming: An Empirical Exploration."

artificially created in lab studies.[55] These are rapid changes in heart rate, sweat, and respiration, and they seem to suggest that our bodies can sense the future when something significant is going to happen, even if we don't know what that future might be. The scientific term used for these predictive physical responses is *presentiment.*

Because of all of this promising evidence, precognition is fast establishing itself as a topic that is at the very least worthy of greater research. It continues to have detractors from mainstream scientists who label it a pseudoscience that attempts to violate the law of cause and effect and linear time. With leading scientists researching consciousness, such as Dr. Stanley Krippner, Dr. Daryl Bem, Dr. Charles Honorton, Dr. Montague Ullman, Dr. Rupert Sheldrake, Dr. Julia Mossbridge, and Dr. Dean Radin, as well as Nobel Prize–winning physicist Dr. Brian Josephson, to name but a few luminaries paving the way ahead, precognition is making firm scientific inroads.

The laboratory evidence was strong enough for Dr. Jessica Utts—who was asked by the US Congress to examine the evidence for precognition based on classified work by the US government and who, in 2016, became the president of the American Statistical Association—to state, "Precognition, in which the answer is known to no one until a future time, appears to work quite well."[56]

The above is just a hint of the science currently out there. In the footnote here, you will find some key studies if you want to delve more deeply, but it is not essential.[57] At the end of the day, your personal experience of

55. Mossbridge and Radin, "Precognition as a Form of Prospection"; Bem, Tressoldi, Rabeyron, and Duggan, "Feeling the Future: A Meta-Analysis of 90 Experiments on the Anomalous Anticipation of Random Future Events."

56. Utts, "An Assessment of the Evidence for Psychic Functioning."

57. All of the studies referenced in the footnotes are worth investigating further, in addition to the following: Honorton and Ferrari, "'Future Telling': A Meta-Analysis of Forced-Choice Precognition Experiments, 1935–1987"; May and Depp, "Entropy and Precognition"; Watt, "Precognitive Dreaming"; Ullman et al., *Dream Telepathy*; Haynes, "Scientists Used IBM's Quantum Computer to Reverse Time, Possibly Breaking a Law of Physics"; Watt et al., "Psychological Factors in Precognitive Dream Experiences"; Radin, "Unconscious Perception of Future Emotions"; McLuhan, "Precognitive Dreaming Should Not Be Dismissed as Coincidence"; and "Why Our Dreams Could Be the Key to Time Travel," BBC.

precognition is what matters most and is what is most likely to convince you. I am flagging the science here because I want you to feel confident that precognition *is* being investigated scientifically, and the landslide evidence from that research is that it exists.

Precognitive potential/ability exists in you and how you experience time.

What Is Time?

No one knows for sure what time is. As is the case with dreams, love, and other invisible but essential forces, time is hard for scientists to define and pin down. It remains an infinite mystery, like life itself.

Most of us think of time as a linear flow of events, from past to present and into the future. The past is remembered, the present is lived in, and the future is unknown. Precognitive dreams and experiences challenge this standard definition, suggesting that the future can somehow be glimpsed, "remembered," in the now. It seems that the field of physics is closer than ever to agreeing. In many physics equations, time can go in either direction, forward or backward, +t or −t. This doesn't match our everyday experience of time as linear, even though the equations work out, does it? While some physicists continue to assert that the linear flow of time is crucial to the workings of the universe, a steady stream of them are concluding that the linear flow of time may be an illusion.

Genius theoretical physicist Albert Einstein (1879–1955), whose dreams famously inspired many of his world-shifting theories such as the theory of relativity, stated that "for people like us who believe in physics, the separation between past, present and future has only the importance of an admittedly tenacious illusion."[58] In other words, we perceive time as linear because infinity is too vast for our brains to grasp.

We live in a series of nows that are static and not linear-flowing in any sense of the word. Our perception of time is also subjective and not the same based on what we are doing. We've all heard the sayings "A watched kettle never boils" and "Time flies when you're having fun." Numerous

58. Venning "Time's Arrow: Albert Einstein's Letters to Michele Besso." Einstein is quoted in a letter he wrote to Besso dated July 29, 1953.

studies have examined how people's perceptions of time are different based on their mental perception of what they are doing.[59] Time has the subjective experience of slowing down or speeding up.

There is also the human experience of timelessness, where people feel like they are in no time. This has been researched, especially in meditation studies where meditators experienced a subjective transcendent state.[60] One common feature of this state was that the meditators experienced a sense of timelessness. Interestingly, this transcendent state was described as being both relaxed and awake and accompanied by feelings of bliss.

Causal loops, like the "Which came first: the chicken or the egg?" scenario, where it is unclear what event causes what, further defy our understanding of time being linear. The same is true of two other approaches that also originate in physics: multiple futures prediction and the near-miss approach. The multiple futures approach suggests that potential futures are constantly being created but then are redirected by your spontaneous reactions in the present. For example, you decide to drop a ball on the floor, but at the last moment you change your mind and catch the ball in your hands before it hits the floor, thereby creating an alternative future for that once-destined-to-hit-the-floor ball. The near-miss theory is similar in that an intuitive hunch helps prepare you so you can swerve away from a potentially unwelcome future possibility.

Here's yet more pause for scientific thought. Quantum theorists tend to subscribe to the theory that the universe is evolutionary. In an evolutionary universe, can the laws themselves, specifically the law of time being linear, or cause and effect, not also evolve?

Mind-blowing, isn't it?

But if you aren't a quantum physicist, what does all this mean?

It means the notion that the future can't have any effect on your present is not necessarily true. There is considerable uncertainty in scientific and philosophical circles about what time is and how it works. This uncertainty can help you embrace the possibility that precognition is a kind of *mental*

---

59. Wittmann, "The Inner Experience of Time."

60. Linares Gutiérrez, Schmidt, Meissner, and Wittmann, "Changes in Subjective Time and Self during Meditation."

time travel into the future. The possibility of physical time travel remains the stuff of science fiction novels and movies.

If you think time is entirely mental and does not or cannot exist in the physical world, then you are in harmony with the likes of great philosophers such as John McTaggart (1866–1925) and St. Augustine of Hippo (354–430).

Psychologists and cognitive neuroscientists also focus their investigations on the mental experience of time as opposed to physical time. They suggest that there is an order to the events you experience in your life, which, when put together, is called the flow of time, temporal flow, or your "stream of consciousness," as psychologist William James (1842–1910) famously put it. They try to understand time and the perception of it by figuring out how the mind creates this sense of temporal flow.

Precognitive dreams and experiences suggest that although waking experiences tell us that a cause moves in a pushing or forward direction towards an effect, there also seem to be hidden mental and sometimes physical pulls from the future influencing the past, known in scientific circles as *retrocausality.*[61]

It is possible that you might already be harnessing these pulls from your future right now, in your body when you are awake and in your dreams at night. That's why listening to physical cues in your waking life and recalling your dreams, as suggested in your precognition-boosting action plan on page 12, can help you get way ahead of your time.

What Is Precognition and Where Does It Come From?

Given that we all have precognitive potential, can science explain what precognition is and where it comes from?

Not fully, but quantum physics, the investigation into subatomic particles, is getting close. It suggests that everything is made up of vibrating energy strands connected by force fields to create the material world. This means that everything you see and experience—whether that be visible, conscious, and material or invisible, unconscious, and precognitive—consists of

---

61. Ferreira, "A Growing Number of Scientists Are Convinced the Future Influences the Past."

the same source material, which is energy. There is also research suggesting that the observer may be able to influence the way this energy operates.[62] Put this all together and it offers a potential explanation for precognitive abilities and the powerful link between your perspective and your life.

Quantum physics is a deeply complex topic best discussed by a scientist and not a dream expert like me, but it does propose that precognition is simply the result of natural physics, an infinite energy that we have yet to fully understand. Precognition both consists of and connects you to the source or energy that is infinite and timeless and encapsulates everything and everyone within and all around you.

The beautiful outcome of awakening your precognition, empowering your inner space, is that it connects you strongly to the invisible energies in the world around you. It makes you less rather than more self-centred. You understand that what is within you is also around you, and you are interconnected with everyone and everything. You are both everything and nothing, a part of something so much greater than yourself. It's liberating and humbling at the same time.

If all this sounds contradictory, get used to it. Embracing opposites and letting go of the restraints of logic is all part of awakening your precognition.

Time Leap

To conclude, let's not forget that there may also be a spiritual dimension to consider here. Precognition is an indicator that your mind, or your essence, soul, consciousness, spark, or whatever you want to call it, can exist outside of time. That timeless essence of you is more infinite than space itself. Compare the over 100 trillion synaptic connections in your brain with the mere 100-plus billions of stars in the Milky Way.

Precognition reminds you that there is so much more to you than meets the eye or than you have allowed yourself to believe or even dream of. Perhaps the future, the infinity you think is out there in outer space,

---

62. Weizmann Institute of Science, "Quantum Theory Demonstrated: Observation Affects Reality."

is already alive and breathing deep within you, hidden in dreams or your inner space.

The answers you are seeking and the future you dream of are not out there at all; they're all within you.

Recommended Resources

The Premonition Code by Theresa Cheung and Julia Mossbridge (Watkins, 2017)

Psychic Dreaming by Loyd Auerbach (Warner Books, 1991)

Memories, Dreams, Reflections by Carl Jung (Vintage, 1965)

Precognitive Dreaming and the Long Self by Eric Wargo (Inner Traditions, 2021)

Opening to the Infinite by Stephan A. Schwartz (Nemoseen Media, 2007)

The Science of Channeling by Helané Wahbeh (New Harbinger, 2021)

Heads-Up Dreaming by Carlyle T. Smith (Turning Stone, 2017)

The Art of Transforming Nightmares by Clare R. Johnson (Llewellyn, 2021)

Lucid Dreaming Made Easy by Charlie Morley (Hay House, 2018)

The Reality of ESP by Russell Targ (Quest Books, 2012)

The Science of Channeling by Helané Wahbeh (New Harbinger, 2022)

The Dream Dictionary from A to Z by Theresa Cheung (Thunderbay, 2023)

The Dream Cure by Theresa Cheung (HarperCollins/Llewellyn, 2024)

Real Magic by Dean Radin (Harmony, 2018)

The Power of Premonitions by Larry Dossey (Hay House, 2009)

Extraordinary Dreams and How to Work with Them by Stanley Krippner (SUNY Press, 2012)

The Committee of Sleep by Deirdre Barrett (Oneiroi Press, 2001)

The Premonitions Bureau by Sam Knight (Faber, 2022)

Spiritual Science by Steve Taylor (Watkins, 2017)

Imaginable by Jane McGonigal (Bantam, 2022)

The Labyrinth of Time by Anthony Peake (Arcturus, 2017)

Your Brain Is a Time Machine by Dean Buonomano (W. W. Norton & Co., 2017)

The Simulation Hypothesis by Rizwan Virk (Bayview Books, 2019)

Dreaming Ahead of Time by Gary Lachman (Floris, 2022)

Transcendent Mind by Imants Barušs and Julia Mossbridge (American Psychological Association, 2017)

Why We Sleep: The New Science of Sleep and Dreams by Matthew Walker (Penguin, 2017)

A Christmas Carol by Charles Dickens (1843)

White Shores podcast, hosted by Theresa Cheung. Launched in 2019 and available on all podcast platforms, *White Shores* is a weekly podcast for dreaming beings having a human experience. Scroll down through the list of episodes and you will find interviews with many of the world's leading scientists, authors, and experts researching and writing about dreams and the science of consciousness, including Julia Mossbridge, Eric Wargo, Charlie Morley, Dean Radin, Helané Wahbeh, Arnaud Delorme, Garret Yount, Raymond Moody, Eben Alexander, Carlyle Smith, Gary Lachman, Lauri Loewenberg, Athena Laz, and Clare R. Johnson, among others.

www.noetic.org: Institute of Noetic Sciences (IONS). Founded in 1973 by Apollo 14 astronaut Dr. Edgar Mitchell, IONS conducts and advances the science of the interconnected universe, reaching new understanding about the nature of reality, dreams, and our extended capacities. IONS welcomes your precognitive dream experiences at this link: https://www.research.net/r/IONS_ExperienceDatabase.

www.spr.ac.uk: Society for Psychical Research (SPR). Founded in 1882, the SPR was the first organisation to conduct scholarly research into human experiences that challenge contemporary scientific models.

www.timemachine.love: Time Machine is a project of TILT: The Institute for Love and Time. Learn to use unconditional love to connect to yourself across time with this free online resource for mental time travellers. By recording a message to your past, present, or future self and sending it off in the time machine until tomorrow, you notice how you change over time.

Acknowledgments

Sincere gratitude to my visionary publisher, Llewellyn, and Bill Krause for their good faith in my dreamwork, and to my wise editor, Amy Glaser, for her good vibrations, to Andrea Neff for her deeply insightful work at the copyediting stage, to Kat Neff and Alison Aten for their advice and support, and to everyone involved in the production and promotion of this book.

Special thanks to my agent Mark Gottlieb from the Trident Media Group for his guidance and positivity and to Gail Torr from Galaxy Media for being a dream to work with. I would also like to sincerely thank Dr. Julia Mossbridge for her remarkable precognitive vision and all of the scientists and dream researchers I have worked with along the way, as well as the powered by dreams experts I have interviewed on my *White Shores* podcast.

Heartfelt thanks also to my family. I could not have written this book without your love and my little soul dog, Arnie, guiding and inspiring me across time.

Most important of all are my readers and listeners. You are the stuff that dreams are made of and a constant source of illumination to me. Thank you from my heart and soul.

Bibliography

Adventure-Heart, Denholm J., Natasha A. Madden, and Paul Delfabbro. "Effects of Vitamin B6 (Pyridoxine) and a B Complex Preparation on Dreaming and Sleep." *Perceptual and Motor Skills* 125, no. 3 (June 2018): 451–62. doi: 10.1177/0031512518770326.

Aron, Elaine N. *The Highly Sensitive Person: How to Thrive When the World Overwhelms You.* Thorsons Classics, 2017.

Atance, Cristina M., and Daniela O'Neill. "Episodic Future Thinking." *Trends in Cognitive Sciences* 5, no. 12 (Dec. 1, 2001): 533–39. doi: 10.1016/s1364-6613(00)01804-0. PMID: 11728911.

BBC. "Why Our Dreams Could Be the Key to Time Travel." Feb. 23, 2022. https://www.bbc.co.uk/reel/video/p08yxrlb/why-our-dreams-could-be-the-key-to-time-travel.

Beidel, Eric. "More Than a Feeling: ONR Investigates 'Spidey Sense' for Sailors and Marines." Office of Naval Research, Jan. 1, 2014. https://www.nre.navy.mil/media-center/news-releases/more-feeling-onr-investigates-spidey-sense-sailors-and-marines.

Beischel, Julie. "Mediumship Research at the Windbridge Research Center by Director of Research, Julie Beischel, PhD." Windbridge Research Center. Accessed Oct. 2024. https://www.windbridge.org/research/mediumship-research.

Bem, Daryl, Patrizio Tressoldi, Thomas Rabeyron, and Michael Duggan. "Feeling the Future: A Meta-Analysis of 90 Experiments on the Anomalous Anticipation of Random Future Events." *F1000Research* 4 (Oct. 30, 2015): 1188. doi: 10.12688/f1000research.7177.2.

Callaghan, Brendan. "Precognitive Dreaming: An Empirical Exploration." Master's thesis, Adler University, Dec. 2019. doi:10.13140/RG.2.2.12592.30725.

Cheung, Theresa, host. *White Shores with Theresa Cheung.* Season 6, episode 4, "Lottery Dreams and Your Fortune with Powerball Winner, Timothy Schulz." March 20, 2022. https://podcasts.apple.com/gb/podcast/lottery-dreams-and-your-fortune-with-powerball/id1475553348?i=1000554608432.

Cheung, Theresa, and Julia Mossbridge. *The Premonition Code.* Watkins, 2017.

Ferreira, Becky. "A Growing Number of Scientists Are Convinced the Future Influences the Past." VICE, March 16, 2023. https://www.vice.com/en/article/epvgjm/a-growing-number-of-scientists-are-convinced-the-future-influences-the-past.

Ficco, Linda, Lorenzo Mancuso, et al. "Disentangling Predictive Processing in the Brain: A Meta-Analytic Study in Favour of a Predictive Network." *Scientific Reports* 11, no. 16258 (2021). doi.org/10.1038/s41598-021-95603-5.

Fisher, Helen L., Suzet Tanya Lereya, Andrew Thompson, Glyn Lewis, Stanley Zammit, and Dieter Wolke. "Childhood Parasomnias and Psychotic Experiences at Age 12 Years in a United Kingdom Birth Cohort." *Sleep* 37, no. 3 (March 1, 2014): 475-82. doi: 10.5665/sleep.3478.

Flaherty, Colleen. "How Mindfulness Helps Grad Students." Inside Higher Ed. November 14, 2019. https://www.insidehighered.com/news/2019/11/15/mindfulness-significantly-benefits-graduate-students-says-first-study-its-kind.

Floyd, Marlys. "How a Mother's Love Transformed a Life." *Southeast Iowa Union*, Aug. 9, 2022. https://www.southeastiowaunion.com/pioneer-republican/how-a-mothers-love-transformed-a-life.

Frankl, Viktor E. *Man's Search for Meaning.* Penguin/Rider, 2004.

Gearan, Hannah. "'Dreams Are Messages from the Deep': Why a Sardaukar Speaks Dune's Opening Line Explained by Villeneuve." ScreenRant, April 18, 2024. https://screenrant.com/dune-movie-opening-line-message-sardaukar-explained-denis-villeneuve.

Hamer, Dean. *The God Gene: How Faith Is Hardwired into Our Genes.* Doubleday, 2004.

HeartMath Institute. "Heart Coherence." Accessed Oct. 2024. https://www.heartmath.org/heart-coherence.

Hill, Napoleon. *Think and Grow Rich.* The Ralston Society, 1937.

Hitchman, Glenn, and Chris Roe. "A Re-examination of Nonintentional Precognition with Openness to Experience, Creativity, Psi Beliefs, and Luck Beliefs as Predictors of Success." *Journal of Parapsychology* 76 (Jan. 2012): 109–45. https://www.researchgate.net/publication/278405744_A_re-examination_of_nonintentional_precognition_with_openness_to_experience_creativity_psi_beliefs_and_luck_beliefs_as_predictors_of_success.

Holmes, Alec. "Carl Jung on Synchronicity," Arts of Thought. Accessed Oct. 2024. https://artsofthought.com/2020/05/30/carl-jung-synchronicity.

Honorton, Charles, Diane Ferrari, and Daryl Bem. "Extraversion and ESP Performance: A Meta-Analysis and a New Confirmation." *Journal of Parapsychology* 62, no. 3 (Sept. 1998): 255–76.

Institute of Noetic Sciences (IONS)."Healing Lucid Dream Pilot Study: Origins of IONS First Experiment on Dreams." Accessed Oct. 2024. https://noetic.org/event/healing-lucid-dream-study.

Jung, Carl. *Memories, Dreams, Reflections.* Vintage, 1989.

Krieger, Jean-Philippe, Mohammed Asker, et al. "Neural Pathway for Gut Feelings: Vagal Interoceptive Feedback from the Gastrointestinal Tract Is a Critical Modulator of Anxiety-Like Behavior." *Biological Psychiatry* 92, no. 9 (Nov. 1, 2022): 709–21. doi: 10.1016/j.biopsych.

Kutsch, Laura. "Can We Rely on Our Intuition?" *Scientific American*, Aug. 15, 2019. https://www.scientificamerican.com/article/can-we-rely-on-our-intuition.

Linares Gutiérrez, Damisela, Stefan Schmidt, Karin Meissner, and Marc Wittmann. "Changes in Subjective Time and Self during Meditation." *Biology* 11, no. 8 (July 26, 2022): 1116. doi: 10.3390/biology11081116.

Lovato, Nicole, and Leon Lack. "The Effects of Napping on Cognitive Functioning." *Progress in Brain Research* 185 (2010): 155–66. doi: 10.1016/B978-0-444-53702-7.00009-9.

"Lucid Dreaming Study Reveals a Huge Decrease in PTSD Symptoms." PTSD UK. Accessed Oct. 2024. https://www.ptsduk.org/lucid-dreaming-study.

Lufityanto, Galang, Chris Donkin, and Joel Pearson." Measuring Intuition: Nonconscious Emotional Information Boosts Decision Accuracy and Confidence." *Psychological Science* 27, no. 5 (2016): 622–34. doi.org/10.1177/0956797616629403.

Luke, David, Deborah Delanoy, and Simon Sherwood. "Psi May Look Like Luck: Perceived Luckiness and Beliefs about Luck in Relation to Precognition." *Journal of the Society for Psychical Research* 72 (Oct. 2008): 193–207. https://www.researchgate.net/publication/31872108_Psi_May_Look_Like_Luck_Perceived_Luckiness_And_Beliefs_About_Luck_In_Relation_To_Precognition.

Macrae, C. Neil, et al. "Turning I into Me: Imagining Your Future Self." *Consciousness and Cognition* 37 (Dec. 2015): 207–13. doi: 10.1016/j.concog.2015.09.009.

Mossbridge, Julia, and Daryl Bem. "Reproductive Hormonal Status as a Predictor of Precognition." March 2018. http://www.koestler-parapsychology.psy.ed.ac.uk/Documents/KPU_1043_Results.pdf.

Mossbridge, Julia, and Dean Radin. "Precognition as a Form of Prospection: A Review of the Evidence." *Psychology of Consciousness: Theory, Research, and Practice* 5, no. 1 (2018): 78–93. doi.org/10.1037/cns0000121.

Mossbridge, Julia, Kirsten Cameron, and Mark Boccuzzi. "State, Trait, and Target Parameters Associated with Accuracy in Two Online Tests of Precognitive Remote Viewing." *Journal of Anomalous Experience and Cognition* 4, no.1 (2024): 88–121. doi.org/10.31156/jaex.24743.

Mossbridge, Julia, Patrizio Tressoldi, et al. "Predicting the Unpredictable: Critical Analysis and Practical Implications of Predictive Anticipatory Activity." *Frontiers in Human Neuroscience* 25, no. 8 (March 25, 2014): 146. doi: 10.3389/fnhum.2014.00146.

Murphy, Jennifer, and Freya Prentice. "Humans Have a 'Sixth Sense', and It's Actually Vital to Our Health." March 29, 2024, ScienceAlert. https://www.sciencealert.com/humans-have-a-sixth-sense-and-its-actually-vital-to-our-health.

Naiman, Rubin. "Dreamless: The Silent Epidemic of REM Sleep Loss." *Annals of the New York Academy of Sciences* 1406, no. 1 (Oct. 2017): 77–85. doi: 10.1111/nyas.13447.

Penberthy, J. Kim, Adam Hodge, et al. "Meditators and Nonmeditators: A Descriptive Analysis over Time with a Focus on Unusual and Extraordinary Experiences." *Journal of Yoga and Physiotherapy* 8, no. 3 (Jan. 2020). doi: 10.19080/JYP.2020.08.555744.

Poetry Foundation. "Locksley Hall" by Alfred, Lord Tennyson. Accessed Oct. 2024. https://www.poetryfoundation.org/poems/45362/locksley-hall.

Rattet, Shelley, and Krisanne Bursik. "Investigating the Personality Correlates of Paranormal Belief and Precognitive Experience." *Personality and Individual Differences* 3, no. 3 (2001): 433–44. doi.org/10.1016/S0191-8869(00)00148-3.

Remmers, Carina, and Thea Zander. "Why You Don't See the Forest for the Trees When You Are Anxious: Anxiety Impairs Intuitive Decision-Making." *Clinical Psychological Science* 6, no. 1 (2018): 48–62. doi.org/10.1177/2167702617728705.

Robson, David. "Intuition: When Is It Right to Trust Your Gut Instincts?" BBC, April 4, 2022. https://www.bbc.com/worklife/article/20220401-intuition-when-is-it-right-to-trust-your-gut-instincts.

Roney-Dougal, Serena, and Jerry Solfvin. "Exploring the Relationship between Tibetan Meditation Attainment and Precognition." *Journal of Scientific Exploration* 25, no. 1 (April 5, 2011). https://journalofscientificexploration.org/index.php/jse/article/view/32.

Saplakoglu, Yasemin. "Sleep Technique Used by Salvador Dalí Really Works." Live Science, December 8, 2021. https://www.livescience.com/little-known-sleep-stage-may-be-creative-sweet-spot.

Schacter, Daniel L., Roland G. Benoit, and Karl K. Szpunar. "Episodic Future Thinking: Mechanisms and Functions." *Current Opinion in Behavioral Sciences* 17 (Oct. 2017): 41–50. doi: 10.1016/j.cobeha.2017.06.002.

Schultz, Timothy, host. *Lottery, Dreams and Fortune.* Podcast. https://www.youtube.com/@TimothySchultz/podcasts.

Sestir, Marc, Ming Tai, and Jennifer Peszka. "Relationships between Video Game Play Factors and Frequency of Lucid and Control Dreaming Experiences." *Dreaming* 29, no. 2 (2019): 127–43. doi.org/10.1037/drm0000102.

Stawarczyk, David, and Arnaud D'Argembeau. "Neural Correlates of Personal Goal Processing during Episodic Future Thinking and Mind-Wandering: An ALE Meta-Analysis." *Human Brain Mapping* 36, no. 8 (Aug. 2015): 2928–47. doi: 10.1002/hbm.22818.

Stowell, Mary S. "Precognitive Dreams: A Phenomenological Study. Part 1: Methodology and Sample Cases." *Journal of the American Society for Psychical Research* 91 (1997): 163–220.

Sundermier, Ali. "99.9999999% of Your Body Is Empty Space." ScienceAlert, Sept. 23, 2016. https://www.sciencealert.com/99-9999999-of-your-body-is-empty-space.

Travers, Mark. "New Psychological Research Says Paranormal Experiences Are the Norm, Not the Exception," Forbes, June 18, 2022. https://www.forbes.com/sites/traversmark/2022/06/18/new-psychological-research-says-paranormal-experiences-are-the-norm-not-the-exception/?sh=2945126022cc.

Utts, Jessica. "An Assessment of the Evidence for Psychic Functioning." *Journal of Parapsychology* 82, Suppl. (2018): 118–46. http://doi.org/10.30891/jopar.2018S.01.10.

Venning, Thomas. "Time's Arrow: Albert Einstein's Letters to Michele Besso." Christie's, Nov. 14, 2017. https://www.christies.com/en/stories

/einstein-letters-to-michele-besso-3ecca787d9be4463a8695269259d6c00.

Walker, Matthew. *Why We Sleep: The New Science of Sleep and Dreams.* Penguin, 2018.

Walton, Alice G. "Seven Ways Meditation Can Actually Change the Brain." Forbes, Feb. 9, 2015. https://www.forbes.com/sites/alicegwalton/2015/02/09/7-ways-meditation-can-actually-change-the-brain/?sh=76831c531465.

Wamsley, Erin J., and Robert Stickgold. "Dreaming and Offline Memory Processing." *Current Biology* 20, no. 23 (Dec. 7, 2010): R1010-3. doi: 10.1016/j.cub.2010.10.045.

Weizmann Institute of Science. "Quantum Theory Demonstrated: Observation Affects Reality." ScienceDaily, Feb. 27, 1998. http://www.sciencedaily.com/releases/1998/02/980227055013.htm.

"When James Dean Met Sir Alec Guinness in September 1955." Posted Aug. 1, 2021, by historyinvid. YouTube video, https://www.youtube.com/watch?v=6B731y12pc4.

Wittmann, Marc. "The Inner Experience of Time." *Philosophical Transactions of the Royal Society of London B: Biological Sciences* 364, no. 1525 (July 12, 2009): 1955–67. doi: 10.1098/rstb.2009.0003.

Index

A to Z of Dream Symbols Listed in the Book

To Write to the Author

If you wish to contact the author or would like more information about this book, please write to the author in care of Llewellyn Worldwide Ltd. and we will forward your request. Both the author and the publisher appreciate hearing from you and learning of your enjoyment of this book and how it has helped you. Llewellyn Worldwide Ltd. cannot guarantee that every letter written to the author can be answered, but all will be forwarded. Please write to:

Theresa Cheung
℅ Llewellyn Worldwide
2143 Wooddale Drive
Woodbury, MN 55125-2989

Please enclose a self-addressed stamped envelope for reply, or $1.00 to cover costs. If outside the U.S.A., enclose an international postal reply coupon.

Many of Llewellyn's authors have websites with additional information and resources. For more information, please visit our website at http://www.llewellyn.com.